DISCARDED

THE
PLAYWRIGHT'S
MUSE

D0226256

DISCARDED

STUDIES IN MODERN DRAMA
Kimball King, *Series Editor*

SOUTH ORANGE PUBLIC LIBRARY

THE PLAYWRIGHT'S MUSE

edited by Joan Herrington

Routledge
New York and London

812
PLA

Published in 2002 by
Routledge
29 West 35th Street
New York, NY 10001

Published in Great Britain by
Routledge
11 New Fetter Lane
London EC4P 4EE

Routledge is an imprint of the Taylor & Francis Group.

Copyright © 2002 by Joan Herrington

Printed in the United States of America on acid-free paper.

All rights reserved. No part of this book may be reprinted or reproduced or utilized in any form or by any electronic, mechanical, or other means, now known or hereafter invented, including any photocopying and recording, or in any information storage or retrieval system, without permission in writing from the publisher.

10 9 8 7 6 5 4 3 2 1

Library of Congress Cataloging-in-Publishing Data is available from the Library of Congress.

The playwright's muse / edited by Joan Herrington
ISBN 0–8153–3779–5 — ISBN 0–8153–3780–9 (pbk.)

CONTENTS

24.95   20-12-11   138

ACKNOWLEDGMENTS

I am grateful to the many people who have supported my work on this book. I have learned much from its contributors and I appreciate the opportunity to bring their work to you. I also extend my thanks to the playwrights who shared their thoughts with us. Theirs are the voices which can shape the future of the American theatre, and we must listen.

In addition, my gratitude goes to my colleagues in the Theatre Department at Western Michigan University for encouraging my work on this book.

Finally, and most importantly, I thank my family: my two daughters, Emily and Sarah, who patiently shared their mother with these pages, and my husband Rick, whose devotion and faith enabled me to complete *The Playwright's Muse.*

INTRODUCTION

Joan Herrington

To study that which inspires the playwrights who inspire us is to dig deeply into the mystery of drama, not to unmask it, but rather to revel in its glory. What we learn about their most fertile imaginations will not enable us to "understand" the playwrights; rather, it will enable us to see, for a moment, our world as these writers see it. What stimulates those first words of dialogue? Which images help form a character? Which events inform the plot? Which heartaches inspire the theme? How does the pulsing world of people, places, and events distill itself in the mind of a writer who then rebirths this world in an extraordinary play?

The most recent recipients of the Pulitzer Prize for Drama present a wide perspective on their art in form and content, tone, and style. These winners have included extraordinary plays of social commentary in a dazzling array of forms: *How I Learned to Drive* (Paula Vogel, 1998) is a frighteningly funny exploration of sexual abuse in which Vogel rejects causal, linear structure in favor of episodic, circular dramaturgy; *Rent* (Jonathan Larson, 1996) is a radical rock opera examining the AIDS epidemic and the dehumanization of society. August Wilson's *The Piano Lesson* (1990) continues his chronicle of a century of African-American history in a lyric drama exploring a race's relationship with its past.

Angels in America: The Millennium Approaches (1993) is Tony Kushner's provocative epic in which reality and fantasy readily intertwine in a complex commentary on sex, religion, and politics. Robert Schenkkan's *The Kentucky Cycle* (1992), a unique series of nine compellingly honest plays, each written in a different style, reveals the darker realities of the history of rural America.

From the most political to the most personal, the list includes exceptional plays which probe the human soul: Donald Margulies's *Dinner with Friends* (2000) is a wry and clever commentary on contemporary relationships, a seemingly straightforward comedy of manners with profound insight on intimacy; Margaret Edson's *Wit* (1999) is a haunting story of redemption before death made all the more unnerving by its metatheatrical approach; and *Three Tall Women* (1994), Edward Albee's brilliant exploration of the life of one woman, is an experiment in perception as the central character is simultaneously manifest onstage at three different ages.

For several writers, the Pulitzer was awarded for a work that specifically characterized career-long artistic pursuits. Wendy Wasserstein is at the height of her comedic form as *The Heidi Chronicles* (1989) examines issues of women's achievement and independence and the ramifications of their pursuit. *Lost In Yonkers* (1991) embodies Neil Simon's successful attempt to redefine his own work by venturing into deeper thematic waters. *The Young Man from Atlanta* (1995) is the culmination of Horton Foote's development of a singular style whose seeming simplicity belies the complexities of his transcendental vision of the American family.

What drives these plays are the writers' relationships with music and painting, their passionate responses to world events, the deep impact of personal drama. The inspirations and influences on the development of these plays are as diverse as the plays themselves.

All of Wendy Wasserstein's most well known plays, *Uncommon Women and Others*, *Isn't It Romantic*, *The Heidi Chronicles*, *The Sisters Rosensweig*, and *An American Daughter*, focus on female characters struggling with difficult personal and professional decisions in an environment that is changing quickly with each new decade. The characters' experiences and conflicts reflect Wasserstein's relationship with the women's movement as it developed over thirty years. The plays explore the conflicts between career ambition and personal fulfillment and are a response to the changing cultural and social positions of women. In her chapter on Wasserstein, Angelika Czekay explores Wasserstein's relationship with the women's movement, recognizing that the visibility and success of her plays has caused her to be "tokenized as one of the central feminist playwrights of the past twenty years." Czekay points out, however, that many feminists have critized Wasserstein for "creating a questionable representation of feminist politics, theory, and activism." Interestingly, this has served not only to redefine the continuing debate on women's issues but also to redefine Wasserstein's plays themselves.

After Wasserstein, the Pulitzer Committee turned to August Wilson, who had won three years earlier for *Fences*. (Interestingly, *The Piano Lesson,* the 1990 Pulitzer winner, had been a finalist the year before.) In naming what he terms his four "Bs," Wilson identifies his artistic muses, pointing toward his creative spark and leading his critics straight to the visual and aural images that inspire him. Playwright Amiri Baraka, Argentinian short-story writer Jorge Luis Borges, and painter Romare Bearden have all heavily influenced Wilson's style and content. But it is his fourth "B," the blues, that serves both Wilson's artistic and his political goals.

Blues music has provided Wilson's play titles, determined his dramatic plots, and powered the underlying emotional content of his work. There is blues music at the heart of all Wilson's plays, in his musician characters, his music industry settings, and the continued presence of song in the plays. Music is integral to the lives of the playwright and his characters. The music finds its way into Wilson's work not only as subject but also as technique—he writes his plays as if he were creating blues: improvising, repeating, leaving open phrases, evoking mood with every note. The plays, like the music, are metaphorical, lyrical, loosely organized.

For Wilson, survival of the blues is central to the survival of the African-American community; the blues link past and present and a shared cultural heritage. But Wilson also focuses his work on the blues because they must be reclaimed by the community, saved from the White co-opting of African-American art, which Wilson fears is strangling a cultural identity. Thus, Wilson simultaneously confirms the value of the blues by placing them within his plays and reminds his audience of their precarious state. The blues are useful to Wilson as a social tool and a political tool, for he believes that "All art is politics. I'm one of those warrior spirits" (Rosen 1996, 31).

In 1991, the Pulitzer Committee recognized the career of Neil Simon, awarding *Lost in Yonkers* the coveted prize. In her chapter on Neil Simon and popular culture, Bette Mandl explores not only what makes Simon write his plays but also what makes him rewrite his plays. Focusing on Simon's consideration of the definition of a writer—or at least the definition of an "important" writer—Mandl follows Simon's efforts to influence popular opinion through his Brighton Beach trilogy as the character of Eugene, himself a writer, learns that you don't have to fulfill the traditional stereotype of the tortured artist in order to make your mark on the literary world; indeed, being "too popular," as Simon puts it, does not necessarily negate the possibility of serious work.

Mandl argues that Simon felt a freedom to expose these perspectives on his own career partially as a response to a changing audience expectation for art. She quotes Michael Lind (1999, 39), who comments, "In the 21st century, the fact that a writer, dramatist, composer or visual artist is as law-abiding, successful and well paid as, say, Shakespeare, Haydn or Raphael will not be ground for suspicion." Indeed, Simon's finger on the pulse of the convergence of high culture and mass culture significantly influenced the themes of his later plays.

Simon started his career with light comedies, which he wrote for the same audiences who had enjoyed his writings for early television. But Simon's own desire to "write darker plays" was eventually satisfied as he redefined the focus of his work not only to please himself, but also to accommodate the ever-changing audiences with whom he felt such close rapport.

A chance meeting with a doctor from Eastern Kentucky was the catalyst for Robert Schenkkan's epic work, *The Kentucky Cycle*. Schenkkan was acting in a play at the Actors Theater of Louisville when an offer came to visit rural Kentucky. The poverty and environmental devastation he saw there compelled him to research the area further. Meditations on the nature of the frontier myths that influence American culture, and anger over the rollback of social programs and environmental protection during the 1980s, impelled Schenkkan to write. One single short play was soon followed by eight more as Schenkkan strove to illustrate the historic forces that set in motion the cyclic patterns of greed, deceit, and the resulting vengeance that corrupt the moral order both in the Kentucky Cumberlands and in America as a whole.

Through a brilliant use of storytelling, by both the playwright and his characters, a purposeful variety of styles among the individual plays in the *Cycle*, and a vision for the staging of his material which would emphasize the ritual dimensions of his stories, Schenkkan inspired in his audience both an empathetic response to his characters' plights and a sense of circumspection intended to ensure that the mistakes of our past were powerfully and clearly portrayed.

Although Tony Kushner has himself acknowledged the influence of writers ranging from Herman Melville to Samuel Beckett, Wallace Stevens to Monty Python, Framji Minwalla contends that the attempt to identify Kushner's most formative mentors would be fruitless. Truly, the great writers whom Kushner names have given him "permission" to write and to experiment with form and language. But Minwalla argues that the most integral focus must be on what Kushner writes, and he explores Kushner's relationship with a most powerful and elusive force: history. Through examination of *A Bright Room Called Day* and *Slavs!*, Minwalla explores contradictions involved in representing history, especially in the way this history creates the present, forcing us to reevaluate our role in shaping the future. He illuminates a playwright who, steeped in a fundamentally disappointing century and burdened by contemporary politics and attitudes, considers the revolutionary possibilities left on our stages in and outside of the theatre.

In his chapter on Edward Albee, Thomas Adler examines *Three Tall Women* as a continuation and culmination of the three-time Pulitzer Prize–winning playwright's career. Adler explores the play as the next in a series through which Albee has undertaken a variety of stylistic experiments—what Albee terms "an act of aggression against the familiar and the 'easy'" (Albee 1980, 100–101). Citing the influence of modern art on Albee's work, Adler promotes consideration of *Three Tall Women* within the cubist tradition, citing its demand that the audience re-conceive traditional conceptual reality and point of view.

Albee also requires reconsideration of perception in his use of the techniques of the memory play with its roots in *Glass Menagerie* or *Death of a Salesman*. But *Three Tall Women* also bears the absurdist mark of Beckett, as it explores a simultaneity of existence that memory facilitates. The loss of such memory and the possibility for change, Alder notes, signal death.

Thus, in *Three Tall Women*, Albee returns to familiar territory in the creation of another of what Adler terms a "death watch" play. Like *Sandbox*, *All Over*, or *The Lady from Dubuque*, *Three Tall Women* reflects Ablee's continuing fascination with, and fear of, death and his profound portrayal of a human spirit as it faces the life it has lived.

Edward Albee was followed by Horton Foote, as the 1995 Pulitzer Prize was awarded for *The Young Man from Atlanta*. Horton Foote has spent his career immersed in the work of many of the most important creative visionaries of this century. From the artists of Stanislavski's Moscow Art Theatre to the great modern dance pioneers of the 1930s and 1940s to the poets of the modernist movement, Foote has consistently sought out artists who believed strongly in a spiritual component of great art and its ability to transcend human limitation. In her chapter, Crystal Brian notes that perhaps one of Foote's greatest influences is the iconoclastic American composer, Charles Ives, who singificantly impacted Foote's ability to combine all of these influences in forging a style uniquely capable of embodying the ineffable.

In considering Foote's style, Brian argues that critics and viewers have focused on Foote's continued regional settings or family-related material, rather than noting the thematic and stylistic issues with which the playwright is most concerned. Truly, Foote is a stylist whose pursuit of a transcendental style has led to him being called "our mystic of the theatre."

Horton Foote's Pulitzer crowned a career that spanned more than sixty years. When Jonathan Larson was awarded the Pulitzer Prize in 1996, audiences knew little about him and his previous work, and they assigned to him the romantic ideal of the artist who arises from nowhere with a brilliant virgin creation. But Larson, who had died from an aortic aneurysm three months earlier, had, in fact, written a brilliant creation that was the culmination of years of experimentation with musical form and content. Driven by his desire to "cultivate a new audience for music theatre," Larson had strived for years to create music and to tell stories that would appeal to younger audiences. He hoped that new trends in dramatic storytelling and play structure and innovations in style would help build the new audience that the theatre so desperately needed.

But equally important to him was to educate those audiences socially and politically, and no work undertaken by Larson neglected this goal. From his collegiate composition of political cabarets through the creation of his first full-length musical based on Orwell's *1984*, Larson attended the inspirational words of Bertolt Brecht and Peter Brook as he used the popular theatre to spread "truth among the greatest number." Although, or perhaps because, *1984* and his next work *Superbia* garnered little commercial support, Larson was encouraged to work outside of the box, facilitating an independence that resulted in a "rock monologue." When the idea for *Rent* was brought to him by playwright Billy Aronson, Larson eagerly took on the project, which had the potential to combine his dual goals. Aronson and Larson soon parted ways, but Larson worked on *Rent* for six years, honing his skills as both a composer/lyricist and a social commentator.

In 1997, no Pulitzer Prize was awarded for drama and no explanation was provided. (The nominated finalists were *Collected Stories* by Donald Margulies, *The Last Night of Ballyhoo* by Alfred Uhry, and *Pride's Crossing* by Tina Howe.) In 1998, however, the Committee returned to recognize the brilliant commentary of Paula Vogel and *How I Learned to Drive*. According to Paula Vogel, if theatre is to capitalize on its unique potential to create an immediate and meaningful exchange between theatre artists and audiences, then it must foster sites of resistance that arise from grappling with difficult issues and experimenting with dramaturgical structures.

Ann Linden examines Vogel's explorations of the political dialogues focused on such highly charged issues as domestic violence and pedophilia. She considers the effectiveness of the plays in terms of their ability to inspire critical discussion through their discouragement of empathetic identification. Whether Vogel is reconsidering another author's work or responding to an element of the current political climate, her personal response to the topic at hand and her desire to experiment with formal elements combine to consistently create plays that Vogel hopes will confront "the disturbing questions of our time" and force us to do the same.

The 1999 Pulitzer Prize inspired a certain amount of hushed criticism as it recognized the very first (and, to date, only) play of Margaret Edson. So what was it that inspired a kindergarten teacher, who had never written a play, to rent an apartment, install a desk, and sit down for the sole purpose of writing a play? The answer is the play itself, for it was "this particular play" that fueled the effort—only this play and none since.

According to Mead Hunter, a series of jobs and interests helped to frame *Wit*. Edson had spent time in the medical profession, mostly in positions that facilitated her observation, and she was a teacher, albeit of a different nature than her central character, and she had a certain familiarity with John Donne. So, Edson researched all of these areas and added the information she had assembled to the story she saw so clearly in her head and wanted others to see on the stage. Still, according to Edson the circumstances and details of that story could all be different, the play after all, is only "about redemption."

Donald Margulies had been a nominated finalist twice in the ten years prior to his receipt of the Pulitzer in 2000. In his chapter, Jerry Patch notes that the play for which Margulies won the Pulitzer, *Dinner with Friends*, "is best viewed as the most recent piece of an evolving mosaic of plays, one with some common thematic threads but an ad hoc variety of styles and strategies." Truly the study of Margulies' career reveals a search for an artistic identity; it is a journey that reflects the impression made on Margulies by writers ranging from Arthur Miller to Franz Kroetz.

While Margulies experimented with an assortment of styles—a mock-musical, stylized naturalism, flights of fancy and realism—he developed his voice as he defined his personal identity. Using his family and their community as the basis for much of his work, Margulies wrote first with the voice of the son about his experiences as a child. *Heartbreaker*, a play written in the mid-1980s with an autobiographical inspiration, likely represented a point at which Margulies the artist reflected the maturation of Margulies the man. (This play later became *Sight Unseen*.) As Margulies has said, "The canvas became bigger because my perspective on the themes is broader" (2001).

Margulies writes from the perspective of an outsider, but like Neil Simon, he is one of the more "mainstream" playwrights of his decade to win the award. Margulies writes from what he knows, with first inspirations and drafts that are heavily steeped in personal experience. But as the plays develop, over weeks or even decades, evolving in their own lives or paving the way to a new work, Margulies broadens their context and their appeal, creating complex explorations of moral questions and cultural conundra.

So why do Margulies, Vogel, Albee, Wilson, and Kushner write plays? Why do these writers not churn out Pulitzer Prize–winning short stories or novels? Many of these writers cite inspiration from writers of other forms; most admit to trying their hand at poetry or fiction. But they write plays because they are driven by a love of the form, sometimes instilled through early childhood trips to the stage, sometimes through an innate recognition of the extraordinary power of the live theatre, always, as Horton Foote puts it, through a profound "inclination toward dialogue (2000)." For these artists, the words and images spinning in their minds already exist as living, breathing beings that must be embodied as such. Overall, the reasoning is remarkably simple. As Edward Albee says, "I write plays because I'm a playwright. I think like a playwright, I walk like a playwright, I smell like a playwright and I write like a playwright (2001)."

Despite their commitment and, truly, their success, these writers continue to face creative struggles: fighting for those first words; finessing the last few. They are challenged by the extent of their creative inspiration. In their interviews, included here separately or incorporated into the individual chapters, they talk of the challenge of getting their stories out of their heads, of digging the good play out of the mass on the paper—and they revel in the struggle. As Foote says, "I just sometimes don't think I'm alive unless I'm writing." Paula Vogel sees a truly unique challenge in writing for the stage:

> I actually think of writing for the stage as *not* writing. I think one writes fiction or poems, but playwriting is really about not writing. It's about structuring, about gaps between the language that are really filled in by the collaborators and the process. It's all about indirection rather than direct statement. It's about not writing. (2001)

Truly, the theatre offers an experience to its creative artists that few other art forms can match. As August Wilson describes:

> It's unique. Of all the written art forms, film, short fiction, poetry, all the great art forms, theatre is unique among them. And I think the thing that's most exciting for me is the audience in the sense that if you write a novel, you may get on the bus, for instance and see some one reading the novel. But that is a solitary act. People read novels on buses, trains, in their bedrooms, their bathrooms. That's a solitary act.

> With a play and an audience it's like having 700 people read your novel at the same time. And I just found that so exciting in that it's a communal experience as opposed to a solitary experience. That's intriguing (2001).

If there is disappointment with the creative world among these writers, it has to do with the state of the American theatre and the place of playwrights in it. (Words such as "wasteland" and "moribund" are abundant in their considerations of the commercial theatre.) Many of the playwrights expressed tremendous concern regarding a lack of opportunity for writers to develop new plays. (In the first half of this past decade, new play development dropped nearly seventy percent.[1]) August Wilson feels that the prevalent attitudes are extremely dangerous to playwrights.

> The trend has generally been to do new plays on the second stage and to give your main stage to productions of Chekhov and Moliere and Shakespeare. I think it should be the exact opposite. If doing a play on the second stage stigmatizes the playwright by signifying that he's not going to be as good as Tennessee Williams or Arthur Miller, that he doesn't deserve the main stage, then that puts all of us in a place where we're not going to write "main stage" writing because we've already been relegated to the second stage. So good, bad or indifferent, this is the play, this is where we are and the playwrights should have access to the stages of the American theatre irrespective of whether they are as good as Arthur Miller or some others. This is what we've got and we still deserve the stages.

Speaking from personal history, these established writers recognize the essential need of playwrights to have productions—and not just readings or workshops—of new plays. But then even with such opportunities, they express concern regarding the "creative environment" in which the playwrights are forced to function. As Albee says:

> They're trying to turn playwrights into the same kind of employees that they've turned movie script writers into—at the beck and call of the director and actors and the producer to alter things if they think that will be more commercial. That's one of the awful things that's happening to playwrights. Even though we have the protection of the Dramatists Guild in our contract, playwrights are still being urged and pushed to compromise, to simplify, to over clarify, to make plays pleasant rather than unpleasant, to use Shaw's phrase. (2001)

Kusher also bemoans the way in which the pressure of pursuing production impacts on the creative process: "In a way, the ruthless demands of stage-time, of modern attention spans, forces all of us playwrights toward the epigrammatic and terse, toward a classical severity; right now I'm hacking page after page off *Homebody* [Kushner's most recent play]."

Certainly many of these playwrights, during the course of their career, have experienced the pressure Albee and Kushner describe or the disenfranchisement inspired by a theatre that prefers dead playwrights. Despite their potential to contribute valuable insight into a production, playwrights are often ignored. Donald Margulies remembers clearly his first Broadway experience with *What's Wrong with the Picture?*:

> If it had been a good production, things might have been different. But it wasn't a good production. It happened on its own scheme, its own terms, and I was rendered essentially ineffectual. I had very little voice or clout; mostly I felt like I was hanging out during rehearsal and previews. (2001)

The extent of the abandonment is frightening and the exceptions are few. But when those exceptions come, they are deeply welcomed, even by the most lauded of playwrights. When the Signature Theatre in New York selected Horton Foote's work to be the focus of their 1993/1994 season, Edward Albee sent him this letter (Foote 1995, xii):

> Dear Horton,
>
> Welcome to the club! You will most probably have a frightening experience with the Signature Theatre Company this coming season.
>
> You will discover that you are working with eager, dedicated, talented, resourceful, gentle and thoughtful people whose main concern will be making you happy. This will be frightening.
>
> Even more, they will succeed in making you happy. This will be even more fightening.
>
> Don't fret about it; just go with it. Have a wonderful season.
>
> Regards,
Edward Albee

Once the production has opened, the seas become even more treacherous in the intensely commercial environment described by Robert Schenkkan:

There's very little meaningful support for new work. It's extremely difficult to get a play produced. If it does not go brilliantly in its first incarnation, the chances of a second are diminished further. To a playwright, the
importance of journalistic criticism to the success of a play is crucial. In
fact, the playwright is very vulnerable to dramatic criticism. It definitely
can impact the success of a play whereas the same is not true of a film
which has a wide opening and as often as not doesn't really depend on the
critical success in order to have commercial success. It's also very difficult,
even if you are very successful, to make enough of an income on a regular
basis to support yourself and a family which means that most writers are
forced into a second career of some sort like teaching. Its a fairly discouraging business that requires a fairly strong stomach. (2001)

Vogel recognizes an even more acute problem for women writers
and writers of color:

I see us taking a step back, primarily with George W. Bush's election. I see
it as a constant struggle which I don't see it getting any better, which distresses me, dismays me. I'm aware that I was possibly the only woman
produced in the last couple of years in theatre companies and that's not a
good thing. I have to say that I also feel like I'm back to square one with
the next play that I do. I think that by and large women playwrights are
not given the same leeway in terms of developing different muscles that,
say, the critics may give a David Mamet.

Women and writers of color are still seen as threats because in
essence, when a woman or a writer of color is defining a play world,
there's another definition of what our society is, and that's very threatening. I think it's always going to be very hard won. I'm hoping it changes,
but I think what has to happen is that the supply of women writers and
writers of color has to increase so that there's a greater demand. I think
the supply always comes first. (2001)

Wasserstein notes, "there are playwrights and they are male. And then
there are women playwrights, black playwrights. . . ."(2001).

For many of these reasons almost all of these Pulitzer playwrights
have played in the world of film and television through adaptations of
their work or independently conceived projects. The appeal is clear and
hasn't changed in seventy years, as Schenkkan notes:

> To read the journals of writers in the 30s and 40s who toiled as play-wrights to make a living, it's very similar to what I hear today: Their most fervent wish seems to be that they can sell the rights of their plays to the movies for a large enough sum to support their playwriting habit for a couple of years. (2001)

Vogel reiterates: "The economic reality is that either one teaches or one writes for other media in order to stay in theatre (2001)."

Still, these writers stick with the stage because, as Margulies says, "it's where my voice can still be the purest it can be as a dramatic writer (2001)." Perhaps it's just the relativity. Neil Simon notes:

> I've found the process of working on a play much more in keeping with the way I wanted to work. I wanted to have more control over my mate-rial than I would have had if I had only done film. When you make a film, you are always listening to the people who run the studio. And there are countless numbers of them on each picture. When you're doing a play, it's basically you and the director. (2000)

Margulies agrees: "Film and television are corporate endeavors that don't allow the purity of the artist's voice to come through. The theatre is a writer's medium completely albeit maybe a dying one" (2001).

All of these playwrights are deeply concerned for the future of their craft. Horton Foote says, "Playwrights increasingly are faced with dimin-ishing audience and places to have their plays done or to make a living at their craft. And it's not heartening (2000)." Even the audiences who do come, often weaned on television, have what Kushner describes as "little patience" for challenging work, making it "hard to be difficult in the the-atre." He notes, however, "that we could create a bigger audience for hard work if we had decent free public education. If we taught people how to read (2001)." Albee agrees that we must "create an audience that wants to see plays that are not destroyed by commerce (2001)." In fact, he demands an overhaul of the entire theatrical community:

> You have to have critics who urge people to see plays that matter. You have to have brave producers who want to do the play that the play-wright wrote. You have to have actors who are more interested in the work rather than themselves. You need a whole bunch of changes that I'm not holding my breath about. (2001)

In the meantime, these writers write, and despite the extraordinary level of recognition their work has achieved, the pressure and stress do not abate: As Margules notes:

> Whenever I start something new I'm filled with the same terror I experienced when I first set out to write plays. That doesn't go away. You don't become imbued with confidence with recognition and success. In fact, it's more terrifying: more pressure, more expectations, you imagine people standing there with their arms folded, waiting. (2001)

August Wilson agrees:

> All those awards, all that stuff, I take them and I hang them on my wall. But then I turn around and my typewriter's sitting there, and it doesn't know from awards. I always tell people I'm a struggling playwright. I'm struggling to get the next play down on paper. You start at the beginning each time you sit down. Nothing you've written before has any bearing on what you're going to write now. It's like a heavyweight fighter. You've gotta go and knock the guy out. It doesn't matter if you're undefeated. There's another guy standing there, and you have to go out again, and you have to duck his punches and do all the rest of whatever it is you do. (Rothstein 1990, A&L 1)

* * *

If you would like your produced play considered for a Pulitzer Prize, you need only ask a friend to sponsor you and to send in the appropriate paperwork. The entry form is very straightforward, asking for name, address, occupation, and place of birth for the writer, and a check in the box for the category in which the work should be considered (distinguished fiction, distinguished play, distinguished book, etc.). The form must be accompanied by a biography and photograph of the playwright and fifty dollars. (Please note that photocopied entry forms are not acceptable.)

You must also send six copies of the play itself. These will be read by a panel of four critics and one academic who will consider your play along with others submitted and others the committee members themselves deem worthy. They read them all *and* attend performances of the plays both in New York and regionally. The award in drama is given to a playwright, but the quality of the production is also weighed in the final decision.

This panel will narrow the competitive field and present to the Pulitzer Board three nominations for the award. (The list of "runner-ups" in the past decade includes, among others, John Guare, Maria Irene Fornes, AR Gurney, Anna Deavere Smith, David Mamet, Richard Greenberg, and Suzi-Lori Parks.) The panel may present its nominations equally or may, in writing, offer the preferences of the panel. The seventeen members of the Pulitzer Board, made up primarily of academics and journalists, must have both read the play and seen a production (live or on videotape) in order to be eligible to vote. For two days, following receipt of the nominations, the Board deliberates and debates. One week after the Board completes its work in the award categories, the winners are announced.

In theory, your chances are as strong as the next writer's. But the competition over the 82 years of Pulitzer Awards has been keen. Fifty-four individual writers have been awarded the prize and several teams of writers (mostly for musicals) have also won. A few writers have won more than once: August Wilson, Thornton Wilder, George S. Kaufman, and Tennessee Williams each won twice. Edward Albee and Robert Sherwood each won three times, and Eugene O'Neill won four Pulitzer Prizes. In twelve individual years, no Pulitzer Prize was awarded in Drama; five of those were between 1963 and 1972; one was in 1997. In 1963, the top contender, *Who's Afraid of Virginia Woolf?* was considered by the Board to be "insufficiently uplifting," a response most likely engendered by its sexual and violent undertones. Thirty years later, with the award to Tony Kushner for *Angels in America: Millennium Approaches*, a revised Board had become less provincial.

It is, of course, possible that your play will not be selected. Then, you must return to your keyboard and try to find solace in the belief that you were just barely edged out by Wendy Wasserstein or August Wilson, by Neil Simon or Robert Schenkkan, Tony Kushner or Edward Albee, Horton Foote or Jonathan Larson, Paula Vogel or Margaret Edson. Or even Donald Margulies—himself a runner-up twice before.

Note
1. See "Theatre Facts," *American Theatre*, 1994, insert.

Works Cited

Albee, Edward. Interview conducted by Joan Herrington. 2001.

Albee, Edward. 1980 The World is Beginning to Resemble Her Art. *Art News,* 79.5, May, 99–101.

Foote, Horton. 1995. Introduction to *The Young Man from Atlanta.* New York: Penguin Books.

Foote, Horton. Interview conducted by Crystal Brian, 2000.

Kushner, Tony. Interview conducted by Framji Minwalla, 2001.

Lind, Michael. Defrocking the Artist. *The New York Times Book Review.* 14 March 1999: 39.

Margulies, Donald. Interview conducted by Jerry Patch, 2001.

Rosen, Carol. August Wilson: Bard of the Blues. *Theater Week* 27 May, 1996: 18–35.

Rothstein, Mervyn. 1990. Round five for a theatrical heavyweight. *The New York Times,* 15 April, Arts and Leisure Section, 1 & 8.

Schenkkan, Robert. Interview conducted by Tom Bryant, 2001.

Simon, Neil. Interview conducted by Bette Mandl, 2000.

Wasserstein, Wendy. Interview conducted by Angelika Czekay, 2001.

Wilson, August. Interview conducted by Joan Herrington, 2000.

Vogel, Paula. Interview conducted by Ann Linden, 2000.

"NOT HAVING IT ALL": WENDY WASSERSTEIN'S UNCOMMON WOMEN

Angelika Czekay

[F]eminism gave me the right to find my own voice. . . . [F]eminism gave me the perspective to see that there weren't enough women's voices being heard. It gave me the belief that my own voice was worth hearing. And that there could be many different women's voices, all that could and should be heard.

—Wendy Wasserstein, "Yes I Am a Feminist . . ."

Though women are often said to write "small tragedies," they are our tragedies, and therefore large, and therefore legitimate. They deserve a stage.

—Wendy Wasserstein, *Interviews with Contemporary Women Playwrights*

My plays are generally about women talking to each other. The sense of action is perhaps different than if I had come of age as a male playwright.

—Wendy Wasserstein, *The Playwright's Art*

Wendy Wasserstein's five most famous plays, *Uncommon Women and Others* (1977), *Isn't It Romantic* (1981, revised 1983), *The Heidi Chronicles* (1988), *The Sisters Rosensweig* (1992), and *An American Daughter* (1997), which have all been produced on and off-Broadway, focus on female characters struggling with difficult personal and professional decisions in challenging, often transitional moments of their lives. The women Wasserstein places center stage are strong, intelligent, well educated, upper middle class, and frequently Jewish. They share her generation's convictions of and frustrations with the social movements and discourses of their times, which is why the author is often called the voice of her generation.

Wasserstein's plays are driven by character rather than plot, but the characters' experiences and conflicts are consistently set against current cultural and political developments. Thus, the characters are exposed as products of cultural and political history rather than results of personal choices. In particular, they can be read with regard to the history of feminism from the late 1960s to the late 1990s. The issue of "having it all"—the female characters' discovery that choosing a career over family invariably jeopardizes personal happiness—is the leitmotif of all of Wasserstein's plays. As the characters are torn between career ambition and personal fulfillment, in other words, *having* to choose either the one or the other, all of Wasserstein's plays also (implicitly or explicitly) engage in a critical dialogue with the women's movement on women's cultural and social positions.

Although Wasserstein has been much maligned by feminist critics for her problematic representations of the women's movement—particularly regarding her Pulitzer Prize–winning play, *The Heidi Chronicles*—a closer look into her major plays testifies to a feminist sensibility and sensitivity that have enabled and inspired her writing. Wasserstein's plays do not necessarily focus on explicitly feminist topics, but they are woman-conscious in their consistent treatment of women's conflicts. While Wasserstein rejects a clear-cut feminist label for herself, scholars, critics, and interviewers alike nonetheless tokenize her within the constraints of female authorship, an aspect that in itself places her within the discourse of gender politics.

In light of the small number of female playwrights in mainstream theatre or, more precisely, the comparatively small number of visible women playwrights in general, this relatively one-sided critical and scholarly categorization of Wasserstein is not surprising. However, Wasserstein is as famous for her feminism in mainstream circles as she is notorious for betraying it in certain feminist circles. From a materialist feminist perspective, several of Wasserstein's plays sell feminism out. Jill Dolan (1996, 50), for instance, astutely remarked that *The Heidi Chronicles* "narrates the uncomplimentary view of the feminist movement promoted by dominant culture." In this play, Wasserstein seems to locate the source of Heidi's problems in the failure of the women's movement to liberate her rather than in her own ambiguity towards the movement and the gender-biased dominant structures that oppress her.

In contrast, other feminist scholars, such as Gail Ciociola (1998), in her comprehensive book-length study of Wasserstein's work, have tried to expand definitions of feminism in order to recuperate Wasserstein. Ciociola offers the notion of "fem-en-actment," a "textual or performance drama that, guided by a feminist disposition, thematically *and* stylistically enacts situations of interest to women, the psychological and social effects of which form the core of that drama" (2). "Feminism," Ciociola suggests, has become "feminisms," a "myriad of different and sometimes conflicting ideas about how women define themselves and their needs" (3). According to her, Wasserstein "seems to favor a pluralistic blend of feminism, [revealing] signs of liberal, cultural, and materialist thinking, and as a whole [advancing] contemporary 'power feminism'" (3). While power feminism, according to Ciociola, promotes "ideas of equality and self-empowerment," it does so "without the benefit of a clear theoretical impulse" (7). It thus lacks a systemic analysis and fails to challenge dominant ideology or raise questions of access and privilege.

Rather than directly engaging in this debate and trying to either refute or recuperate Wasserstein as a feminist playwright, this chapter examines her plays as her ongoing dialogue and critical engagement with the women's movement. This dialogue is exposed through the experiences, conflicts, and choices of her female protagonists who grow in age from play to play and thus always remain of the same— Wasserstein's own—generation. Read chronologically, her plays give voice to upper middle-class women from the baby boomer generation. Born in the 1950s, they came of age in the uproar of the late 1960s, were caught between the two conflicting discourses of gender conservatism and women's liberation of the 1970s, moved through the major shifts of the feminist movement and the feminist backlash of the 1980s, and then arrived at what has been termed a postfeminist era in the 1990s. According to their age, the main characters in her earlier plays, *Uncommon Women* and *Isn't It Romantic,* concentrate on the hopes and outlooks for their futures. In contrast, the protagonists of her later plays, *The Sisters Rosensweig* and *An American Daughter,* tend to reflect, in retrospect, on past choices and directions their lives have taken (Savran 1999, 291). Set up as a flashback chronology and juxtaposing the forward and backward perspectives of its protagonist, *The Heidi Chronicles* formally occupies a place in between her earlier episodic plays and her later realist ones. Thus, as Wasserstein takes inventory of women's positions in society against the backdrop of the feminist movement throughout the past three decades, her characters reflect the gender politics of their times.

Furthermore, Wasserstein historicizes each play's present by integrating references from contemporary cultural, political, and feminist history. To mark the historicity of women's experiences, she juxtaposes different time periods, either by inserting flashbacks (as in *Uncommon Women*), by mapping out a chronology (as in *The Heidi Chronicles*), or by contrasting characters from different generations (as in *Isn't It Romantic*, *The Sisters Rosensweig*, and *An American Daughter*). This dramaturgy allows her to frame the personal within the larger context of the political and, thus, offers gendered experience as a historical category.

In this context, Wasserstein's use of comedy—critics call it her trademark—becomes a crucial stylistic means through which the characters express their social critique along with their personal emotions. Praised for their poignant wit, Wasserstein's plays are frequently described as funny with "serious undertones" (Wasserstein 1996, 383). While comedy makes her plays entertaining and, as Wasserstein suggests, fosters "a community with the audience" (386), it also allows her protagonists to vent their frustrations, anger, and pain in a socially acceptable form for women. Wasserstein imbues her characters with humor that, on the surface, deflects from their outrage but that also creates a visible subtext, which highlights the social and personal pressures they face. Thus, comedy in her plays often functions as a form of politicized speech, a distancing device that prevents the characters from being subsumed by self-pity or categorized as victims. Christopher Bigsby contends that Wasserstein uses comedy as "a way of taking the heat out of things," which, he suggests, "would seem to imply a disengagement" from the issues at hand. In contrast, Bigsby (1999, 342) stated, "her autobiographical element implies an engagement." He convincingly argued that "the tension between the two [aspects] is definitional of her work."

In many ways, Wasserstein's plays are based on her own life. As she remarked in an interview: "My plays tend to be semi-autobiographical or come out of something that's irking me" (Wasserstein 1996, 262). Many of her characters can be traced to the author's upbringing, her college experiences, and her family and friends. Several of the protagonists, such as Janie Blumberg and Heidi Holland, resemble Wasserstein herself in their perceptions and conflicts. Their thoughts, questions, and hesitations reflect the author's own observations and opinions of the current cultural and political climate. Likewise, Wasserstein has always regarded herself as an outsider, as do many of her characters, which is reflected in their position as somewhat removed from the plays' action (*Bachelor Girls* 1990, 194). As David Savran (1999, 290) put it in his introduction to an interview with the author, her main characters are "slightly detached from the world in which they move" and "as much spectator as actor."

The upper middle-class social milieu in which Wasserstein's plays are consistently set also reflects the author's experiences, since Wasserstein was privileged through her upper middle-class background and her Ivy League education. As Ciociola (1998) accurately pointed out:

> Wasserstein does not pretend to speak for all women. . . . Her main char-
> acters are not every woman, but college-educated and career-driven
> "uncommon women" determined to "fulfill their potential" even when
> they have not reached certainty about the direction of that potential. (3–4)

Born in Brooklyn in 1950, Wendy Wasserstein grew up on Manhattan's Upper East Side. Her parents regularly took the children to plays and musicals. Wasserstein attended the all-girls' Calhoun school and later the elite Mount Holyoke College as a history major. After graduating from Mount Holyoke in 1971, Wasserstein returned to New York and earned her M.A. in creative writing from the City University of New York (CUNY) in 1973, the same year during which her first play, *Any Woman Can't*, was read off-Broadway. Upon graduating from CUNY, Wasserstein rejected an offer from the Columbia School of Business and instead attended the Yale School of Drama where she wrote two satires that, like *Any Woman Can't*, signify early attempts to critically engage with dominant gender representations.

Originally produced in 1975 at Yale as Wasserstein's M.F.A. thesis production, *Uncommon Women and Others* was to become her first professional play. Wasserstein refined some of the gender-specific themes

and issues raised in her student plays by presenting an all-woman perspective to explore the impact of the rising women's movement on individual women's lives. The play is based on Wasserstein's own college
years and was inspired by her realization that women were not represented in theatre history:

> I remember when I first wrote *Uncommon Women*, which is a play about
> a reunion of Mount Holyoke graduates, I was a student at Yale and we
> were studying a lot of Jacobean drama. To me, basically, it was men kiss-
> ing the skulls of women and then dropping dead from their poison, and I
> thought to myself, "Gee, this is really not familiar to me. It's not within
> my realm of experience." I . . . thought, "I want to see an all-female cur-
> tain call in the basement of the Yale School of Drama." (1996, 264)

Episodic in structure, the play features a group of five female students
who meet for a reunion lunch at a New York restaurant in 1978, six years
after they have graduated from the all-women's college, Mount Holyoke.
They reminisce about their lives, compare former hopes and illusions to
later achievements and disappointments, and share their pasts, presents,
and futures. The restaurant encounter frames the play in the beginning
and the end, but most of the seventeen scenes take place in collective flashbacks to the characters' senior year at the college in 1972.

Uncommon Women is set against the backdrop of the radical political changes in the mid-1970s. The college scenes include numerous references to the political climate and popular culture of the time, from
Cambodia to Judy Collins, the Beatles, James Taylor, and EST. In particular, by featuring discussions about birth control, *Ms.* magazine, and
women's history classes, the play zooms in on this first generation of
female college students exposed to the newly burgeoning rhetoric of
feminists such as Friedan, Greer, and Millett. "*Uncommon Women*,"
Wasserstein (1998) said, "is in a way about feminism. It's . . . filtered
through the people who were participating in it at that time" (268). The
play captures the characters' perceptions and confusions during this
period when the "women's liberation movement" began to critique sexism, misogyny, and power relations in the patriarchy and challenged
women's traditional roles along with the conventional institutions of
marriage, motherhood, and family.

At the same time, as the play outlines, Mount Holyoke, founded in

1837 and originally conceptualized to give women the same access to education that young men had at Yale and Harvard, still trains women in proper behavior and "Gracious Living" with high tea hours and candlelight dinners. A male voice-over, citing the inaugural address of a former Mount Holyoke president and articles from the 1966/1967 college bulletin, opens most of the scenes to describe the college's traditional values: "The college produces women who are persons in their own right: Uncommon Women who as individuals have the dignity that comes with intelligence, competence, flexibility, maturity, and a sense of responsibility. This can happen without a loss of gaiety, charm, or femininity" (*Uncommon Women*, reprinted in Wasserstein 1991, 7). "They will be part-time mothers, part-time cooks, and part-time intellectuals (Wasserstein 1991, 23).

Simultaneously confronted with two conflicting ideologies, Wasserstein's college students have to negotiate a new stance for themselves without the privilege of having any role models. Through a range of characters, the college scenes depict the students' struggles to find and define their positions vis-à-vis the confusions and contradictions of the times, which, the play suggests, are the flip side of newly assumed attitudes of self-awareness and self-realization along with newly available professional options for women. On one end of the spectrum there is Kate, the overachieving career woman, who gets accepted into Harvard Law School after she graduates (Wasserstein 1991, 64). On the other end there is Samantha, the "prefeminist prototype, whose cheerful disposition and unassuming manner seem so suited for the traditional role of good wife" (Ciociola 1998, 29). As Wasserstein contended:

> The Women's Movement has had answers for the Kates of the world (she becomes a lawyer), or the Samanthas (she gets married). But for the creative people, a movement can't provide answers. There isn't a specific space for them to move into. (Wasserstein 1987, 424)

Consequently, Wasserstein places the other three of the five main characters, Holly, Muffet, and Rita, somewhere in the middle of the spectrum. With only vague dreams for the future, they remain undecided about what to do after they graduate. Rita, a radical feminist, summarizes the dilemma of her generation—and the play's main theme—when she says to Muffet on graduation day:

Well, God knows there is no security in marriage. You give up your anatomy, economic self-support, spontaneous creativity, and a helluva lot of energy trying to convert a male half-person into a whole person who will eventually stop draining you, so you can do your own work. And the alternative—hopping onto the corporate ladder—is just as self-destructive. If you spend your life proving yourself, then you just become a man, which is where the whole problem began, and continues. (Wasserstein, 1991, 66)

Rita's statement describes her future as a catch twenty-two situation and signifies the loss of a women's support system, which the play has so carefully laid out during the college scenes.[1] Being lifted out of the security of this female community after graduation, the individual woman gets catapulted into the reality of a male value system, which leaves her the alternative to either live with a man or "become" one. While feminist values, which the characters alternately embrace or challenge, have become part of their daily thought processes, they remain unclear on how to apply them to their future lives.

The college scenes are book-ended with the women's reunion in 1978 after about a decade of feminist activism and politics. With this framing device Wasserstein places the two perspectives and times into a dialogical and historical relationship, allowing the women to take inventory and compare their former outlooks at graduation with the turns their lives have taken in the ensuing years. Mount Holyoke had already discontinued "Gracious Living" when the women graduated in 1972 (Wasserstein 1991, 66), but six years after college, the women's lives have not taken earth-shattering courses and are still largely characterized by confusion and dissatisfaction. Each of them expresses that she is missing out on something because of the choices she made, either professionally or personally. Kate, for instance, now a successful lawyer, had to sacrifice her relationship because she is "committed to [her] work" (69). Samantha, living the most traditional lifestyle within the group, is still married and expecting a baby, but thinks she has not "done very much of anything important" (70). Holly has changed graduate schools twice and is now going for a master's degree in history, but is ultimately "still in transition" (9). Each of the women implicitly judges herself in light of "having it all." Together, the women represent retrospective facets of a feminist discourse, commonly established during their college years and perpetuated in their present lives, in which seemingly new career options were easily transmuted into self-imposed expectations of "having it all."

Nonetheless, during the reunion the women also rediscover a sense of community, which goes far above and beyond a sentimental "those were the days, my friend" nostalgia. They express a genuine, mutually accepting, and nonhierarchical support for each other's choices and a continued sense of solidarity and friendship. Like the first act, the play ends on a hopeful note, summarized by Rita's much quoted motto: "When we're forty we can be pretty fucking amazing . . . When we're . . . forty-five, we can be pretty fucking amazing" (Wasserstein 1991, 72). The predicted age for this personally and professionally fulfilled future, however, keeps being projected into the future. Wasserstein refrains from privileging one choice over another, celebrating instead women's increased rights to have choices. *Uncommon Women* represented a theatrical "landmark" with its exclusive portrayal of "contemporary women's issues" and perspectives off-Broadway (Balakian 1999, 217), highlighting "experiences that had never before been staged" (Cage 1988, 69).

While the subject position in *Uncommon Women* is multifaceted and represented through a spectrum of characters, in *Isn't It Romantic* (commissioned and first produced by the Phoenix Theatre in New York in 1981 and revised in 1983), Wasserstein recreates two of the characters from the earlier play and examines their lives after graduate school. She thus shifts the emphasis away from a group of women onto the individual. Janie Blumberg, the play's protagonist, is a Jewish, intelligent, plump, funny, but self-deprecating writer who resembles Holly from *Uncommon Women*. Harriet Cornwall, Janie's long-term friend from high school, resembles Kate in demeanor, attitude, and even looks. She is ambitious, career-oriented, and successful. Both characters are well-educated, upper middle class, and, similarly to the college graduates during their reunion meeting, in their late twenties.

The play, composed of two acts and a total of thirteen scenes, takes place in 1983 in different locations in Manhattan after Janie and Harriet have just moved back to their hometown. By exposing their struggles to negotiate their positions within inner as well as outside expectations—mainly revealed through interactions with their mothers and their boyfriends—Wasserstein returns to her exploration of women's self-definitions but adds themes of mother–daughter and male–female relationships. If the main characters in *Uncommon Women* are interpellated by conflicting discourses on a more abstract level, in *Isn't It Romantic*, Wasserstein personifies such discourses and contradictory messages through secondary characters and their articulation of expectations.

Accordingly, the structure and dramaturgy of *Isn't It Romantic* differ significantly from the earlier play. Instead of contrasting different time periods, *Isn't It Romantic* contrasts different locales, showing the characters in various circumstances, environments, and conversations. The enclosed, safe, and arguably utopian world of the dorm room, in which women *talk* about their pasts and futures, has been replaced by the outside "real world," in which they *live* the present. Both plays are episodic in structure, offering momentary insights into the characters' lives. *Isn't It Romantic,* however, shifts the focus from the subjective level, exposing experiences through the characters' perceived and told realities, memories, and thoughts, to a more objective one, displaying their actual experiences.

This shift in form moves the play closer to psychological realism in its effect and highlights the protagonist's struggle between internalized feminist values and outside demands. In an interview, Wasserstein explained:

> The play is about her [Janie's] difficulty in communicating. She is so verbal, and yet she can't talk. It's a play about speech—about the ability to speak and not to speak at the same time, which comes from the pressure women are under to be a good girl, a smart girl, and a warm girl simultaneously. (Wasserstein 1987, 420)

The play addresses the different psychological and social pressures imposed on Janie by introducing a number of personal relationships in which she at first looks like a ping pong ball bouncing back and forth between contradictory expectations until she gradually learns to resist them and liberate herself.

Tasha Blumberg, Janie's mother, for instance, modeled after Wasserstein's own mother, Lola, is incorrigible in trying to run her daughter's life. In contrast, Harriet's mother, Lillian, is a high-ranking businesswoman with little time for Harriet's personal life. While Tasha Blumberg is pushing Janie to start a family, Lillian is mainly concerned with her daughter's professional life. Lillian, however, knows that success has its price; she left her husband for her career. She cautions Harriet, who dreams of having a wonderful husband, children, and a career, that the notion of "having it all" is a fantasy of her daughter's generation (Wasserstein 1991, 133):

> You think the women who go back to work at thirty-six are going to have the same career as a woman who has been there since her twenties? You think that someone who has a baby and leaves it after two weeks to go back to work is going to have the same relationship with that child as someone who has been there all along? . . . You show me the wonderful man with whom you're going to have it all. You tell me how he feels when you take as many business trips as he does. You tell me who has to leave the office when the kid bumps his head on the radiator. . . . (134)

The contrast of the two generations and their different values and convictions allows Wasserstein to chart a double historical perspective on women's positions, which contrasts feminist ideals on the one hand with lived reality on the other. Thus, rather than explicitly engaging feminist debates, she integrates popular feminist rhetoric as an accepted public discourse "of Harriet's generation," against which the two mothers set their established lifestyles, their life experiences, and their opposite values. These are represented through Tasha's praises of the nuclear family and domesticity and Lillian's celebration of a career in which there is "no room for a man" (Wasserstein 1987, 423).

Ironically, though not surprisingly, both Janie and Harriet opt for the exact opposite of what their mothers foresee for their futures. Janie ultimately dumps "her mother's dream come true," the Jewish doctor she had been dating, but also the fulfillment of her own romantic desires. Harriet decides to marry a man she has only known for two weeks despite her earlier assertion that she "never respected women who didn't learn to live alone and pay their own rent" (Wasserstein 1991, 104). Although Janie feels betrayed and abandoned by her friend's ad hoc decision, she realizes that she made the right choice for herself. As the curtain closes, Janie tap dances, "beautifully, alone" (153). As in *Uncommon Women*, the play's ending suggests a celebration of women's choices and self-empowerment, although Janie's is less a choice that finds outside support than a wistfully isolated one. The women's community of the late 1970s has been replaced by the forced individualism of the 1980s, jeopardizing, the play suggests, friendships among women.

Although the play is focused on Janie's development as an individual, *Isn't It Romantic* represents a continuation of Wasserstein's dialogue with feminism and her increasingly ambivalent position. On the one hand, the play celebrates women's liberation and their independent choices. It critiques the sexism of the 1980s as well as the traditional expectations of women in their immediate environment of family and friends, who, for the most part, have not yet liberated their views. On the other hand, Wasserstein seems to attribute women's increased anxiety over "having it all" to the women's movement itself. "What's troublesome from my point of view about the Women's Movement," she said in an interview, "is that there are more check marks"(Wasserstein 1987, 420). Wasserstein critiques what she identifies as a shift from the rhetoric of liberation, suggesting that women *can* "have it all," to what she perceives as a prescription that they *must* "have it all."[2]

Wasserstein's equivocal representation of the women's movement reached its peak with the production of her most famous play, *The Heidi Chronicles*. Originally produced as a workshop by the Seattle Repertory Theatre in April 1988, the play moved to Playwrights Horizons in New York in December 1988. About three months later, it premiered at the Plymouth Theatre on Broadway, where it enjoyed a highly successful run and was soon granted numerous awards and prizes, including the Pulitzer and the Tony.

Over a decade after *Uncommon Women* had been praised for its groundbreaking "all-woman curtain call," *The Heidi Chronicles*, as the first Broadway-produced play on feminism, triggered heated controversies among critics and scholars with vehemently divided responses. While the mainstream patted itself on the back for accepting a supposedly feminist play first into the Broadway repertoire and then into the canon, feminist critics commented scathingly on its content and message and were equally infuriated by its celebratory reception in the mainstream.[3] Given such strong reactions, the play's content and its reception can hardly be disentangled. Yet, it seems safe to assume that had the play not towered on Broadway, with Heidi's lament "I feel stranded" echoing through the U.S. theatre world as *the*—not one—representation of feminism in the mainstream, reactions and critiques might have been more moderate. From today's perspective, over a decade after *Heidi* was initially staged, however, it perhaps matters less whether and for whom *Heidi* was or is a pro- or antifeminist play than what the play continues to represent.

The Heidi Chronicles traces the life of art history professor, Dr. Heidi Holland, through a quarter of a century: from her high school years during the students' movement in the mid-1960s, through the beginnings of feminism and consciousness-raising groups in the 1970s, to the careerism and yuppie lifestyle in the 1980s Reagan years. The chronology of the two-act play is framed through the opening prologues of both acts, which feature Heidi lecturing to her students at Columbia University, and the closing scene, showing her as a single mother with her adopted baby, all set in 1989, the play's present. The remaining ten scenes are arranged as chronological flashbacks and follow Heidi though different locations from 1965 to 1987 in two- to three-year intervals. On a formal level, *The Heidi Chronicles* is Wasserstein's most complex play.

Similarly to *Uncommon Women* and *Isn't It Romantic*, Wasserstein concentrates on moments of transition in the characters' lives. As in her previous plays, she focuses on her protagonist's observations, perceptions, and choices, but in *The Heidi Chronicles* she does so with more of an eye to the pivotal political and cultural developments that characterize twenty-five years of American and feminist history. The large leaps in time provide a more fragmentary vision of the characters' lives and, as Christopher Bigsby argued, "eliminate psychological development" (1999, 347), pointing instead to the larger social significance of the events portrayed and their impact on the characters. In contrast to both her earlier and her later plays, these jumps also defy a unified portrayal of a specific cultural *moment* in favor of a distinguished historical *period* and social *movement*.

By viewing the baby boomers from their teenage years to their forties, *The Heidi Chronicles* translates Wasserstein's statement that "people are products of the time in which they came of age," intertwining the personal with the political (Wasserstein 1996, 388). Changes in attitude and lifestyle are shown as being produced by shifting social and cultural values. Thus, the play chronicles cultural history and personal histories side by side, each commenting on and constructing the other. This double perspective—formally, quite an ambitious endeavor—allows Wasserstein to express her own sentiments on the developments of past decades through her characters, especially Heidi. However, as opposed to foregrounding her historicization of the past as individual and subjective, Wasserstein also pays careful attention to historical detail by inserting popular music, current fashion, and references to political and cultural events in order to evoke specific cultural moments. The problems are no longer presented as merely those of a single character but become representative of a whole generation, which adds a level of universality to the play's frame that disguises its subjective element and thus makes it so problematic and susceptible to criticism.

The prologue to the first act introduces Heidi as a feminist art historian invested in the excavation of artists left out of traditional historical accounts. Heidi uses the slides she presents to her students to segue into her own history, establishing the link between the personal and the political and framing subsequent scenes as a retrospective of personal memories. The first act, spanning the decade from the mid-1960s to the mid-1970s, demonstrates Heidi's involvement with contemporary political movements and outlines her encounters with male sexism on the one hand and emerging feminist politics on the other. It also introduces the main characters, Peter Patrone, a gay male pediatrician, and Scoop Rosenbaum, with whom Heidi has an affair early in the play. These men become Heidi's closest friends and her most sophisticated conversation partners. By introducing two male characters as her protagonist's "soul mates," Wasserstein deviates from her other works, in which intimate friendships are consistently displayed with other women.

One of the early scenes portrays Heidi's "visit"—both literal and symbolic—to a women's consciousness-raising group in Ann Arbor in 1970. This is Heidi's only direct encounter with organized feminism in the play and the only scene that displays a women's community. Wasserstein depicts this meeting by satirizing its rituals and rhetoric through ironic exaggeration. Given the scene's general tone, the meeting's actual conversations allude only tangentially to the important historical function of consciousness raising in this early phase of radical and liberal feminism. Fran, for instance, the only lesbian, is ridiculed and stereotyped. Her repeated phrase "either you shave your legs or you don't" (Wasserstein 1991, 178) serves as a radical feminist stand-in metaphor of women's resistance to male gender prescriptions. The phrase is contrasted to Heidi's "all people deserve to fulfill their potential" (181), summarizing her—and Wasserstein's—self-declared, middle-ground "humanism," with which she distances herself from the politics and rhetoric of the meeting (180).

In an essay in *Bachelor Girls* (1990), ironically entitled "The Razor's Edge," Wasserstein remembered her own participation in a consciousness-raising group in 1970, in which one of the women "simplified all political stances with one sweeping agenda. . . . 'Body hair is the last frontier.' The good . . . persons fell on the furry side" (137). While the remainder of Wasserstein's essay dealt with her own ambiguity toward body hair, she significantly chooses this one phrase to both ridicule early radical feminism and tokenize it within the play's only representation of lesbian sexuality. Likewise, she marks radical feminism as outside the realm of heterosexuality and thus as inapplicable to Heidi as a political stance. Given this isolated, derisive representation of the early women's movement, there is little surprise when the last two scenes of the first act depict Heidi as privileging her personal relationships with Peter and Scoop over her political alliances with women. In these last two scenes, Peter comes out to Heidi as gay and Scoop marries an unassuming housewife, so that the first act ends by completing the picture that "good men are either gay or married."

Act two explores the 1980s as a decade of individualism, ambitiousness, careerism, and materialism, which, as the play suggests, is a historical consequence of the preceding "me decade" (Ciociola 1998, 58). In particular, the act explores different variations on women who are "trying to have it all," replacing grassroots feminist politics of liberation, emancipation, and solidarity with materialism, consumerism, and ambitious professional lives. Heidi's high school friend, Susan, for instance, undergoes a metamorphosis from "shepherdess" for a women's health and legal collective in Montana to high-powered TV executive in L.A., adapting her attitudes, aspirations, and agenda according to the shifting cultural values around her. As she tells Heidi, "I'm not political anymore. I mean, equal rights is one thing, equal pay is one thing, but blaming everything on being a woman is just passé" (Wasserstein 1991, 226).

In the play's culminating moment, Heidi's luncheon alumnae speech, "Women, Where Are We Going?", addresses this loss of politics and sisterhood in a decade where trendy status and flashy appearance have become the primary values. Heidi starts out by inventing a fictive day in the life of Ms. Superwoman, who goes from work to an aerobics class, takes one of her children to a drawing-with-computers class, the other to a swimming-for-gifted-children lesson, prepares grilled chicken for her investment banker husband, writes ten pages of her new book, returns the leftover chicken to a church that feeds the homeless, and "does it" with her husband in the kitchen before turning off the light. What then follows is Heidi's real-life description of her experiences in a locker room before her own aerobics class, which portrays her as feeling self-conscious, inept, and isolated while eavesdropping on the conversations of three generations of women around her. She ends her speech abruptly with her often quoted and much criticized statement: "It's just that I feel stranded. And I thought the whole point was that we wouldn't feel stranded. I thought the point was that we were all in this together" (232).

Heidi's speech is based on Wasserstein's initial idea for the play:

> I wrote this play because I had this image of a woman standing up at a women's meeting saying, "I've never been so unhappy in my life." . . . Talking to friends, I knew there was this feeling around, in me and in others and I thought it should be expressed theatrically. (quoted in Mandl 1999, 6–7)

While Wasserstein correctly identifies a shift in social values and cultural development from one decade to the other, she fails to seek its causes in a system that so readily adopted and marketed the new career woman image and simultaneously tokenized feminism as the cause for the supposed crises of America's women.[4] Instead of analyzing the backlash against feminism as a result of the rhetoric of the Reagan years, Wasserstein attributes the problems to the failure of the women's movement, thereby subscribing to the dominant view promoted by the media in the 1980s.

Parallel to the end of act one, the play's final two scenes are dedicated exclusively to Heidi's personal relationship with her two male friends. Both scenes end with mutually nostalgic, intimately emotional moments, during which Heidi replaces the loss of sisterhood with the comfort of her male friends—in Peter's words, her "family" (Wasserstein 1991, 238). Her final encounter with Peter could signify a utopian moment, encompassing the notion of community through the symbolic expression of feminist alliances with gay males. However, within the play's construction of its protagonist's history alongside the history of the women's movement, there is a default solution in which Heidi seeks personal comfort—as opposed to political alliance—after feminism has failed her. The play's last moment shows Heidi in a rocking chair with her adopted Panamanian daughter, a dramaturgically unmotivated image that has provided much fodder for a feminist critique. Wasserstein, who had believed for almost a decade that her own "greatest regret of life" would be childlessness (Wasserstein 2000, 92), not surprisingly constructs a strong final image in which her protagonist finds personal fulfillment in traditional motherhood. Wasserstein does acknowledge that as a spectator, she too might "have gotten angry" at the play's final image, but ultimately thought that adoption "was the right choice . . . for Heidi as a person" (Wasserstein 1995, 267).

Feminist criticism has targeted *The Heidi Chronicles* not only for its ending but also for its essentialist representation of women and women's communities, Heidi's condescending attitude about other women characters, her indecisiveness and victim status, and Wasserstein's unfavorable representation and indictment of the women's movement (Cianciola 1998, 73–80). Even from today's perspective, the play is problematic because of its high visibility and representational value as well as its integration into the canon of dramatic works. In her review of the original Plymouth Theatre production in New York, Gayle Austin (1990) cautioned:

> The biggest danger to women posed by the play is its future influence. As *Heidi* enters the canon of plays that are widely produced, it will be published, anthologized, criticized, and taught as a prime example of the work of a woman playwright. . . . Scenes from the play will echo through audition halls for decades to come. The "I thought we were all in this together" monologue will be memorized and repeated, enacted and absorbed by thousands of aspiring young actresses. In this way, the play will become part of a system that oppresses women and so highly rewards their creative expressions when they aid in its purposes. (108)

Wasserstein acknowledges critiques such as Austin's, but suggests that the problem lies less in her individual representation of feminism in *The Heidi Chronicles* than in commercial underrepresentations of plays by women: "One woman . . . can't write that one play, that one movie. You can't put that kind of weight on something. . . . There should be more plays by and about women . . . Suddenly you become a spokesperson . . . (Wasserstein 1999, 303).

Like Gayle Austin, Wasserstein is uneasy with the fact that *The Heidi Chronicles* may become a tokenized symbol of feminist theatre and promotes the production of more plays by women in order to amplify a diversity of women's voices and experiences.

Nonetheless, in her next two plays, *The Sisters Rosensweig* and *An American Daughter*, Wasserstein reacts to the vehement feminist criticism of *The Heidi Chronicles* by constructing stronger and older female characters. Unlike the younger characters in her earlier plays who are actively engaged in the quest for "having it all" in their futures, her protagonists in these last two plays reevaluate their pasts and the resulting personal and professional achievements in the present. In *The Sisters Rosensweig*, the author examines yet another version of sisterhood, both literally and symbolically, but ties her exploration of gender identity to questions of ethnicity, cultural heritage, and assimilation. In contrast to her first three works, this play, written and set in the early 1990s, concentrates on mature, middle-aged, established women at critical moments of reflection and transition, as they sort through their lives and identities. While they share the contemplation of their futures with their earlier counterparts, these older characters more frequently ask questions regarding their past decisions.

In addition, the play deviates in form and dramaturgy from Wasserstein's earlier episodic style, which portrays its protagonists through snapshot images. *The Sisters Rosensweig*, realist in form, "complete with unities of time, place, and action," is set in the traditional living room (*The Sisters Rosensweig* 1993, ix). Metaphorically, Wasserstein replaces her previous heroines' changes of locations with inner journeys and reflections. The author explained her aspirations:

> *The Sisters Rosensweig* seems a combination of *Isn't It Romantic* and
> *Uncommon Women*. But those other plays are episodic, and this was a deliberate decision not to be episodic. Also, I decided not to write another play
> about my generation. Even though it has autobiographical materials, the
> focus of the play is not me. I wanted to do all those things and also evoke a
> fondness for plays that I love, including Chekhov. (Wasserstein 1997b, 169)

Like *The Heidi Chronicles*, *The Sisters Rosensweig* was a major Broadway success. The play was originally produced in a workshop before it opened in April 1992 at the Seattle Repertory Theatre. In October 1992, it was revised and staged at the Lincoln Center, before it moved to the Barrymore Theatre on Broadway in March 1993, where it ran over 500 times. While the play's self-consciously employed form of

Chekhovian realism, its quick-witted comedy, and its focus on family relations make it accessible and entertaining to mainstream audiences, Wasserstein's choice of characters and conflict testifies to her continuing gender awareness. *The Sisters Rosensweig* broke theatrical ground by concentrating on a nontraditional cast of three middle-aged women. Aware of the representational impacts of her success, the author commented:

> Feminism has affected me more in my writing than in a specifically political way. Sitting down to write a play that has three parts for women over forty, I think, is political. . . . *The Sisters Rosensweig* had the largest advance in Broadway history, therefore nobody is going to turn down a play on Broadway because a woman wrote it or because it's about women. (Wasserstein 1997b, 172)

Set over the course of a weekend in August 1991, the two-act play features three upper-class Jewish sisters from Brooklyn who pursued very different lifestyles and now meet in London to celebrate the fifty-fourth birthday of the eldest. Wasserstein may not have wanted to write another play about her generation, but the play's characters are nonetheless largely modeled on her and her two older sisters (Franklin 1997, 67). Sara Goode, in whose apartment the action takes place, emigrated to London with her daughter, Tess, five years previously to leave her Jewish-American heritage behind. For this purpose she has kept her English last name from one of her two ex-husbands, assumed a British accent, and named her daughter after the English novel *Tess of the D'Urbervilles*. As the first woman to run a Hong Kong Bank, she is a successful, efficient businesswoman but has basically given up on any serious romantic involvements. Her sister Gorgeous, a practicing Jew, is forty-six and married to an unemployed attorney. She supports her husband and children by hosting a radio show in the United States. The youngest sister, Pfeni, forty, has had a somewhat casual relationship with a bisexual theatre director. She is a journalist, a "wandering Jew" (*The Sisters Rosensweig* 1993, 103), who flew in from Bombay for the birthday celebration. Much of the play revolves around the women's relationships with each other and with the men in their lives, but concentrates on the sisters' spiritual journeys of coming to terms with themselves, each other, and their Jewish heritage.

Wasserstein locates this reconciliation in the family history, the celebration of common memories, and the growing bond between the sisters.

Moreover, in contrast to previous works, Wasserstein wanted to end a play with the outlook of a successful relationship as opposed to showing her heroine alone when the curtain closes (Wasserstein 1996, 386). Thus, she provides the fifty-four-year-old Sara with a sweeping love affair, thus undermining the intersecting stereotypes of age and gender.

Wasserstein also recycles the generational contrast from *Isn't It Romantic* to underpin the historicity of Sara's past by having Tess write "biographies of [her] parents' early years for [her] school summer project" (*The Sisters Rosensweig* 1993, 4). She collects her mother's and aunts' memories, which for her signify important personal, cultural, and historical testimony. Tess's character also resonates with the search for identity. At the end of the play, she asks Sara: "Mother, if I've never really been Jewish, and I'm not actually American anymore, and I'm not English or European, then who am I?" (106). Wasserstein has often considered herself an outsider, which made it crucial for her to write a play about Jewish identity:

> I had the idea for *The Sisters Rosensweig* while I was living in London, writing *The Heidi Chronicles*. I guess while I was there I felt very much American and very much Jewish and ethnic. And a lot of my life—going to Mount Holyoke and Yale—has been sort of being a Jew within . . . an outsider. (Wasserstein 1996, 384).

In a final bonding moment with Tess, Sara responds to her daughter's school interview questions: "My name is Sara Rosensweig. . . . I was born in Brooklyn, New York" (107). Sara's statement highlights her reconciliation with her past and her heritage as parts of her identity. By foregrounding ethnicity along with gender, Wasserstein takes her exploration of women's identities and positions a step beyond that of her earlier plays. While Wasserstein always integrates Jewish characters, none of the early plays focus on cultural heritage as a crucial aspect of defining identity.[5]

Wasserstein's next play, *An American Daughter*, was first produced as a workshop at the Seattle Repertory Theatre, before it simultaneously opened in April 1997 in Seattle and at the Lincoln Center on Broadway to mixed reviews. Like *The Sisters Rosensweig*, *An American Daughter* is a well-made realist play, divided into two acts with four scenes each. It focuses on middle-aged, professionally and personally established characters and takes place over the course of two weekends in September 1994. While *The Sisters Rosensweig* outlines family relationships only in their personal aspects, however, *An American Daughter* skillfully combines the private and the public, the personal and the political spheres, thereby adding a critical political dimension. The plot revolves around the protagonist Lyssa Dent Hughes's nomination for Surgeon General and its ensuing scandal. As Wasserstein indicates in the play's preface:

> My intention with *An American Daughter* was not to overhaul but to widen the range of my work: to create a fractured fairy tale depicting both a social and a political dilemma for contemporary professional women. In other words, if Chekhov was the icon of *The Sisters Rosensweig*, then Ibsen would be the postfeminist muse of *An American Daughter*. (*An American Dughter* 1997, viii)

Similarly to its predecessor, the play is set in the living room, traditionally characterized as realism's private, but also as women's domestic, sphere. In this play, however, it is redefined to provide a link as well as a juxtaposition between the private and the public, signified through the invasion of various press representatives as well as a TV interviewer, complete with his camera team. "If Lyssa were a man," Claudia Barnett (1997) argued, "this play might be set in an office or a restaurant," but although the play's focus is on her as a public figure, Lyssa "never leaves her home" (520). In her role as mother and wife, she is pushed to the margins off-stage (the kitchen, the dining room, and the upstairs), but even in her public persona she is confined to the domestic space of her home (the living room), which still situates her within dominant gender constraints.

An American Daughter is a play of ideas, "a deliberate mix of genres and disciplines" (Frank 1999, 161). It is also Wasserstein's least autobiographical work (*An American Daughter* 1997, xi). The play examines the gender politics and biases in the post (liberal) feminist 1990s when women had supposedly achieved equal access to education and equal rights to top-notch careers, including political ones, and thus offers a new angle on the "having it all" theme. Rather than focusing on her protagonist's negotiation of an either/or choice, *An American Daughter* illustrates the professional struggles of a heroine who already "has it all," thereby questioning the very notion on both a societal and personal level. Lyssa is a self-confident, ambitious, and career-oriented female character somewhat familiar through such characters as Kate (*Uncommon Women*) and Lillian Cornwall (*Isn't It Romantic*). However, Wasserstein's earlier plays relegated the Lillian Cornwalls to secondary characters who lost or sacrificed their personal relationships with men for their careers.

In contrast, *An American Daughter* casts a follow spot on a female character who has both a successful career *and* a family and who, as the daughter of the conservative senator from Indiana and the great-grand-daughter of U.S. President Ulysses S. Grant, is also a public figure. An advocate of healthcare reform and a promoter of pro-choice reproductive rights, Lyssa is forty-two when she is nominated by a Democratic president to become Surgeon General. The play highlights the gender bias and media coverage of her nomination, which is jeopardized when a casual remark by first her husband and then by the family's archconservative, gay male friend Morrow reveals to the press that Lyssa ignored an earlier jury duty notice. In addition, she herself makes a seemingly derogatory public remark about her mother as being "the kind of ordinary Indiana house-wife who took pride in the icebox cakes and cheese pimento canapés" (*An American Daughter* 1997, 45). Opinion polls indicate that this off-hand comment turns the women in the heartland against her. After two disas-trous television interviews irreparably damage her public image, Lyssa withdraws her name from the nomination at the end of the play.

An American Daughter foregrounds the gender politics surrounding women in public office and contains numerous allusions to recent polit-ical events. In her preface to the written text, Wasserstein indicates that the play was inspired by the "nannygate" affair surrounding the attor-ney general nominee, Zoe Baird, during the first months of the Clinton administration. When she was discovered to have hired illegal aliens for childcare, Zoe Baird withdrew her name from consideration for the position (*An American Daughter* 1997, ix). In an interview, Wasserstein attributed the critiques of Baird's mistake to the gender bias that high-powered, publicly known women face:

> I'm not exactly clear how it's different from men, but I think it is. Look at Zoe Baird. Women resented her when it came out that she had a nanny, and she wasn't paying Social Security taxes. Do they even ask men these questions? There's this perception that some women just have too much. (Berson 1997)

Wasserstein also cited Hillary Clinton, then wife of the presidential nominee, who had publicly stated that she did not want to "stay at home and bake cookies" as an inspiration for this play (*An American*

Daughter 1997, ix). Ms. Clinton was critiqued for being arrogant and condescending, and her next public appearance showed her wearing a headband and dutifully holding her husband's hand (ix).

Wasserstein points to the double standard with which women in the public eye are measured and spectacularized when Lyssa—like Hillary—is judged on her attitude, appearance, and privileged status as opposed to her knowledge and abilities as a health expert. Thus the misplaced court notice for jury duty is less the reason for her downfall than the remark she made about her mother. As her husband, Walter, astutely points out to her:

> It's the women of America who are furious with you, Lizard. You're pretty, you have two great kids, you're successful, you're admired, you're thin, and you have a great soul. Face it, Lizard, in the heartland that means you're one prissy privileged ungrateful-to-her-mother, conniving bitch. (*An American Daughter* 1997, 64)

Rather than placing the blame exclusively on the "ordinary Indiana housewives," however, which would arguably be problematic in terms of the play's representation of class and class distinction, Wasserstein indicts the media and their perpetuation of a female image that represents *"being it all."* As the incident and the national scandal that follows it make clear, for a woman, success is defined as professional expertise *in addition to* her traditional domestic responsibilities as wife and mother. Consequently, the spin doctor whom Lyssa's father hires to coach her for her final television interview instructs her to construct a self-image for the cameras in which she comes across as a working mom who has "great family values" (*An American Daughter* 1997, 66). Lyssa agrees to "wear feminine attire" and a headband for the TV cameras (70), but in the interview's final furious moments, she stands up for her beliefs even if it costs her the nomination. To the interviewer's relentless questions, Lyssa responds by addressing the media's incitement against women in public office:

> There's nothing quite so satisfying as erasing the professional competency of a woman, is there? . . . And anyway, it would be all right if she were a man and cold. That man would be tough. No one would give a damn what he felt about his mother! But a woman? A woman from good schools and a good family? That kind of woman should be perfect! And if she manages to be perfect, then there is something distorted and condescending about her. (92)

Lyssa's unwillingness to give up her principles in order to put a positive spin on her media persona, constructed along dominant gender prescriptions, critiques liberal politics along with the double standard of a society that is still reluctant to accept a woman's access to power and political office. In the play's final moment, Lyssa resorts to going upstairs, a space that has been represented by the disembodied voices of her children up to this point. This act indicates her withdrawal into her family, but rather than signifying a defeat it reflects Lyssa's intent to "rise and continue" (105).

As in her other plays, Wasserstein contrasts her protagonist to several other women characters who provide variations on the desire to "have it all." Quincy Quince, an opportunistic, flashy journalist in her late twenties, represents a shift towards a neofeminist attitude during the 1990s. As author of the bestseller, *The Prisoner of Gender*, Quincy turns gender consciousness into a fashionable, even sexy commodity to further her personal fame. Wasserstein's unfavorable treatment of the character suggests less a critique of feminism in general than that of a new generation of ambitious young women who strive for their own version of "having it all" by sucking up to men in power positions.

Moreover, for the first time, she includes an African-American woman as her "response to the on-going discussion of diversity" (Wasserstein 1998). Dr. Judith Kaufman, Lyssa's long-term best friend, is a forty-two-year-old African-American Jewish oncologist who specializes in breast cancer treatment and, like Lyssa, advocates the improvement of women's healthcare while struggling with the knowledge that breast cancer research is vastly underfunded (*An American Daughter* 1997, 31). After a failed marriage with a closeted gay doctor and years of unsuccessful in-vitro fertilization treatments, Judith wants her "time back" (31). She is so desperate about not being able to "make life or stop death" that she tries to drown herself in the Potomac during Tashlick, the Jewish festival of regrets, at the end of the first act (57). At the end of the play, simultaneously with Lyssa's failed nomination, Judith's "final quest for fertility collapse[s]" (98). Nonetheless, she recovers a positive outlook, concluding that she has "time [. . .] for friendship now" (99) and affirming her solidarity with Lyssa. For Wasserstein, Lyssa and Judith are "two sides of the same person" (quoted in Faingold 1998). Their continuous dedication to women's healthcare is indicative of early feminist idealism. Both characters are voices of a feminist generation that grew up without role models; both are representatives of its successes and its failures.

As her most overtly political play, *An American Daughter* represents a political shift in Wasserstein's oeuvre. Her humanism prevails in her earlier plays, often preventing her protagonists from taking a political stance. Through Lyssa's active political engagement, *An American Daughter* offers a focused perspective on the twisted moral value system of a society that privileges performativity and sensation over content and principle. Unlike Holly Kaplan, Janie Blumberg, and Heidi Holland, Lyssa is strong-willed and determined to stand up for herself, an aspect that, as for Sara Goode, can be attributed to her maturity and age. It may also be due to her position as a player rather than an observer. This in turn may be the result of a less autobiographically influenced script or, more precisely, a shift from autobiographically modeled characters to a focus on the playwright's political opinions.

Although the visibility of women playwrights has increased since the 1989 production of *The Heidi Chronicles*, Wasserstein's concern that she has been positioned as a scapegoat representative of feminist and women's issues is still well taken. Given her success and high visibility as a mainstream contemporary American playwright, it is almost impossible to read her plays, as I have attempted in this chapter, without an eye to her representations of what the mainstream labels as feminist or postfeminist. It is therefore not surprising that *Uncommon Women*, her most overtly woman-conscious play, was not staged on Broadway and that *An American Daughter*, her angriest and most overtly political play, had a very short Broadway run.

Nevertheless, both Wasserstein's ambivalent, even critical position on the women's movement and her representation of only privileged, well-educated, upper middle-class, and (with the exception of Judith) white characters are problematic from today's feminist perspective. Yet, her plays consistently concentrate on women and women's issues. They generally present women in subject positions making active choices and feature themes and plots motivated by these choices and decisions. They further engage in a dialogue with the feminist movement and they explore the impacts of popular feminism on upper middle-class women. And though the characters in her five major plays all take a critical stance toward the women's movement, they also acknowledge—like the author herself—that feminism gave them the right to speak and the strength to make decisions independent of others. In their contentiousness for feminist critics on the one hand and in their sheer entertainment value, created by colorfully drawn characters for mainstream audiences, on the other, Wasserstein's plays still provoke strongly divided reactions. These, in turn, encourage productive, even passionate debates and explorations of issues still crucial to women in contemporary American society.

As *An American Daughter* shows, "having it all" is still a relevant, though contestable, goal for American women today. Although the content of the very notion keeps being redefined, even in the twenty-first century society still offers no satisfying ideological or material basis for women to "have it all." Though from diametrically opposite perspectives, Lillian Cornwall and Lyssa Dent Hughes would certainly commiserate over the double standards professional women still face in American society. Likewise, they would surely agree that it is not the feminist movement that has set these standards. In an interview over a decade ago, Wasserstein responded to an interviewer's question of whether her women characters can "have it all": I know there are women who have careers *and* babies. They work very hard. More credit to them. But the whole notion of "having it all" is ridiculous. It's a ridiculous phrase (Wasserstein 1987, 422).

In her earlier plays, Wasserstein pervasively directed her frustration at what she critiques as programmatic prescriptions by the women's movement. In *An American Daughter,* she identifies society's double standards as the basis for gender-biased politics and acknowledges the material impacts of what was once so ground-breakingly phrased as "the personal is political."

In 1999 at the age of 49, Wendy Wasserstein gave birth to a daughter. In December 2000, her new play, *Old Money,* opened at New York's Lincoln Center. It seems as if in her own life Wasserstein may have solved the very conflict with which her heroines could not come to grips for the past three decades. While being a single mother, she continues to pursue her professional commitments and, in a manner of speaking, has managed to achieve one version of "having it all," although it is ironically the one that was met with such vehement criticism when presented in the final scene of *The Heidi Chronicles*. While she still may not "know everything" (Wasserstein 1987, 424), it seems that, at least by her own standards, at the age of fifty, Wendy Wasserstein is "pretty . . . amazing."

Notes

1. Several critical accounts emphasize the play's careful depiction of female friendships and an inclusive community of women, particularly with regard to the final scene of the first act, in which the women playfully speculate on whom they would marry if they could marry each other and engage in a communal dance. In that scene, as throughout *Uncommon Women,* Wasserstein uses comic strategies to enhance this notion of female community formation. See, for instance, Susan L. Carlson, "Comic Textures and Female Communities 1937 and 1977: Clare Boothe and Wendy Wasserstein," *Modern Drama* 27.4 (1984) 564–73; Miriam M. Chirico, "Female Laughter and Comic Possibilities: *Uncommon Women* and *Others*," *Wendy Wasserstein: A Casebook*, ed. Claudia Barnett (New York and London: Garland, 1999) 81–105; and William C. Boles, "'We've All Come a Long Way': the Role of Women in *Uncommon Women, Top Girls* and *My Mother Said I Never Should*," *Wendy Wasserstein: A Casebook*, ed. Claudia Barnett (New York and London: Garland, 1999) 57–80.

2. Even for a 2001 New York production of *Isn't It Romantic,* over twenty years after the play was originally staged, reviewers continued to note that Wasserstein locates her critique and the reasons for her characters' dilemma in the feminist rhetoric as it was popularly perceived at the time of her writing. See Bruce Weber, "Wasserstein's Women Try Holding on to Love and Independence," review of *Isn't It Romantic, New York Times* 19 Feb. 2001, B5.

3. For critical feminist readings of *The Heidi Chronicles*, see, for instance, Jill Dolan, *Presence & Desire. Essays on Gender and Performance* (Ann Arbor: University of Michigan Press, 1996); Helene Keyssar, "Drama and the Dialogic Imagination: *The Heidi Chronicles* and *Fefu and Her Friends*," *Feminist Theatre and Theory*, ed. Helene Keyssar (New York: St. Martin's Press, 1996) 109–36; Gayle Austin, "Rev. of *the Heidi Chronicles*.," *Theatre Journal* 42.1 (1990): 107–8; Helene Keyssar, "When Wendy Isn't Trendy: Wendy Wasserstein's *the Heidi Chronicles* and *An American Daughter*," *Wendy Wasserstein: A Casebook*, ed. Claudia Barnett (New York and London: Garland, 1999) 133–60. For more positive accounts, see, for instance, Ciociola (1998), *Wendy Wasserstein: Dramatizing Women, Their Choices and Their Boundaries*; Jan Balakian, "*The Heidi Chronicles*: The Big Chill of Feminism," *South Atlantic Review* 60.2 (1995): 93–101.

4. For an astute, detailed account of the backlash against women's rights in the 1980s and its representation through the media, see, for instance, Susan Falludi, *Backlash: The Undeclared War Against American Women* (New York: Anchor Books, 1992).

5. While the focus of my discussion is on the representation of gender and feminism in Wasserstein's work, there are several excellent analyses that focus on her representation of Jewish identity in *The Sisters Rosensweig*. See, for instance, Glenda Frank, "The Struggle to Affirm: The Image of Jewish-Americans on Stage," *Staging Difference: Cultural Pluralism in American Theatre and Drama*, ed. Marc Mauford (New York, Washington, DC/Baltimore, San Francisco: Peter Lang, 1995) 245–57; and Stephen J. Whitfield, "Wendy Wasserstein and the Crisis of (Jewish) Identity," *Daughters of Valor: Contemporary Jewish American Women Writers*, ed. Jay L. Halio and Ben Siegel (Newark: University of Delaware Press, 1997) 226–46.

Works Cited

Austin, Gayle. 1990. Review of *The Heidi Chronicles*, by Wendy Wasserstein. Plymouth Theatre, New York. *Theatre Journal* 42.1: 107–8.

Balakian, Jan. 1999. Wendy Wasserstein: A Feminist Voice from the Seventies to the Present. In *The Cambridge Companion to American Women Playwrights*, ed. Brenda Murphy. Cambridge, UK: Cambridge University Press, 213–31.

Barnett, Claudia. 1997. Review of *An American Daughter*, by Wendy Wasserstein. Lincoln Center Theater, Cort Theatre, New York. *Theatre Journal* 49.4: 520–1.

Berson, Misha. 1997. "Daughter" Comes Home: Wendy Wasserstein Rewards Seattle for Birthday with Another Play. *The Seattle Times,* 24 April. from http://www.seattletimes.com/extra/bruuse/html197/alterwass-042497.

Bigsby, Christopher. 1999. Wendy Wasserstein. In *Contemporary American Playwrights.* Cambridge, UK: Cambridge University Press, 330–68.

Case, Sue-Ellen. 1998. *Feminism and Theatre.* New York: Methuen.

Ciociola, Gail. 1998. *Wendy Wasserstein : Dramatizing Women, Their Choices and Their Boundaries.* Jefferson, NC: McFarland.

Dolan, Jill. 1996. *Presence & Desire. Essays on Gender and Performance.* Ann Arbor: University of Michigan Press.

Faingold, Norma. 1998. Wendy Wasserstein Confronts Strong Women, Tough Choices. *Jewish Bulletin* 4 September from http: www.jewishsf.com/bk980904/etwendy.htm

Frank, Glenda. 1999. Three American Daughters: Wendy Wasserstein Critiques Success. In *Wendy Wasserstein: A Casebook*, ed. Claudia Barnett. New York and London: Garland, 161–77.

Franklin, Nancy. 1997. Profile: The Time of Her Life. *The New Yorker,* 14 April, 62–71.

Mandl, Bette. 1999. Women's Movement: The Personal as Political in the Plays of Wendy Wasserstein. In *Wendy Wasserstein: A Casebook,* ed. Claudia Barnett. New York and London: Garland, 3–11.

Savran, David. 1999. Introduction: Wendy Wasserstein. In *The Playwright's Voice: American Dramatists on Memory, Writing and the Politics of Culture*, David Savran. New York: Theatre Communications Group, 289–92.

Wasserstein, Wendy. 1987. Interview with Kathleen Betsko and Rachel Koenig. In *Interviews with Contemporary Women Playwrights*, ed. Kathleen Betsko and Rachel Koenig. New York: Beech Tree Books, 418–31.

———. 1988. Interview with Esther Cohen. *Women's Studies: An Interdisciplinary Journal* 15.1–3: 257–70.

———. 1990. *Bachelor Girls,* 1st ed. New York: Alfred A. Knopf.

———. 1991. *The Heidi Chronicles and Other Plays.* New York: Vintage Books.

———. 1993. *The Sisters Rosensweig,* 1st ed. New York: Harcourt Brace Jovanovich.

———. 1995. Interview with Leslie Jacobson. *The Playwright's Art: Conversations with Contemporary American Dramatists,* ed. Jackson R. Bryer. New Brunswick, NJ: Rutgers University Press, 1995. 257–76.

———. 1996. Interview with Jan Balakian. *Speaking on Stage: Interviews with Contemporary American Playwrights*, ed. Philip C. Kolin and Colby H. Kullman. Tuscaloosa: University of Alabama Press, 378–91.

———. 1997a. *An American Daughter.* New York: Dramatists Play Service.

———. 1997b. Wendy Wasserstein: The Art of Theatre XIII. Interview with Laurie Winer. *The Paris Review* 39.142: 164–88.

———. 1997c. Yes, I am a Feminist &. . . . *Ms.* September/October, 42–49.

———. 1998. Wendy Wasserstein. *New Tradition Compendium.* Retrieved 9 Feb. 2001 from http://www.ntcp.org/compendium/WENDY.html.

———. 1999. Interview with David Savran. In *The Playwright's Voice: American Dramatists on Memory, Writing and the Politics of Culture,* David Savran. New York: Theatre Communications Group, 293–310.

———. 2000. Annals of Motherhood: Complications. *The New Yorker,* 21 & 28 February, 87–109.

INTERVIEW WITH WENDY WASSERSTEIN

Interview conducted by Angelika Czekay
in February 2001

Angelika Czekay: I know you have written in other forms, such as screenplays, articles, and essays, but why have you chosen to write for the theatre? Is there something about the form of dialogue that is particularly intriguing to you?

Wendy Wasserstein: I love the theatre. I grew up going to plays. I grew up in New York, and my parents took me to Broadway plays and off-Broadway plays on Saturdays. And my parents still love going to the theatre, so it was very much, I think, a product of my childhood. And also that I was always sort of funny and shy. So what better thing than to write funny plays, so that someone else acts in them.

AC: How would you describe your writing process?

WW: I think about my ideas for a while. I tend to think of them when I'm finishing the previous play. So they stay on my mind for a while. And then I have to clear out my calendar to have enough time to start writing a play because there are certain things you have to do to make a living—especially supporting a baby now. So, I think of things, and then I set out time and say, okay, now I'm going to write a play. And I start writing it. I tend to write from character. And I guess situation, too. I mean, for the more recent plays like *Old Money*. I sort of wanted to write about New York now and New York seventy-five years ago. I thought that was interesting. A lot of the times the structure changes. *The Heidi Chronicles* is an episodic play and so is *Isn't It Romantic*, whereas *The Sisters Rosensweig* is really a well-made Boulevard comedy.

AC: As is *An American Daughter*.

WW: Yes, they are both sort of well-made plays. So that's what interests me, and I think a lot of the time the content does dictate the form. I think *Old Money* is a sad play. It's a funny play, but it's sad. It's about a man who's dying. It's in some ways very much about that. So I guess I wanted to do that form of going forward and backwards because I was trying to go for the rhythms of what's the pattern of life.

AC: You employ at least two different historical perspectives in your plays, whether that's done through a contrast in generations or whether it's achieved through a direct juxtaposition in time periods. In *Uncommon Women*, the girls look back to their college years, and *Heidi* is a chronicle. In *Isn't It Romantic*, you contrast two different generations, similarly to *Sisters Rosensweig* and *An American Daughter*. Is there something that's particularly interesting to you about this kind of historicity?

WW: I was a history student at Mount Holyoke. I've always been interested in, "How did we get here?" A lot of my plays are about personal choices given the times you live in. And, how is one influenced, especially Heidi, by one's own times? So, in that way, there is that generational contrast. And I like that. Maybe it's my idea of family that you would have people on stage of various generations. Not so much in *The Heidi Chronicles*. *The Heidi Chronicles* is about a specific generation.

AC: Your earlier plays, in particular, are more episodic, yet they function to some extent like realism. Could you talk about why you prefer the form of realism for your plays?

WW: You know, there just was a revival of *Isn't It Romantic* in New York that, I think, is reviewed in today's *New York Times*. What's interesting is that in that play, which is really an autobiographic Boulevard comedy, I think the naturalistic form makes it specific. You know, these are these people, this is the time they've lived in. Here are the specific benchmarks. So that those girls are all talking about "having it all" and that they make jokes about Jean Harris killing diet doctors. It somehow feeds into that and their choices.

AC: So then, do you think there is a particular relationship between realism and comedy?

WW: Yes, I do. Although you can always do "name-brand comedy" and people will laugh because that's what's current. So, I think there is.

There are different forms of comedy. There's nothing I admire more than Lucille Ball and physical comedy. I can't do it, but I think it's fantastic. It makes me really laugh. The sort of comedy I do is character-driven. It'll always come out of either you wouldn't anticipate this person would do this, or, absolutely, that's exactly what this person would do. One of my favorite things is Doctor Gorgeous in *The Sisters Rosensweig* returning the Chanel suit, because it's such a moment of dignity from this comic character. And the realism that that comes from is that she has no money. She is living in a world where she's totally pretending she does, and she doesn't. So then you get into the question of what are the economic pressures that this person is under.

AC: Music often provides an allusion to a certain time period in your plays. Could you talk about the role of music, particularly with regard to establishing a time period and setting a cultural frame?

WW: There are two things. First of all, the music itself helps me write. So, whatever play I am working on, sometimes when I stop writing I sit and listen to the music, and I find it relaxing. Or I'll drive around with the music on from that time period. So, for instance, when I was writing *An American Daughter*, I was listening to the Beach Boys, because Walter is obsessed with the Beach Boys. In *Old Money*, they sing old New York songs after the ball. And in *The Sisters Rosensweig*, Sara was a singer. So, I think, one thing it has to do with is just my own artistic process. I like to listen to music. It's a kind of an excuse not to write because I'll have to listen for the play. [Laughs] And I also think it does very much—which they use all the time in television and film now—evoke a specific period. Hearing Aretha Franklin sing "Respect" during *The Heidi Chronicles*, you know exactly what that is. Any time you put on Janis Joplin you know exactly what the time period is.

AC: Speaking of other media, unlike other playwrights you have not chosen to integrate slides or film sequences very frequently in your plays. Could you comment on the reason for this?

WW: Well, they did the transitions in *The Heidi Chronicles* with slides, and I thought that was very well done by Dan Sullivan, especially on Broadway. But I like plays because I like dialogue. I like writing dialogue. I like actors coming on and working with it. I really enjoy it.

AC: Do you have a target audience in mind when you're writing a play, perhaps people from a specific generation?

WW: No, I don't. When I went back and saw *Isn't It Romantic* I was very happy that there were these parts for women, and that it exists. I do think about women being able to come to the theatre and see something approximating their lives on stage.

AC: Do you mind being categorized as a woman playwright?

WW: No, I don't. I am a woman playwright. But what is hard is that there are playwrights, and they are male. And then there are women playwrights, black playwrights . . .

AC: Do you shape your plays with an eye to their producibility?

WW: You know, it's such a gamble whether a play will do well or not or get produced, or, God knows, get a good notice. Who knows? I really see plays as pieces of art. I do. I see them as something I am lucky enough to do, and I am lucky enough that someone will produce them somewhere, I hope. So, I don't look at it in terms of producibility. I mean it's unlikely I would write a play for forty people with elephants. [Laughs] Or chickens falling from the sky.

AC: Are you doing commissioned work?

WW: I haven't done commissioned work in a while. I've done my last few plays for Lincoln Center. So, I haven't, because to make a living I also write for television and film. So I look at that as commissioned work.

AC: So, you can't live off being a playwright?

WW: No.

AC: I would like to talk a little bit about the production of your plays. Ideally, what working relationship would you like to have with the director?

WW: I worked on three of my plays with Daniel Sullivan, who is a great director, I think. First of all, you want to respect them. I also think when they start dealing with the text it should be going where you want it to go. You know that the work they're asking you to do is the work that you agree will help the text. You don't want to be in a situation where you think you're taking dictation. I think that's a problem. But I've really enjoyed working with Dan all these years. And I just worked with Marc Brokaw, who I thought was excellent, on *Old Money*. And I worked with Derek Anson Jones, who directed *Wit*. We revamped *An American Daughter* at the Long Wharf Theatre. That was very satisfying because I always felt badly about *An American Daughter*. That was the play that got not even mixed but sort of mean notices, except for Linda Winer. And it's one of my favorite plays. It's a very strong play. Of all of them in a sense it's the angriest.

AC: And it's also the most political one in terms of integrating current politics and a critique of the media.

WW: Yes, I think so, too. And it's not a gentle play, and it's not a lovable play. You don't want to embrace it.

AC: You say you've had a good relationship with the director in terms of the work in process. What does a good relationship with the director then mean for you?

WW: It means that they helped me shape the text. And I am someone who works a lot in rehearsal. I will cut and change a play a great deal. And I think the guidance is very good. I am there at the rehearsal all the time. I cut the play. I listen to it. I think that's fun.

AC: Do you have a good relationship with the whole production team, for instance, with the designers?

WW: Yes, designers are my favorite people in the theatre because I am not very visual at all. So that they're visual and textual I find fascinating. They're actually personally my close friends.

AC: Have you ever been shocked when you saw one of your plays produced?

WW: Yes, of course. Not so much the productions I have been involved with, but you can go out of town and see a play that's just horrifying. Chris Durang saw a play of his *History of the American Film*, and in the second act everyone took off their shirts. [Laughs] You can't say in the text that nobody takes off the shirt. Who would dream of such a thing? I was thinking in the theatre you probably make no money and can be publicly humiliated, but, what's great about the theatre is, it will be yours. The theatre is where the playwright is most respected in America as opposed to movies, for instance. It is a writer's medium. You know, I'll never forget, in *The Heidi Chronicles*, Joan Allen coming up to me and saying: "Do you mind if I say an 'a' instead of a 'the' here?" and you think, "Wow, thanks!"

AC: That says a lot about the authority of the playwright, even if it doesn't translate into being paid for it. What do you experience emotionally when you see a premiere of one of your plays, such as *Old Money* recently?

WW: Well, it's sort of overwhelming. [Laughs] I've given birth, and I've produced plays, and producing plays is harder. And I had pre-eclampsia. [Laughs] Because you care so much, and it's so public, and it's there, and you've got to come through. And if it doesn't work, you feel awful, and if it does work, and it's not appreciated or if it does work, and it is appreciated, it's just an overwhelming sense of delivery.

AC: Are you then very aware of the audience around you?

WW: Yes, but it's more like during these things you just think, "Can I do this to the best of my ability?" That's really what I think. It's like an endurance test.

AC: But at least at that point you have seen rehearsals and the dress rehearsal, so you know what the product will look like. You just don't know how the audience will react.

WW: Yes, and if it'll connect or not. And if it doesn't connect you sort of don't quite know what to do.

AC: I also wanted to ask you about your perceptions of the state of American theatre. Are there any new impulses you can identify?

WW: I think there is very good writing going on in American theatre. I do. And, people always say, from a variety of voices. That it isn't any more the sort of White male theatre that it was thirty years ago. I think that's a good thing. I also think the more there are 500 television channels and the internet and God knows what else, the more precious the theatre becomes because it is an intimate community, and it is a voice, and it is an idea. And in our world now, who knows what's genuine? And who knows what's a genuine idea? What's been spun, and what's being told? In the theatre at least you're in this room with live people, and it's the voice of one author and something can happen there. You know, there is that human excitement if it works.

AC: Do you also think theatre functions as a medium to convey a political message? To engage the audience on that level?

WW: The theatre is not television. Not as many people will ever see my plays in one night. But what you can do with theatre because it's not a big business initially—even when it is big business it's not big like the other things—you can begin to say things that then sort of filter into the culture. I think that's a good thing.

AC: Where do you see your own work in the current cultural moment?

WW: Certainly there are many more women, especially young women, writing plays. Because there were me and Marsha Norman and Beth Henley and Paula Vogel, that's encouraged new generations of young women to write plays, and I think that's good.

AC: I know you also teach playwriting. Has that shaped your own work?

WW: Yes it does. You start realizing that you're a craftsman. At least, you can sit down with someone young and say, "Look, if you did this, this is a way to clarify this."

AC: Do you think one can teach playwriting?

WW: I think what you can teach is for students to have confidence in their voice and try to find it and not imitate someone else. It's not like in movie writing where you have to have a subsidiary character come on page 10. But you can at least say, if you're writing parallel scenes, then we have to see the parallel somewhere. You can sort of teach them to be able to look at their work more craftily.

AC: I was also wondering how having a daughter has impacted you in terms of topics or ideas. It seems as if you have now what so many of your characters were struggling with in terms of "having it all."

WW: [Laughs] It does make you think about the future. It makes you think about life. It not just about my daughter being born, it's also knowing people who died, too. So what I know is very different than, say, what Janie Blumberg knew in *Isn't It Romantic.* This is not to say that Janie isn't a wise girl. It's just that I'm older.

AC: What I find interesting about your plays is that you are always the same age as your central characters. So, they always have your historical view. In this sense your plays can be read as a chronology of the past thirty years. Will you continue writing from this perspective?

WW: [Laughs] I know. I am not quite sure. I am working on two musicals now, actually. And maybe that has to do with my daughter.

AC: Is that where you see your own work going from here?

WW: I'm not quite sure where my work is going. I have avoided autobiographical work for a while. And I think it might go back to autobiographical work. As a friend of mine says, I was born into a lot of material.

BIRTH, BAPTISM, AND RESURRECTION: AUGUST WILSON AND THE BLUES

Joan Herrington

An amalgam of work songs, group seculars, field hollers, sacred harmonies, proverbial wisdom, folk philosophy, political commentary, ribald humor, elegiac lament, and much more.

—Houston Baker, on the blues

August Wilson discovered the blues in 1965 when he came upon a copy of Bessie Smith's "Nobody in Town Can Bake a Sweet Jellyroll Like Mine" and put it on the turntable. That moment reshaped the young writer's future:

> Suffice it to say it was a birth, a baptism, a resurrection, and a redemption all rolled up in one. It was the beginning of my consciousness that I was representative of a culture and the carrier of some very valuable antecedents. With my discovery of Bessie Smith and the blues I had been given a world that contained my image, a world at once rich and varied, marked and marking, brutal and beautiful, and at crucial odds with the larger world that contained it and preyed and pressed on it from every conceivable angle.
>
> I turned my ear, my heart, and whatever analytical tools I possessed to embrace this world. I elevated it, rightly or wrongly, to biblical status. I rooted out the ideas and attitudes expressed in the music, charted them and bent and twisted and stretched them. I tested them on the common ground of experience and evidence and gave my whole being, muscle and

bone and sinew and flesh and spirit, over to the emotional reference provided by the music. (Wilson, *Three Plays*, 1991).

For twenty years following this epiphanal moment, August Wilson mined the blues for inspiration of theme and style. In October 1984, *Ma Rainey's Black Bottom* opened on Broadway. The play offered a unique voice in the theatre; the voice, like the music which inspired it, was an "an amalgam of work songs, group seculars, field hollers, sacred harmonies, proverbial wisdom, folk philosophy, political commentary, ribald humor, elegiac lament, and much more" (Baker 1984, 5).

For Wilson, who plans to chronicle a hundred years of African-American history by writing one play set in each decade of the twentieth century, the inclusion and celebration of the blues are essential. For him, survival of the blues is central to the survival of the African-American community: Wilson includes the blues because the music itself is a chronicle of 400 years of history, and the community must know its history; he includes the blues because it is a direct link to the past in its reaffirmation of a shared cultural heritage with roots in two continents; and he includes the blues because it must be reclaimed by the community, saved from the white co-opting of African-American art, which Wilson fears is strangling a cultural identity. In his battle to reaffirm a people, the blues are Wilson's weapon of choice.

Wilson claims that his historical chronicle "is entirely based on the ideas and attributes that come out of the blues" (Goodstein and Rosenfeld 1990, C 1+). At the core of his work is the belief that "in a world dominated by white culture the black must be strong enough not only to survive but to reestablish his own identity and heritage which flows unbroken from an African fountainhead" (Nelson 1995, 5). The blues have historically carved the route to the fountainhead. It exists in the Americas as the contemporary incarnation of the African storyteller who maintained the stories and myths of the community, who stoked the collective memory of the community, which Paul Carter Harrison (1984) has noted is vital to its well being:

> Certainly it can be argued that the African-American experience is not
> monolithic nor otherwise without its diversity; however, the psychic
> response to the dislocations shared in American history binds the collec-
> tive unconsciousness into an ethos that strives for material and spiritual

cohesion. The stories and gestures that codify collective experience are framed ideologically by myths which serve to preserve the essential metaphors of the cultural world view. (292)

In the African tradition, the established myths and their accompanying life lessons are passed orally from one generation to the next, in story and eventually in song. Wilson calls on the blues and its accompanying myths, incorporating it actively into this work, to reestablish a cultural connection he sees as dangerously lacking in twentieth-century African Americans. Because the blues arose from the need to reestablish in a new world a cultural connection to a previous one, it offers tremendous power for cultural affirmation:

> Irrespective of African adaptation to the Eurocentric priorities of dominant culture, marginalization prompted African Americans to probe the recesses of ancestral memory for recognizable African values, linguistic techniques, and aesthetic constructions that could be cultivated as a source of ethnic reaffirmation. (Harrison 1984, 292)

The same marginalization that shaped the blues has hundreds of years later shaped the unique drama of the playwright so committed to its inclusion in his work. Wilson's plays consistently bring traditional African elements into contemporary African-American culture to provide, as the music does, a link that promotes cultural reaffirmation.

The development of the blues through the years, its incorporation of African tradition into a musical form reflective of a new and difficult world, inspired the titles of Wilson's plays, influenced his dramatic plots, and strengthened the underlying emotional content of his work. There is blues music in the inspiration of all of Wilson's plays: two Wilson plays examine the commercial world of music; *Ma Rainey's Black Bottom* and his early one-act, *Homecoming,* both chronicle the passion and exploitation of the performers; Wilson took the title and story of his play *Joe Turner's Come and Gone* from an old blues song. In that play, Herald Loomis, newly freed from a seven-year internment, searches for his wife, from whom he was separated. He also searches for his "song," or sense of self, lost in the enslavement. *The Piano Lesson* has at its core a musical instrument that bridges past and present worlds and that has the history of a family carved in its legs. Wilson named his play *Two Trains*

Running after a blues song. He remembers the words as "two trains running, neither going my way" (Interview 1994). And it is the dream of a career in music which destroys the flamboyant Floyd Barton in *Seven Guitars*. Wilson's characters rise out of the music, they live the stories contained in the music, and the music is an integral part of their everyday lives. Some are professional musicians; some sing in the privacy of their homes. Some revel in the music to share a joyous moment; others quietly hum a song that soothes their mind. All use it to find strength in a shared community.

In its earliest incarnation among the slaves in the Americas, the African-based music was an outlet for frustration, an opportunity for celebration, and a ritual that could empower its participants. Early music of the enslaved people utilized the West African tradition of antiphonal singing, wherein a singer sings a verse, often improvised and always changing, and is answered by a chorus whose response is always the same.

In the mid-nineteenth century, as the promise of freedom deteriorated into the denial of opportunity, the music changed; the two vocal parts of antiphonal singing were consolidated for a single voice. The individual bluesmen of this time were reminiscent of their African counterparts, the griotes who commented musically on local events with humor and improvised verse.

In the early part of the twentieth century, the blues were a vital part of African-American life, and it became the bluesman's role to voice the truths, ironies, joys, heartbreak, and suppressed anger of the community. Still oppressed by society and still denied freedom of expression, African Americans continued to use their music to feed the spirit. Bluesman Memphis Slim says: "Blues is a kind of revenge . . . things we couldn't say. . . . I mean we sing" (Lomax 1990). This underside of blues as "revenge" continued even as the music became popular across America. Songs were recorded and played again and again. In the 1910s and 1920s, the blues were developed for large, and largely White, audiences, a move which divided the path of the music into that which still served the community and that which was taken from the community.

Ma Rainey's Black Bottom (1985) examines the simultaneous power of the blues to heal the soul and threaten its survival. Ma understands that "The blues help you get out of bed in the morning. You get up knowing you ain't alone. There's something else in the world.

Something's been added by that song. This be an empty world without the blues" (83). But she clearly sees the realities of their production:

> As soon as they get my voice down on them recording machines, then it's just like if I'd be some whore and they roll over and put their pants on. Ain't got no use for me then. I know what I'm talking about. (79)

Music is integrated throughout *Ma Rainey,* and Wilson skillfully provides examples of its many uses. At the end of Act I, the character Levee tells the horrifying story of the rape of his mother by eight White men. A response comes from Slow Drag, who plays his bass and sings an old blues song of revolution:

> If I had my way
> If I had my way
> If I had my way
> I would tear this old building down. (71)

As Ma waits to begin the recording session, she sings to herself, relieving her physical pain, but more importantly, her stress. Throughout the play, the band is trying to record a version of "Ma Rainey's Black Bottom," a song of defiance, veiling a powerful challenge with seemingly harmless lyrics.

Although the blues were popular across racial lines at this point in their history, Ma Rainey notes: "White folks don't understand the blues. They hear it come out but they don't know how it got there. They don't understand that's life's way of talking. . . . You sing 'cause that's a way of understanding life" (82). The blues facilitates understanding by bringing the past into the present. This is a crucial exercise for Wilson, who believes that to know where you are, you must know where you've been. As Memphis says in *Two Trains Running*: "If you drop the ball you got to go back and pick it up. Ain't no need to keeping running, cause if you get to the end zone it ain't gonna be a touchdown" (1993, 109). As Robert Ellison noted, the blues keeps the history alive:

> The blues is an impulse to keep the painful details and episodes of a brutal experience alive in one's aching consciousness, to finger its jagged grain and to transcend it, not by the consolation of philosophy but by squeezing from it a near-tragic, near-comic lyricism. (Pereira 1995, 9)

Through the two plays that followed *Ma Rainey, Fences* and *Joe Turner's Come and Gone,* Wilson incorporated the music and its traditions as characters sing in celebration and lament, often rediscovering themselves through connection to song. But it is in *The Piano Lesson,* written in 1985 and winner of Wilson's second Pulitzer in 1988, that the music comes again to center stage, physically and spiritually.

Wilson's process of writing *The Piano Lesson* followed the path he had forged with earlier work.

> I generally start with an idea, something that I want to say. In *The Piano Lesson* the question was "Can one acquire a sense of self-worth by denying one's past?" So then, how do you put this question on stage, how do you narrate it? Next I got the title from a Romare Bearden painting called *The Piano Lesson.* His painting is actually a piano teacher with a kid. . . . From the painting I had a piano, and I just started writing a line of dialogue and had no idea who was talking. First I had four guys moving the piano into an empty house.
>
> While writing *The Piano Lesson* I came up with the idea of tracing the history of the piano for a hundred and thirty-five years, with the idea that it had been used to purchase members of this family from slavery. But I didn't know how that was going to tie in. I knew there was a story, but I didn't know what the story was. I discovered it as the characters began to talk. (Savran 1988, 294)

In the inception of this work, Wilson combined his love of the music with a vital energy he had taken from the painter Romare Bearden—the second of four "B's" that Wilson claims as the primary influences on his work. (Blues, Bearden, Baraka, and Borges.) Wilson found the concrete core of a play in an image created by Bearden, an artist most well known for his textural collages. In Bearden's canvas *The Piano Lesson,* Wilson encountered an artistic challenge:

> What I saw was Black life presented on its own terms, on a grand and epic scale, with all its richness and fullness, in a language that was vibrant and which, made attendant to everyday life, ennobled it, affirmed its value, and exalted its presence. In Bearden I found my artistic mentor and sought, and still aspire, to make my plays the equal of his canvasses. (Schwartzman 1980, 8)

Wilson and Bearden both portray African Americans trying to meld past and future, to reconcile African and contemporary American culture. Such issues are the backbone of *The Piano Lesson,* described as Wilson's "noisiest play," filled with shouts, chants, and drum beats; it is a play deeply dependent on the blues (Wolfe 1999, 108). *The Piano Lesson* focuses on a struggle between brother, Boy Willie, and sister, Berniece, over the sale of an heirloom piano. The piano was previously owned by the Sutter family, who held Boy Willie and Berniece's family enslaved. The slave owner acquired the piano in a trade: he traded Berniece and Boy Willie's father and grandmother for the musical instrument. Berniece and Boy Willie's grandfather, mourning the loss of his wife and son, carved portraits of his family into the piano legs.

Boy Willie wants to sell the piano to buy a piece of the property where his family had served as slaves. His eye is only on the future. Berniece refuses to part with the instrument even though she is unable to play the piano; she fears that to do so is to raise the spirits embodied within it:

> I used to think those pictures came alive and walked through the house. Sometimes late at night, I could hear my mama talking to them. I said that wasn't going to happen to me. I don't play that piano because I don't want to walk them spirits. They never be walking around in this house. (70)

At the end of *The Piano Lesson,* however, when Boy Willie is struggling for his life against Sutter's ghost, Berniece finally understands that the only way to save him is to call upon her heritage, thereby empowering herself with its strength. At the end of the play, Berniece plays the piano and chants a plea for assistance. Repetitive and ritualistic, it is an age-old plea, spoken by her forefathers, and in it is the power to defeat the ghost of the slave trader.

The action of *The Piano Lesson* revolves largely around the presence of a ghost. Indeed, ghost stories are sprinkled throughout the play. This was not Wilson's first play to include a presence from another world; Wilson's characters battle not only ghosts, but death (in *Fences*) and God (in *Ma Rainey*) and Jesus Christ (in *Joe Turner's Come and Gone*). Qun Wang (1999) recognized that Wilson's use of the blues facilitates the unworldly presence:

> Similar to the blues, Wilson's use of metaphors in his plays is accurate,
> precise, and powerful. It demonstrates the writer's awareness that to poet-
> ize the dramatization of the African-American experience is to identify
> images that can bridge the gap between the visible and the invisible,
> between permanence and the impermanent, and between the physical
> world and metaphysical world. (30)

Wilson's explorations of metaphysics reflect the acknowledged
influence of Argentinean short-story writer Jorge Luis Borges, who continually questions man's place within a larger continuum. Borges shares
with Wilson a characteristic described by Wole Soyinka in *Myth,
Literature, and the African World* (1976) as "the deep-seated need of
creative man to recover [an] archetypical consciousness" (43).

The issues of destiny and of man's relationship with the universe
relate directly to Wilson's examination of connections to cultural history
as a key to the future. It is thus that Wilson ties the blues and Borges
together. Levee in *Ma Rainey's Black Bottom,* Troy in *Fences,* Berniece
in *The Piano Lesson,* and Loomis in *Joe Turner's Come and Gone* all
exist without an opportunity to pursue their dreams. In anger, they have
closed themselves off to their cultural heritage. Their inability to
acknowledge their connection to an archetypal consciousness is ultimately destructive. In *The Piano Lesson,* Berniece is emotionally crip-
pled, filled with hate and rage; she cannot begin to approach her
heirloom piano, alive with the spirits of her ancestors. In *Joe Turner's
Come and Gone,* Loomis denies his history and is therefore forced to
wander, endlessly enslaved, despite his release from captivity by Joe
Turner. This ever-present message in Wilson's work reflects his underlying philosophy that individual strength and transcendence are achieved
only through connection to a larger continuum. It is a connection the
blues facilitates.

For Wilson, the connection is vital for the survival of the entire
African-American community, and the struggle is greatest in the twentieth century, which has been characterized as neglectful of the past.
"History, like the blues, demands that we witness the painful events of
our prior lives; and that we either confront these painful events or be
destroyed by them" (Larry Neal, quoted in Plum 1993, 563). In *The
Piano Lesson*, Wilson reveals his belief that history is not a burden, as

Berniece initially perceives it, but rather a source of positive energy that can empower the entire African-American community.

Wilson's unique combination of theater, music, and visual art creates drama within an African context described by Soyinka (1976) as intended to "reinforce by observances, rituals, and mytho-historical recitals the existing consciousness or cosmic entanglement in the community, and to arbitrate in the sometimes difficult application of such truths to domestic and community undertakings" (54). His plays rarely guide toward external solution. Instead, they focus on the need for the individual to become part of the community and thus to heal himself and the community. The art reveals conflict and struggle not within what Soyinka identified as the traditional Western context, which sees "human anguish as viable only within strictly temporal capsules," but rather within the African context, "whose tragic understanding transcends the causes of individual disjunction and recognizes them as reflections of a far greater disharmony in the communal psyche" (46).

Of all Wilson's plays, *The Piano Lesson* most clearly defines Wilson's remedies for a healthier community. Like *Ma Rainey, The Piano Lesson* is heavily laced with the blues and variations on the music. As Boy Willie's Uncle Doaker irons, he sings a song he learned while working on the railroad. Wilson writes that the song provides a rhythm for his work and it makes the ironing less burdensome.

Wilson also includes selections from the blues that recognize the humor in everyday life. They are sung by Boy Willie's other uncle, Wining Boy, who is himself a bluesman who has lost his taste for the music through its exploitation at the hands of White men. Wining Boy has had a troubled life on many fronts, and his music reflects his complaints:

Tell me how long

Is I got to wait

Can I get it now

Or must I hesitate

It takes a hesitating stocking her hesitating shoe

It takes a hesitating woman wanna sing the blues

Tell me how long

Is I got to wait

Can I kiss you now
Or must I hesitate. (101)

New to *The Piano Lesson* was the prison work song, music prominent in the historical period in which the play is set (1930s) and that still
retained much of its African roots. These collective work songs in which
all the participants sing, clap, and dance together are found throughout
Africa, but most likely came to America through Africans from the sub-
Saharan, savannah regions, where group farming was common. These
inland people were sold into slavery by conquering western Africans or
even by their own tribes.

This type of work song, with its free-flowing, "hollering" qualities,
is skillfully incorporated by Wilson. Boy Willie and his friend Lymon
have come up North to retrieve the piano. They have come to the home
of Boy Willie's sister, Berniece. As they relax, Boy Willie and Lymon
remember the trouble they have left behind in the South and the days
they spent working on the Parchman Farm, reputed to be the most ruthless of all the southern work farms. Part of their memory is the songs
they sang to ease their load.

Go 'head marry don't you wait on me oh-ah
Go 'head marry don't you wait on me oh-ah
Might not want you when I go free oh-ah
Might not want you when I go free well
O Lord Berta Berta O Lord gal oh-ah
O Lord Berta Berta O Lord gal well
Berta in Meridan and she living at ease oh-ah
Berta in Meridan and she living at ease well
I'm on old Parchman, got to work or leave oh-ah
I'm on old Parchman, got to work or leave well. (39–40)

Boy Willie and Lymon, joined by Boy Willie's uncles, stomp their
feet and clap to keep time. "Oh Berta" is a typical Mississippi Valley
work gang song, sung by hundreds of men as they worked in the fields
or cleared the land of trees. The music in *The Piano Lesson* creates linkages; it is "a connective force that links the past with the present, and
the present with the future" (Plum 1993, 561). Without such linkages,
Wilson believes the African-American community is suffering.

Music finds its way into Wilson's work not only as subject but also as technique. Wilson's approach to writing is akin to creating blues music. He writes the basic story, the underlying melody is there, and then he improvises on his theme, discovering the power of the music and bringing to life its mystical elements. The plays are metaphorical, lyrical, loosely organized. The structure of Wilson's plays is similar to a blues scale, progressing for a few notes, then slipping into disappointment, often rising again. Sometimes the plays end in despair; sometimes the disappointment is overcome and the plays end in exuberance.

But it is not how the story ends that is of greatest interest as a Wilson story unfolds; rather, it is how the story is told. The dialogue does not consistently advance the plot; the plays do not necessarily follow traditional dramatic structure, with clear causal progression; nor do they definitively "end." As Harrison (1984) noted, "Wilson, as blues raconteur, orchestrates his tale with a recursive language that allows words, mood, and potential resolution to shift and reappear almost improvisationally, at least, creating an unanticipated suspension of closure in the event" (305).

Wilson has received some criticism for this quality of his work, particularly among mainstream theater critics. And in the commercial productions of his work, even his colleagues have prodded Wilson to provide greater closure to his work. *The Piano Lesson* originally concluded with Boy Willie endlessly fighting Sutter's ghost and Wilson was satisfied: "In the original ending, I never said what happened to the piano. To me, it wasn't important. The important thing was Boy Willie's willingness to engage the ghost in battle. Once you have that moment, then for me, the play was over" (Interview 1994). But director Lloyd Richards, and others who worked on the play's development, encouraged Wilson to "keep the lights on" a little longer and to provide an ending with greater closure. Ultimately Wilson followed this advice.

Not everyone supported Wilson's revision of *The Piano Lesson*; Michael Feingold, dramaturg at the O'Neill Playwrights Conference where Wilson developed *The Piano Lesson*, was disappointed with the final addition:

> I was very unhappy when I saw the pat ending. The first ending—the one the O'Neill staged—was the right one. With Boy Willie endlessly fighting

off the ghost, and his sister and the minister endlessly playing the piano, singing their hymn. There's an impulse there of something which does not end. And, therefore, the play cannot end. (Interview, 1994)

Feingold is not alone; many have lauded Wilson's impulse to create open-ended structures as testaments to an African artistic tradition and to question the potential loss of cultural identity in the process of mainstream dramaturgy. Expressing concern over artistic assimilation, Paul Carter Harrison bemoaned what has slipped away. "Lost," wrote Harrison, "is the aesthetic appreciation of discontinuity—rather than linear continuity—as a rhythmic device in the expressive mode of African socialization, including the polymorphic orchestration of off beats, counter beats, and breaks in music and storytelling" (295). Harrison argued that Wilson has returned something integral to his art form and the African-American community, reclaiming an essential element of community history:

> Wilson brings to the American theater, then, the oracular voice of the poet as a communal griote and has reaffirmed a kinship with the tradition of blues narratives, advancing the aesthetic strategies of polyrhythm and repetition, choric call 'n' response, double entendre and improvisation, signifyin' text that resists closure, and the reenactment of experience by the narrator/trickster figure whose self-parodic tactics allow him to suspend the painful consequences of reality. (302)

Wilson gravitates to the blues form because he is a storyteller and because he loves to hear a good story. As he sits in coffee shops, contemplating his next play, he awaits the voices of his characters, telling him their tales, surprising him, inspiring him. Then, he carefully allows them to tell their stories to us.

> Blacks do not have a history of writing—things in African were passed on orally. In that tradition you orally pass on your entire philosophy, your ideas and attitudes about life. Most of them were passed along in blues. You have to make the philosophy interesting musically and lyrically, so that some one will want to repeat it, to teach it to someone else as soon as they've heard it. (Wilson, quoted in Savran 1988, 295)

Wilson spends hours listening to people talk and then brings to the stage monologue and dialogue immediately recognizable in its music. His ear is finely tuned to the rhythms and repetitions that characterize ordinary Black speech, and his use of them invests his writing with a mixture of poetry and song. Wilson's dialogue includes both the call and response of the original antiphonal music and the lone voice of the later bluesman. His theater contains the history of the blues. His "memory has fashioned a vernacular voice that resonates, with archetypical sonority, the rhythms of West African 'talking drums,' and the riffs of Delta blues guitars" (Harrison 1984, 292).

From *Ma Rainey*, the Wilson play most directly connected to the music in both its form and dramatic setting, through *Fences* and *Joe Turner's Come and Gone*, and onto *The Piano Lesson*, Wilson continued to feed the spirit of his drama with the music he so loved. While its presence is felt in the later plays, *Two Trains Running* and *Seven Guitars*, the music is noticeably absent in *King Hedley II*, which premiered in 1999. It is the darkest of all Wilson's plays, and perhaps, through its lack of song, it offers the greatest warning to its audience, revealing a community far removed from any cultural connection.

Ruby, mother of the title character, King Hedley, used to sing. In fact, her need for the music forced her to leave her only son in the hands of another woman who raised him while she was on the road. It was her life: "I know how to press shirts on the machine. But mostly I just worked at singing. That's the only kind of work I know how to do" (King Hedley II 1999, 56). But Ruby has quit singing—she doesn't tell us why.

King Hedley II is more about guns than guitars. It deals with abortion and drive-by shootings. It reveals continued injustice, rampant racism, the presence of an apocalyptic God, and Aunt Esther, a character first introduced in *Two Trains Running*. In *Two Trains*, the unseen Aunt Esther has the power to "make you right with yourself" (*Two Trains*, 1993, 24). She is described as being 322 years old, and she is the bearer of powerful myths, old remedies, and words of wisdom. She is the source and an important symbol for Wilson, who has said: "Aunt Esther suggests that your experience is alive, that there is a repository of wisdom and experience a person can tap into" (Lyons, 17). In *King Hedley II*, Aunt Esther dies.

The play's anger and frustration clearly reflect Wilson's current outlook on culture and the African-American community. Indeed, examination of recent comments by Wilson on his sociopolitical agenda aids in understanding the selection of the artists and art forms that so heavily influence his drama. The preservation of Black culture is vital to Wilson, who states: "Those who would deny black Americans their culture would also deny them their history and the inherent values that are a part of all human life" ("Ground on Which I Stand," 1996, 16). He is thus compelled not only to create one avenue of black culture himself, but also to contain within it other venues. He celebrates the history of this culture and offers it as a model for the rebirth he sees as essential for survival of the community:

> The . . . tradition occurred when the African in the confines of slave quarters sought to invest his spirit with the strength of his ancestors by conceiving in his art, in his song and dance, a world in which he was the spiritual center and his existence was a manifest act of the creator from whom life flowed. He then could create art that was functional and furnished him with a spiritual temperament necessary for his survival as property and the dehumanizing status that was attendant to that. ("Ground," 1996, 16)

Wilson values his role as keeper of cultural flames. He has consistently maintained, first in his plays and lately in public comments, that these flames are endangered by a continual co-opting of Black cultural experience by the White artistic community, including but not limited to greedy record producers or well-meaning theatre directors. And so, Wilson has essentially provided a second home to other expressions of Black culture within his plays, partially in an effort to protect their integrity.

> So much of what makes this country rich in art and all manners of spiritual life is the contributions that we as African Americans have made. We cannot allow others to have authority over our cultural and spiritual products. We reject, without reservation, any attempts by anyone to rewrite our spiritual labors, and to become the cultural custodians of our art, our literature and our lives. To give expression to the spint that has been shaped and fashioned by our history is of necessity to give voice and vent to the history itself. ("Ground," 1996, 72)

Wilson has made clear his belief that African-American culture has suffered as the White community has come, over the course of this century and most actively in the last 30 years, to "embrace" Black culture and ultimately to "dominate and control art" ("Ground," 1996, 71).

Throughout his plays and in other public forums, Wilson has continually commented on this experience as it applies to music, particularly the blues. His early one-act play *The Homecoming* (n.d.) makes it clear that not only the music but the very life of African Americans has been stolen. The action of the play occurs while two friends of the fictional blues singer Blind Willie await the return of his dead body by train. They tell his story:

> He was doing right nice for a while too. Shucks, he'd sing four songs and make him a hundred dollars . . . And after he sing all his songs . . . they didn't need him no more. Nossir. They had his voice trapped in one of them fancy recording machines and they could hear him sing anytime they wanted to . . . then they put him out of that fancy hotel. Made like they never seen him before. Called the police on him when he went down to their office to get his money he made on them records they was selling all over Harlem . . . Blind Willie starved to death . . . That's right. Froze to death on somebody's doorstep. (14)

In *The Piano Lesson*, Boy Willie has a potential buyer for the piano because a White man is trying to buy up all the musical instruments in the "colored houses." And the theme is reiterated by *Ma Rainey* who, as noted earlier, reflects the same understanding of her own expendability, as an artist and as a human being. As Margaret Glover (1988) noted, "His music gave the black man a place in the white man's world but at the cost of losing his rights to that music, and the part of himself he put in it" (69).

Wilson speaks out against false ownership, commenting on the current relationship of the blues with White culture:

> This is the one contribution everyone admits that Africans have made. But the music has been pulled so far out of context that it's no longer recognizable. Any attempt to claim it is met with tremendous resistance. The music is ours, since it contains our soul, so to speak—it contains all our ideas and responses to the world. We need it to help us claim this African-

ness and we would be a stronger people for it. It's presently in the hands of someone else who sits over it as custodian, without even allowing us its source. (Savran 1988, 305)

Wilson lays blame on both sides. He feels the music has been co-opted and is somehow held just out of reach. But simultaneously, he feels the African-American community is, perhaps, not extending its arms far enough or firmly enough to reclaim what it has lost. For Wilson, assimilation continues to be a threat: "The fact is, we act differently, we think differently, we face the world differently—and it is our difference that makes us unique. We must embrace our culture or we will lose ourselves and disappear" (Taylor 21).

There is no music in *King Hedley II,* which ends with gunshots as a mother accidentally kills her own son, pursuing a cycle of death and destruction. The play is set in the 1980s, a decade Wilson views as a low period in the pursuit of cultural affirmation. The drama is oddly quiet. After a long series of plays intended as a call to hear the music, *King Hedley* is burdened by the silence of its absence.

August Wilson is the bluesman, our griote. "We discover in his work an authentic reclamation of the blues voice—dredged up from the oral and musical traditions of black life . . ." (Harrison 1984, 316). For Wilson, the blues are a social tool and a political tool, for he believes:

All art is politics. I'm one of those warrior spirits. The Battle since the first African set foot on the continent of North America has been a battle for the affirmation of the value and worth of one's being in the face of this society that says you're worthless." (Rosen 1996, 31)

The blues are his armory, his source.

Works Cited

Baker, Jr., Houston. 1984. *Blues, ideology, and Afro-American Literature: A Vernacular theory.* Chicago: University of Chicago Press.

Feingold, Michael. 1994. Interview, January.

Glover, Margaret. 1988. Two Notes on August Wilson: Song of the Marked Man. *Theatre,* summer/fall, 69–70.

Goodstein, Laura, and Megan Rosenfeld. 1990. August Wilson: Writing Plays from the Blues. *Washington Post,* 13 April, C 1+.

Harrison, Paul Carter. 1984. August Wilson's Blues Poetics. In *August Wilson Three Plays.* Pittsburgh: University of Pittsburgh Press.

Lomax, Alan. 1990. *Blues in the Night.* Recorded interview with blues singers Big Bill Bronzy, Memphis Slim, and Sonny Boy Williamson. Salem, MA: Rykodisc.

Lyons, Bonnie. An Interview with August Wilson. *Contemporary Literature* 40.1 (Spring 1999): 1–21.

Nelson, Don. 1988. August Arrives. New York *Daily News,* 6 March, 5.

Pereira, Kim. 1995. *August Wilson and the African-American Odyssey.* Urbana: University of Illinois Press.

Plum, Jay. 1993. Blues, History, and the Dramaturgy of August Wilson. *African American Review* 27.4: 561–7.

Rosen, Carol. 1996. August Wilson: Bard of the Blues. *Theater Week,* 27 May, 18–35.

Savran, David. 1988. *In Their Own Words, Contemporary American Playwrights.* New York: Theatre Communications Group.

Schwartzman, Myron. 1990. *Romare Bearden, His Life & Art.* New York: Harry Abrams, Inc.

Soyinka, Wole. 1976. *Myth, Literature, and the African World.* London: Cambridge University Press.

Wang, Qun. 1999. *An In-Depth Study of the Major Plays of African American Playwright August Wilson—Vernacularizing the Blues on Stage.* Lempeter, UK: Edward Mellen Press.

Wilson, August. n.d. *The Homecoming,* unpublished property of August Wilson.

———. 1984. Preface. *August Wilson Three Plays.* Pittsburgh: University of Pittsburgh Press.

———. 1985. *Ma Rainey's Black Bottom.* New York: Plume Books.

———. 1990. *The Piano Lesson.* New York, Penguin Books.

———. 1991. *Three Plays.* Pittsburgh: University of Pittsburgh Press.

———. 1993. Two Trains Running, New York: Penguin Books.

———. 1994. Interview conducted by the author, February.

———. 1996. Quoted in Regina Taylor. That's Why They Call it the Blues, *American Theatre,* April, 18–23.

———. 1996. "The Ground on Which I Stand." Keynote address to the Theatre Communications Group National Conference, reprinted in *American Theatre,* September.

———. 1999. *King Hedley II,* unpublished property of August Wilson.

Wolfe, Peter, 1999. *August Wilson.* New York: Twayne Publishers.

INTERVIEW WITH AUGUST WILSON

Interview conducted by Joan Herrington
in December 2000

Joan Herrington: When did you write your first play?

August Wilson: My very first play, 1973.

JH: What other kind of creative writing had you been doing at that time?

AW: I was writing short fiction and poetry.

JH: What made you decide to write a play?

AW: It was actually an event I witnessed—this guy getting killed. This guy came out of a bar and he was standing on the sidewalk looking up and down the street, and then a hand came out of the door with a gun, and just as I was walking, about 20 feet away, the guy fell down; he'd been shot. And a crowd of people gathered around him and there was a woman who I later found out was a nurse, and she was down on the ground and she was pounding on this guy's chest trying to revive him. Then this guy standing there says, "Baby ain't no need you doing that, that man dead. His brain's laying right there." And she looked on the car and saw that this brain matter was lying on the hood of the car and she got up and walked across the street to this bar. A crowd of people gathered around the body but I followed her. There was something about the way she was pounding on his chest which intrigued me so I went into the bar with her and she said to the bartender, "The niggers are killing each other these days." And he says, "Yeah I heard, is he dead?" And that became the first line of the first play I ever wrote—1973.

I brought the guy into the bar. The same guy who she was pounding on his chest and she says, "Where did you come from." And he says,

"Down the street, lady did you forget?" And she looks at him and says, "Forget about what?" He says, "About everything. Long dancing and wet afternoons, memory lake, something scratching against the silence. All the mean shit we done together." And she says, "I don't know you." So they begin talking and you don't know if she knows him or not and that was the beginning and that was my first effort at writing a play.

JH: Why did you decide to write that as a play instead of a short story, since you'd been writing short fiction?

AW: I have no idea. I think it was just those first two lines. When I followed her that's what she said and I think I got the idea that this guy comes into the bar. I don't know why I wrote it as a play. It was exciting, though.

JH: Was it more exciting to write a play than a short story?

AW: Absolutely.

JH: Was it more difficult?

AW: No. It just flowed. You can do anything in this kind of play. All I had to do, if I got stuck in writing a certain portion of the dialogue, was just change it and they start talking about something else. So you could always keep it alive simply by making changes.

JH: So you felt writing in that format gave you greater freedom than writing fiction?

AW: Oh sure. In the fiction you need a beginning, middle, end, and the way short stories are structured you have the whole thing worked out in your head before you start. You don't have the freedom to just suddenly change and go off on a new path using dialogue in a different direction.

JH: Did you feel that a play needed to have a beginning, middle, and end?

AW: Sure, but you can arrive at the end by circuitous route and I guess at the time I thought you had to go straight forward, more linearly to achieve the structure of the short story. But I found out with the play you can do anything and arrive at the end. I still look for different ways of getting there.

JH: How long between that one and your next play?

AW: I don't know exactly. That was a one-act play and then I wrote this very long and very confusing full-length play in which I was trying to take a spiritual reality and a reality and blend them both together. I had these people leaving the South and going north to Chicago and yet they were stuck in this timeless railroad yard, always ducking the rail wardens. So you witness a baby being born and 19 years later, they're still going to Chicago in the morning. They were always going and there were all sorts of things happening in the landscape.

And then there was a corresponding landscape in Alabama with the same characters and they did the same things but they played out differently in the end. It was a large, confusing play but every play I've ever written is contained in that large play I was writing then.

JH: Had you gone back to writing fiction in between those two plays?

AW: Yes.

JH: So why did you return to the dramatic form for the railroad story?

AW: I was writing it as a short story and that short story had a lot of dialogue in the sense that there was a character, a grandmother, and she had to explain to her grandson the history of these events that we had already witnessed and took place in this train yard. They were long passages of dialogue so I started writing it as a play.

JH: Is there anything that you were sorry to give up that the fiction form allowed you to do that the playwriting form did not?

AW: No, I felt released. I felt that playwriting was boundless where the short story writing was restricting. And again it was a bad play because I was trying to put too much into it. So it wasn't entirely satisfactory but I wrote it and that's cool.

I was still developing as a playwright and then in 1976 I wrote a play called *Ma Rainey's Back Bottom*. I was working originally just with Ma Rainey and men in the studio. But they kept making reference to the band that was in the band room. And it never occurred to me to make those guys characters. I didn't know how to make them talk or anything, in 1976. So I went back to the play in 1980. I'd already written *Jitney* and I'd become a playwright and it was easier to do.

JH: Did you continue to write poetry?

AW: Oh yes, poetry and short fiction. Then in 1977 I moved to St. Paul and I got a job as a script writer at the Science Museum of Minnesota. They had a theatre troupe that was attached to the anthropology floor, so I wrote tales of the northwest Indians. And these actors would go out and act these out for the school kids at three o'clock in the afternoon.

So I had started writing regularly in a script form but at that time I actually wrote more fiction because the job freed me up to write. So I wrote a lot of short stories in between writing these little projects.

JH: Were any of them published?

AW: No.

JH: When you write short fiction you have complete control. It's yours. You describe all the characters, you can define their speech. When you started writing dialogue for actors, and they started interpreting it, how did you respond to that?

AW: Well the first time they didn't say it like it was in my head it kind of threw me at first since I thought they would say it like I heard it. Then I said to myself, "They're never gonna get it like it is in my head. But they do say the words and they don't ad lib—they don't make up stuff, so it's my words." And if you don't like how that guy says it, find a guy who you like. That's what casting was all about for me when I started out. I don't care what kind of actor you are, do you understand the words, can you say the words close to the way I heard them in my head?

We were casting *Ma Rainey* and a guy came in and he read it and I said, "Let's get him." Lloyd [Richards, the director of the production] said, "That guy can't act." But he could approximate the language the way it was in my head. I didn't know if he was a good actor or not. I couldn't tell. But Lloyd says, "No, you don't want to cast him."

JH: Did you continue to try to find actors who sounded like what you heard in your head?

AW: No, I gave that up. I don't try it anymore. I've found that if you get the right actors, they bring a lot to it and they'll actually embody the character and develop it and make that stuff that's on the page so much fuller and richer. I trust them.

JH: I noticed in reading the early draft of *Jitney* that you had provided many more stage directions for the actors than you had in later drafts.

AW: Yes, I did that early on. *Jitney* was written in 1979, and it was my first full-length, realistic-style play, and I wrote things like "angrily." Later I learned to let the actors find that.

JH: Aside from the freedom to change the direction with dialogue and move about more freely, what is there about playwriting that appeals to you more than writing in other forms?

AW: It's unique. Of all the written art forms, film, short fiction, poetry, all the great art forms, theatre is unique among them. And I think the thing that's most exciting for me is the audience in the sense that if you write a novel, you may get on the bus, for instance, and see someone reading the novel. But that is a solitary act. People read novels on buses, trains, in their bedrooms, their bathrooms. That's a solitary act.

With a play and an audience, it's like having 700 people read your novel at the same time. And I just found that so exciting in that it's a communal experience as opposed to a solitary experience. That's intriguing.

But it's a very difficult art form and its history goes all the way back to the Greeks, and there are certain principals like Aristotle's *Poetics*. There are breakthroughs that people made: the well-made play, Ibsen, and all of this. So that becomes exciting because you have a whole body of predecessors, and both their triumphs and their failures are yours in a sense. I just found a home there. I found it liberating.

JH: You say it's hard to write a play. What is the hardest part for you?

AW: Trying to find out how to tell the story, exploring the different ways to do that. For instance, with the play I'm working on now, I know the story but I must decide how to tell it. Do I use this aspect? Is this an important part of telling the story? Do I need the scene in which the history of this particular character is revealed, do you need this for that to be clear?

There are different ways to tell the story and the playwright selects a certain way. You can give another playwright the same story and he will select different things to tell the story. Some parts that I may choose to dramatize, he may want as the backstory and he won't even have that in the play. So there are different ways of doing it.

The thrilling part is when you make discoveries, and it's generally stuff that's been sitting right in front of you for a long while. When I was writing *King Hedly II*, I didn't know that I was going to kill Aunt Esther. But when I was writing the play a character came in said, "You know that little old lady that lived up the street, she died." I didn't know it was Aunt Esther at the time. Then I found out it was Aunt Esther and this was devastating to me. I don't think I could work on the play for a month. I had to digest it. It was a discovery, and I had to consider whether it made sense.

I came to the conclusion that it was correct because she represents a link with the past, and if you don't value it you lose it. There was no way it was there in 1985 [when the play is set], with all these kids running around, with the condition of black America at that time, all that chaos. So you say, "What happened?" Well Aunt Esther died. You lost that connection with your tradition and your past. You no longer know who you are. If you had that connection, you couldn't go and kill someone over $15 worth of narcotics because everything your ancestors have taught you says you don't do that. But if you've lost that connection then you don't know.

So that was important. I said, "OK, I'm correct. I'm not just killing her for no reason." So then I had Aunt Esther die but in the reviews no one mentioned Aunt Esther's dying and to me that's important. So I reread the play and I'd buried it inside the play—a little incidental thing inside the play. So I said, "I know what I'll do, I'll start off the play with her funeral so nobody can miss it."

The hardest part is after you've written a play, finding the play that you have written. It's there but you have to go in and find it. It's just difficult to write a good play. It's also very exciting.

JH: When you write fiction, is the way you're going to tell the story clearer to you? Is it less of a process of discovery?

AW: No, it's discovery also. It's a similar kind of process actually. But I think I know more where I want to go with the fiction than with the plays. And there are more tools at my disposal with narrative fiction.

JH: What's the most frustrating thing about writing a play?

AW: I don't pay enough attention to the time elements in the play. I'll have a scene, and someone will ask me, "When is this scene? Is it three days later? Is it the next day or is it three weeks later?" And I'll say, "It doesn't matter, it's just the next scene."

But then writing the next scene you find that you have to put it in a time frame—you find out you need to know when it is. But it's simply that I'm not paying attention, I'm writing in the heat of the moment and don't think. Sometimes the characters exit and I want them to come right back on in a different costume but I have not given them the chance to change costume because I'm starting the scene with the same character that just exited. Someone has to point that out to me because I was only concerned with how the scene should start.

I just did that in this play. I put some changes in and I wasn't fully cognizant and when we put it up on stage we said, "Wait a minute. She has to change her clothes." And I said I should have known better.

But I wouldn't call it frustrating. I don't know that there's anything frustrating about the process. There are parts I enjoy more than others, but I don't think I've ever been frustrated.

JH: What do you enjoy the most?

AW: I write in twenty-minute spurts. Sometimes you go and it's not there. Other times you find out you're doing something and it's just good, it's going good. When you're there, at that moment, that's the joyous part.

I've found myself right in the middle of moments and stopping. I want to keep on going but I don't have the stamina to continue so I just take that for now. But in actuality you don't know if you're ever going to get back in that place again. I wish I hadn't stopped some of those times, but in those twenty minutes, half an hour, I'm so emotionally drained, I just don't have anything to go forward and continue. Even if it's really going good and I know it's the best writing I've done in the past two weeks and this is the moment and all I have to do is keep going for a little while longer and maybe I'll get some more stuff. But I just don't have the emotional stamina to push it.

So I come back to it two or three days later. People ask me if I write everyday, and I say, "No, man, I don't." But I'm processing every day and when it feels right to do something then I'll do something in a half-hour. That's good for three days. And then I'll think about where this half-hour of work I did is going to lead. So I'm actually getting ready to do the next twenty minutes whenever it happens.

JH: How do you feel about playwriting in America now?

AW: It's an exciting time. Because it's the only time we have. You can talk about the golden age of American playwriting, Williams, Miller. But in the end you realize that for those few names we know there are 500 other guys out there writing whose names we don't know.

I do think the difference in contemporary playwriting is that we have an influence the playwrights of the 1940s didn't have, and that's the influence of television. And I don't think contemporary playwrights have absorbed that influence or know how to use it. So what you have is a lot of plays which are basically sitcoms because that's what the writer grew up on and that's what he knows. But that's not it. This can influence what you write but you have to take that and aspire to create literature. We have this separation between literature and playwriting, and playwriting has come to be viewed more as the practice of a craft than the creation of literature, so we have a lot of "craft literature" where the writer is not aspiring to write the best play that's ever been written but just aspiring to write a good play, well executed. We have a lot of that. But we have to acknowledge and absorb the influence of television so we can get rid of it.

Another thing that is important is that theatres do new plays. The trend has generally been to do them on the second stage and to give your main stage to productions of Chekhov and Molière and Shakespeare. I think it should be the exact opposite. If doing a play on the second stage stigmatizes the playwright by signifying that he's not going to be as good as Tennessee Williams or Arthur Miller, that he doesn't deserve the main stage, then that puts all of us in a place where we're not going to write "main stage" writing because we've already been relegated to the second stage. So good, bad, or indifferent, this is the play, this is where we are, and the playwrights should have access to the stages of the American theatre irrespective of whether they are as good as Arthur Miller or some others. This is what we've got and we still deserve the stages.

I think in the last five years, more and more theatres are doing new plays on the main stage than in my casual observation I discerned previously, which I think is a good thing. The Goodman is a perfect example, with Rebecca Gilman. Then you have some theatres like South Coast Rep, which always did new plays. But we have to have access to the theatres in order to develop as writers. Given that, five years down the road, you're bound to have better writing.

There's an awful lot of bad plays that are being written and there's a few good plays which are being written also. There's a ratio, and you have to go through some bad plays in order to get to the good ones. There are some playwrights who are writing bad plays, me being one of them. So if the playwright is talented, and has to do some more work and then he'll come up with a good play, give him the chance. But he'll never come up with a good play if he doesn't have opportunities to develop his talent by having productions. You can't do it with workshops. You can have workshops. You can sit there in rehearsal, but it doesn't matter until you see the play before an audience. It's the only time I really see it. I watch it in rehearsal and I make some changes, but then we put the thing up onstage and we do the first preview and the second preview and that's when I start working. I don't know how you see it other than with an audience. Fortunately this is like my fifth production of *King Hedly* and I'm still sitting here and making changes. I don't know how you develop a play other than by having opportunities to see it onstage. I find playwriting exciting, I find it challenging. I'm glad I discovered it.

BROADWAY BOUNDARIES: NEIL SIMON AND POPULAR CULTURE

Bette Mandl

When his first play, *Come Blow Your Horn*, opened in 1961, Pulitzer Prize–winning playwright Neil Simon discovered that he had a gift for rewrites. After seeing a performance, he "could reread a script later that night and tell exactly how, where, and to what degree the audience responded, as well as what worked and what needed rewriting" (Simon 1996, 63). Simon would ultimately write and rewrite his way to becoming "the most successful playwright in the American theatre" (Bryer 1996, 58). Having begun his career with writing for early television figures such as Sid Caesar and Phil Silver, Simon has created plays that have resonated with a succession of audiences for forty years. If, as Michael Kammen (1999) said in his study of popular culture in America, "the history of cultural taste levels in the twentieth century has increasingly been one of fluidity, blending, and the attendant blurring of boundaries" (xvi), then Simon's enduring relationship with audiences suggests how attentive he has had to be to all the modulations of response that such movement implies.

Simon has long been aware that commercial success evokes ambivalent responses from reviewers and academics. He describes being "*too* popular" as "an unpardonable sin, at least if you had any thoughts of trying to be accepted by that lofty circle of writers who decide who does and who does not get into the Pantheon" (1998a, 3). He also recognizes that the comedic form he is identified with is a complicating factor: "Woody Allen once remarked that to write comedy is like eating at the children's table . . . In many quarters, to write comedy brings you poularity and success. To write drama brings you respect" (1996, 192–193). Enjoying fame for works such as *Barefoot in the Park* (1963), *The Odd Couple* (1965), and *The Sunshine Boys* (1972), Simon desired to enlarge the scope of his work: "I knew that eventually I wanted to write darker plays, although not drama. I wanted to write comedies the way that dramatists wrote drama . . . It was not something I could just leap into. I would have to grow into it" (1996, 192–193).

Simon ultimately did rescript his own role in the theatre. As William A. Henry III (1986) described it, Simon felt

> the urge for a deeper resonance between present and past, between work and an inner sense of self. And so he subtly but surely changed careers. America's master joke meister moved away from the neatly rounded, readily palatable social comment that had made him the world's most popular living playwright.

Simon had periodically ventured into deeper waters with such works as *The Gingerbread Lady* (1970) and *Chapter Two* (1977). He would continue to try his hand at shaping plays that went beyond the comedies he was most closely identified with, while the audiences he knew best were increasingly developing a taste of their own for more serious material. The trend was gaining momentum during the 1980s and into the 1990s, as Simon was effecting his own transformation. Books by writers like Toni Morrison and Kazuo Ishiguro were appearing on bestseller lists and museum attendance was steadily increasing toward an all-time high. Commenting on a trend that seems to be accelerating at the Millennium, Pico Iyer (1996) suggested that "in certain respects the country around us seems to be dumbing up, presenting us on a daily basis with texts and thoughts that give no indication of a nation suffering from attention deficit disorder" (99). While intense debates rage about the mass marketing of high culture, all seem to agree that we have moved beyond a time when "high culture stood smugly apart, secure in its elitism" (Kakutani 1996, 30).

A writer like Simon, gifted at rewrites and fully in tune with the audience, was likely to benefit from what might be seen as a new intermediate space that was opening near the end of the century between formerly separated cultural worlds. Simon's aspirations as a popular playwright in transition were a perfect match for the needs of an evolving audience. By the time Simon received the Pulitzer Prize for *Lost in Yonkers* in 1991, he had created a distinctive theatrical amalgam for a new aesthetic context with the Brighton Beach Trilogy. The first play of the trilogy, *Brighton Beach Memoirs* (1983), was both critically acclaimed and the "highest-profit making play in the history of the New York theater" (Simon 1999, 198). Simon had indeed grown into the new role he had envisioned for himself, retaining his distinctive comic voice while treating serious matters in a way that a widening audience increasingly appreciated. Kammen (1999) described "a pattern of change that has . . . emerged since mid-century in the blurred relationship between taste publics for high culture and mass culture" (125–126). It is Simon's triumph in the theatre that he forged a position at the cusp of these taste publics.

The blurring of the boundaries between high art and popular culture inevitably leads to new ways of seeing the role of the artist. In a *New York Times* piece, Michael Lind (1999) suggested that there is some advantage in "the fading of the religion of art": "In the 21st century, the fact that a writer, dramatist, composer or visual artist is as law-abiding, successful and well paid as, say, Shakespeare, Haydn or Raphael will not be ground for suspicion" (39). There is a clear confluence of Simon's own relationship to the public and such shifts in attitude that make way for reconceptions of art and the artist. Simon's own increasing awareness of the conventions that have prevailed, and his challenges to them as he moved into a new relationship with them in recent years, have added a significant dimension to a long career that has comprised work in television and film as well as theatre. Leslie Fiedler (1982) has suggested that the "myth of the 'serious' writer" lodged in the collective psyche is that of "an alienated male, condemned to neglect and poverty by a culture simultaneously commercialized and feminized" (29). It was to Simon's considerable advantage that its exclusivity was being challenged in a variety of quarters. The Brighton Beach trilogy, and especially his young jocoserious persona, Eugene Jerome, who addresses the audience throughout the trilogy, provided Simon with an opportunity to seize the day and tailor a portrait of the artist to fit his own dimensions.

The inflections that characterize the Jewish immigrant lower middle-class world of Eugene sets him at a distance from the traditional artist-as-hero, but the classic paradigm remains a strong influence as he develops his sense of self. Early in *Brighton Beach Memoirs* (1984), in the midst of a characteristically exasperating exchange with family, Eugene announces to the audience, "One day I'm going to put all this in a book or play. . . . I'm going to be a writer like Ring Lardner or somebody" (10). In *Long Day's Journey into Night*, Eugene O'Neill's Edmund Tyrone identifies with such literary figures as Baudelaire and Swinburne and is thereby powerfully linked to the Romantic and Modernist conceptions of the artist. Eugene Jerome, in his sense of a calling and his immersion in family turmoil, reminds critics of Edmund,[1] but by providing his engaging protagonist with models of a very different stripe, as well as one-liners, Simon demands that we expand our aesthetic categories. He locates Eugene in a world very like the one familiar to him from his own youth, where the forms of popular entertainment are the lure. Eugene is not unaware of the traditional myth: "How am I going to become a writer if I don't know how to suffer?" (77), but he has an alternative lineage to claim as the stage and the media beckon. In *Brighton Beach Memoirs*, Eugene senses the glamour of Broadway when his cousin, Nora, is tempted to leave high school for an opportunity to perform in a musical. He pictures his family life as fodder for a radio show: "WEAF presents dinner at Brighton Beach starring the Jacob Jerome Family and featuring tonight's specialty liver and cabbage, brought to you by Ex-lax, the mild laxative" (42). Eugene passes through his adolescent rites of initiation as the domestic drama of the Jeromes proceeds, while, as Walter Kerr (1983) noted, "Mr. Simon lets us watch the comic mind growing up" (3).

Simon thinks back to responses to *Brighton Beach Memoirs* when he talks about creating the trilogy: "It got a middling review from Frank Rich of *The New York Times,* but he said at the end of it, 'One hopes that there is a chapter two to *Brighton Beach*'" (Simon 2000, 200). Steven Spielberg then suggested that "the next play should be about my days in the army. I was already thinking about that, and I started to write *Biloxi Blues*." (200–01). In *Biloxi Blues* (1986), where Eugene is a private in the army, he continues to see himself as the would-be young writer, recording his observations faithfully in his notebook. Unlike Arnold Epstein, "a fellow Jew" (40) and a rebel, Eugene is far from closely familiar with Tolstoy or Dostoevsky or Melville. As he says to

Epstein, who urges him to be like them in not merely watching the action, "Yeah. I have to read those guys." We sense that "those guys" will not become his literary mentors. Eugene understands that his work will inevitably be unlike theirs, but he does see a commitment to writing as his vocation and it remains at the center of his experience. When some of his secret and candid appraisals of his bunkmates are read aloud, they cause a stir and are all too persuasive when his guess that Epstein is a homosexual almost leads to an arrest. Eugene feels he "learned a very important lesson that night. People believe what they read. Something magical happens once it's put down on paper . . . Responsibility was my new watchword" (71). The name of O'Neill is briefly mentioned during a romantic interlude the young hero has with Daisy Hannigan at a USO dance, reminding us of this young Eugene's resemblance to the Father of Modern Drama, as well as of the distance between them.

In *Broadway Bound* (1987), Eugene takes his first steps into the world that he has longed to enter with his older brother Stan. The names of those who are involved in work that Eugene and Stan admire form a distinctively alternative pantheon: Abe Burrows, Jack Benny, Ed Sullivan, Arthur Godfrey, Edward R. Murrow. In *Broadway Bound*, Simon intended "to show the anatomy of writing comedy—with the older brother teaching Eugene, which was the case with my brother Danny and me" (Simon 2000, 197). When the brothers ultimately manage to get a humorous autobiographical skit onto a radio show, Eugene has some crucial lessons to learn about making the private public. His mother is pleasantly uncomprehending when responding to the character she has inspired, "She reminds me of someone, but I can't think who" (*Broadway Bound* 1987, 66). His father, however, feels betrayed by his sons:

> I will never forgive either one of you for ridiculing me in front of my neighbors, in front of my friends. You know what I thought when I heard it? . . . I thought it was their way of getting back at me for hurting their mother. (72)

Since Jack has been having an affair and is planning to leave Kate, he has reason to wonder at his sons' motives. Eugene also has to tally in his socialist grandfather's estimate of his contribution. When Eugene explains that "the point" was "to make people laugh," Ben says, "That's not a point. To make people *aware*, that's a point. Political satire, that's what you should have written. You could change half the world with political satire. Think about that some time" (68). Eugene has much to glean from the reactions to his pilot project. No doubt he, too, will one day have a talent for rewrites that take audience reaction into account, even when he remains determinedly on his own path.

Just before Jack leaves Kate at the end of *Broadway Bound* (1987), Eugene urges his mother to retell her story of how she was singled out by George Raft when he was a rising star stopping in at a neighborhood dance. As she relives the memory, Eugene says: "This is a movie. There's a whole movie in this story, Ma. And one day I'm going to write it" (84). Then he dances with the initially reluctant Kate, who enters fully into the moment. Eugene confesses to the audience: "Dancing with my mother was very scary. I was doing what my father should have been doing with her but wasn't" (89). He had not only displaced the father at this point, but had also taken the part of George Raft, the star of the scenario, one more step in the creation of his identity. The dance was as important for Eugene as it was for Kate because it allowed him to take a risk he felt was vital to his self-conception:

> Intimacy is a complex thing . . . You had to be careful who you shared it with . . . But without it life was just breakfast, lunch, dinner and a good night's sleep. Most people would settle for that. Most people do . . . I was determined not to be most people. (89)

Eugene has summoned up the strength to engage in the quest that will set him apart, just as he has staked his claim to his particular arena, with its show business aura.

Broadway Bound caps Simon's creation of the dramatic equivalent of a Bildungsroman with an autobiographical hero. As Simon commented about the response to Eugene's asides there, "The audience listens attentively because it knows this character is going to become a very successful writer who will write the play the audience is seeing" (quoted in Henry 1986). If O'Neill accustomed us to learning about the life of the artist through the staged productions of his work, then Simon extends the project here. In tune with the Zeitgeist of an era absorbed in "real life" stories, Simon was ready to deal with his early experience more directly: "*Broadway Bound* comes closest to being really autobio-graphical. I didn't pull any punches with that one. My mother and father were gone when I wrote it, so I did tell about the fights, and what it was like for me as a kid hearing them" (Simon 2000, 203). Even the mem-ory of dancing with either George Raft or George Burns, since the story was told with variations, was his mother's own. Simon managed to incorporate all of his major themes in this one play: "the abandoned child, a father with a failing heart (my father died of one) and a mother dying of cancer . . . Always abandonment in one form or another" (Simon 1999, 171).

The endeavor of writing a work that immersed him in such personal confrontations seems to have been cathartic, and led him to the step he had always envisioned taking. His next play, *Lost in Yonkers* (1992), which once more introduced elements central to his most profound con-cerns, was "the play I was waiting all my life to write" (Simon 1999, 261). In *Lost in Yonkers*, two young brothers, Jay and Arty, who remind audiences of Eugene and Stan in the Brighton Beach Trilogy but who are not drawn directly from life, develop courage and resilience in their harsh grandmother's home. Their mother had recently died and their father sets off across the country to earn money for their support. With World War II[2] as a distant but crucial backdrop, they learn to conjure up "moxie" under the tutelage of their uncle Louie, a genial Hollywood-style gangster figure, while their Aunt Bella, an avid movie-goer, strug-gles to transcend her mental and emotional limitations and free herself from the tyrannical maternal grip. The play pleases both Simon fans and those who might not otherwise have ventured his way. Acknowledging his own accomplishment in *Lost in Yonkers*, Simon reports that he could hardly believe he was its creator when he watched a scene performed at a tribute in his honor: "I listened in awe at the power of the words, and silently I said to myself, 'God I wish I could write like that.' No one said you had to be sane to be a playwright" (Simon 1999, 125). The idea of "a Neil Simon play" was being broadened.

After winning the Pulitzer Prize, Simon continued his saga of the writer's life in two of the plays he has written. In *Jake's Women* (1994), a Simon-like writer, albeit a novelist, remains preoccupied with the loss of his beloved first wife, modelled after Simon's first wife, Joan Baim, who died of cancer at the age of thirty-nine. Anxious about the possible breakup of his second marriage, a marriage much like Simon's marriage to Marsha Mason, Jake is as immersed in imaginative visions of his experience as he is in his daily reality. He spends his time conjuring up the dramatis personae of his life in order to have conversations with them, allowing them to both bolster him and reproach him. His sister, for example, tells him, in words he provides her, "I think you're afraid to lose control in a relationship with a woman. To let a woman in so close . . . that she'll gobble you up and you'll lose whatever you think you are. You always have to be the master, Jake" (*Jake's Women* 1998b, 199). Ultimately, he manages to move forward by arranging a meeting, in his own vivid fantasy realm, between the wife who didn't live long enough to talk with her grown-up daughter and the daughter who yearns for the lost mother. While he is trying to resolve issues around the marriage, however, Jake is also reflecting on what it has meant to him to be a writer: "I don't observe because I choose to, I'm not alone because I prefer it. I'm not a writer because I'm good at it . . . I write to survive" (224).

Laughter on the 23rd Floor (1993) vividly brings into the foreground Simon's long history of connection to the world of entertainment and continues to add brushstrokes to the portrait of the artist as a popular culture figure. The Simon character in the play, Lucas, addresses the audience much as Eugene does in the Brighton Beach trilogy: "I guess this is what I've dreamed of my whole life. There was no comedy show in all of television that equaled *The Max Prince Show*. Not in 1953, there wasn't . . . An hour and a half review every Saturday night, completely live. And now I was actually a writer on it" (*Laughter on the 23rd floor* 1998c, 234). New and on a four-week contract, watching more than participating in the uproarious activities around the Sid Caesar–like Max, Lucas is shy but learning his craft avidly. Max, somewhat disordered by alcohol and pills, is capable of monumental ire against the tyrannies of McCarthy and is as paternal as he is irascible toward the talented writers who work for him. Simon gives us an insider's view of the birth of TV comedy in this play, as Max struggles to keep his show going. Lucas explains, "The quality was still there but the ratings weren't. America wanted comedy closer to their own lives. Julius Caesar wasn't as familiar to them as kids named Beaver and fathers who knew best" (287). With Lucas as the guide, Simon once more gives us a way of seeing "the comic mind growing up" (Kerr 1983, 3), very much as if Eugene and Stan were engaged in their next great adventure, as in fact Neil and his brother Danny actually were at that time in their careers. Simon reminisces happily about that phase of his life:

> We screamed about everything; we were all 25, 26 years old, angry about the world, in love with the world. It was for me, creatively aside from doing some of the plays, the most fun I ever had; because I was around the funniest people in the world: Sid Caesar, Carl Reiner, Mel Brooks, Larry Gelbart, and a number of others. We were in stitches all day long. (Bryer 1997, 230)

In his memoirs *Rewrites* (1996) and *The Play Goes On* (1999), and in his interviews, Simon continues to develop a seamless representation of a distinctive kind of artist. He talks of his own accomplishments with gently self-deprecatory references to canonical writers, while situating himself effectively in the borderland that he has claimed as his own. He tells an anecdote, for example, about the opening night of *Broadway Bound*, when he could not muster up a celebratory mood (and ultimately feared he was having a heart attack):

> Not to make any comparisons, but I couldn't imagine Eugene O'Neill sitting in a restaurant on the night that *Long Day's Journey into Night* opened, a play so searing he asked that it not be performed until twenty-five years after his death. (Simon 1999, 247)

He also compares himself with Hemingway, employing Simonesque humor to make the contrast vivid. He describes what he calls

> a vast difference between Hemingway and me, which any voting member of the Nobel Prize for Literature committee could tell you. He had a life. I had a career. I envied his life, but I would have been ill-suited to live it. I would never shoot a lion; I'd get no kick out of bringing down a tiger; an antelope's head on my wall wouldn't thrill me at all; and I'm sure I'd get sick at a bullfight as well. (Simon 1998a, 2)

The evidence mounts of the playwright's persistent and effective pressure toward a new aesthetic, and even a new corollary ethic. He dares to question the tenet that, as Hemingway put it, "The writing of a book . . . should destroy the writer" (2). Both in the plays and around them, Simon makes room in American literature for the kind of artist he is, by revisioning what an artist can be. Meditations on his "place" pervade his autobiographical reflections:

> So often I thought that in choosing me the gods picked the wrong man to work in the same field as Shaw and Ibsen and Kaufman and Hart. They were giants; I was not. The irony is, I never felt inferior while in the act of writing. On the contrary, in my little room, and even while in the theatre, I felt as strong and as capable as most of my peers. (Simon 1999, 121)

Simon knows himself to be original, the creator of forms at which he excels, and he guides us toward applying standards that are appropriate to an appreciation of them. He regularly shares his own perceptions of where he should be located in the history of theatre, making self-assessments that are simultaneously prods to ways of seeing his work:

> Those writers who go to the deepest and darkest of agonies are the ones who have lived there as well: O'Neill, Chekhov, Tolstoy, Beckett. The rest of us are not so brave, or perhaps not so damaged and broken, so we do not soar . . . I wish I could go deeper, further, but then again I think I do. I make the effort if not the entire journey; but the effort exhausts me as much as the farthest journey I would take. (Simon 1999, 142)

This blend of the deferential and the directive contributes to the particular flavor of his interviews and memoirs and plays a significant role in clarifying how Simon might be situated in the history of theatre.

Still fully involved in his odyssey, and coping with the demands of an increasingly bottom-line-focused Broadway, Simon continues to develop plays that balance the comic and the tragic. As Ben Brantley (2000) said of Simon's latest play, *The Dinner Party*, "It's heartening to see that at 73 he is asserting his right to explore new territory while holding on to beloved staples of the classic Simon style" (2). The rewrites that have marked the legendary career of "one of our most prolific and durable playwrights" (Weber 2000, 3) will warrant increasing attention as we continue to rewrite our own understandings of the relationship of playwright and audience in the decades leading to the twenty-first century and beyond.

Notes

1. For works comparing Simon and O'Neill, see, for example, Frank, Glenda, "Fun House Mirrors: The Neil Simon-Eugene O'Neill Dialogue." In *Neil Simon: A Casebook,* ed. Gary Konas. New York: Garland Publishing, 1997: 109–125, and Bloom, Steven, "The Lingering (Comic?) Legacy of Eugene O'Neill." *The Eugene O'Neill Review* 20, Spring and Fall 1996: 139–146.
2. See my essay on the influence of WW II on *Lost in Yonkers:* "Beyond Laughter and Forgetting: Echoes of the Holocaust in Neil Simon's *Lost in Yonkers.*" In *Neil Simon: A Casebook,* ed. Gary Konas. New York: Garland Publishing, 1997: 69–77.

Works Cited

Brantley, Ben. 2000. "The Dinner Party": A Fine Meal, Please Pass the Vitriol. *New York Times on the Web,* 20 October, Arts page.

Bryer, Jackson R. 1996. Neil Simon. *Speaking on Stage: Interviews with Contemporary American Playwrights,* ed. Philip C. Kolin and Colby H. Kullman. Tuscaloosa: University of Alabama Press, pp. 58–81.

———. 1997. An interview with Neil Simon. In *Neil Simon: A Casebook,* ed. Gary Konas. New York: Garland Publishing, pp. 217–232.

Fiedler, Leslie. 1982. *What Was Literature? Class Culture and Mass Society.* New York: Simon & Schuster.

Henry III, William A. 1986. Reliving a Poignant Past. *Time,* 15 December, 72–78.

Iyer, Pico. 1999. In Fact, We're Dumbing Up. *Time,* 24 May, 99.

Kakutani, Michiko. 1996. The Trickle-Down Theory. *New York Times Magazine,* 22 September, 28 & 30.

Kammen, Michael. 1999. *American Culture, American Tastes: Social Change and the 20th Century.* New York: Knopf.

Kerr, Walter. 1983. Seeing a Comic Mind Emerge. *New York Times,* 3 April, 3.

Lind, Michael. 1999. Defrocking the Artist. *The New York Times Book Review,* 14 March, 39.

O'Neill, Eugene. 1955. *Long Day's Journey into Night.* New Haven, CT: Yale University Press.

Simon, Neil. 1984. *Brighton Beach Memoirs.* New York: Samuel French.

———. 1986. *Biloxi Blues.* New York: Samuel French.

———. 1987. *Broadway Bound.* New York: Samuel French.

———. 1992. *Lost in Yonkers.* New York: Samuel French.

———. 1996. *Rewrites: A Memoir.* New York: Simon & Schuster.

———. 1998a. Introduction. In *The Collected Plays of Neil Simon. Vol. IV.* New York: Simon & Schuster, pp. 1–6.

———. 1998b. *Jake's Women.* In *The Collected Plays of Neil Simon. Vol. IV.* New York: Simon & Schuster, pp. 157–229.

———. 1998c. *Laughter on the 23rd Floor.* In *The Collected Plays of Neil Simon. Vol. IV.* New York: Simon & Schuster, pp. 231–298.

———. 1999. *The Play Goes On.* New York: Simon & Schuster, 1999.

———. 2000. Interview with James Lipton. *The Paris Review: Playwrights At Work,* ed. George Plimpton. New York: Modern Library, pp. 192–230.

Weber, Bruce. 2000. Simon's Hotel Rooms, Decorated with Nostalgia. *New York Times on the Web,* 16 June, Arts page.

INTERVIEW WITH NEIL SIMON

Interview conducted by Bette Mandl
in September 2000

Bette Mandl: Has winning the Pulitzer Prize for Drama in 1991 for *Lost in Yonkers* had an impact on the way you are seen by your critics or audience?

Neil Simon: The seventy-fifth anniversary of the Pulitzer Prize was the lucky year for me because I won it that year. They usually don't get together to have a yearly function at which the Pulitzer Prizes are handed out. You get a telegram saying, "Congratulations. You just won the Pulitzer Prize for drama." At the time of the seventy-fifth anniversary, all those who had won the Pulitzer and were able to make it to Columbia University gathered there, and Russell Baker spoke. He said, "From now on every time you see your name in print it will be proceeded by 'Pulitzer Prize winner'." So, in that respect, yes, it has had an impact. I've written thirty-one plays, and about thirty-one movies. But I'm always referred to as "the playwright, Neil Simon."

BM: And that is more important to you.

NS: Infinitely. I've found the process of working on a play much more in keeping with the way I wanted to work. I wanted to have more control over my material than I would have had if I had only done film. When you make a film you are always listening to the people who run the studio. And there are countless numbers of them on each picture. When you're doing a play, it's basically you and the director. Almost completely. There will be some input from the producer, but the key people are the director and yourself. And I have had the opportunity of sitting in at every single rehearsal and coming in the next day with rewrites on every play that I've ever done. You can't do that with a film. If you go on the set and they shoot it, you don't go home and rewrite it. They say, "Sorry, we've done that. We have to move on to the next piece."

BM: I can see why you would want to maintain artistic control. You talk about your work, the long hours of writing and your devotion to your craft in the same way that writers of drama do. Do you see comedy writing as a very different kind of activity?

NS: I don't really think I write comedies anymore. Occasionally I do, but once I got past plays like *The Odd Couple*, I've only taken a few detours off the road to do something like *Rumors* because I enjoy the process. Basically, I never say I want to write comedy as if I were Tennessee Williams writing a drama. I feel I was sort of putting those plays together. And I stopped calling plays comedies. I used to write on the manuscript, "A new comedy by . . . " I stopped doing that and started saying, "A new play by . . . "

BM: An interesting shift.

NS: Chekhov used to use the term "comedy." Where the expression "a new comedy" came from I don't know. What else would it be, "an old comedy"?

BM: I remember your saying that the Pulitzer Prize was an award that you didn't expect to get, even though you had, of course, already gotten numerous awards.

NS: Well, yes I did. I think the reason I didn't think I was going to get it that year was because it was up against *Six Degrees of Separation*. Frank Rich of the *New York Times* had already written his review for that play saying it was John Guare's masterpiece, and his review of my play was not nearly that good.

BM: You have always made wonderfully direct connections with your audiences through the years, even when critics like Frank Rich offered qualified praise.

NS: It's always hard to talk about yourself and say why you are, in a sense, successful with audiences. It may be the reason that sometimes you're not successful with academics or critics, who feel that if you have such a good rapport with an audience, there must be something wrong. I ceased trying to fight that a long time ago. But I don't think I would have the career I had if I didn't have a lot of very good reviews.

Even Frank Rich said in a review, which was not overwhelmingly good, of *Brighton Beach Memoirs,* that one hopes there would be a chapter 2, and when there was—*Biloxi Blues*—he loved it and gave it the only great review he had ever given any of my plays.

As for the Pulitzer Prize, I had been so successful early on with *Barefoot in the Park* and *The Odd Couple* and *Plaza Suite* and plays like that, which were so popular with audiences, I rarely thought of getting a Pulitzer Prize. But my plays began to take a deeper turn, darker turn, starting with *Plaza Suite* and *The Gingerbread Lady.* I was specifically trying to change the style of my writing. Apart from occasional comedies, the plays just naturally got darker. I was never sure whether *Lost in Yonkers* is a dark play or not. This was not an autobiographical play, by the way. It seemed to audiences that it was.

BM: The two young boys did make me think of The Brighton Beach Trilogy.

NS: Well, I didn't even have two boys in *Lost in Yonkers* when I started it. I just had one boy. When the father, at the beginning of the play, has to go in and talk to the grandmother about leaving his son with her and Bella so he could go and make some money to pay back his debts, I had no one for the boy to talk to. I needed someone there.

I said, "Well nothing wrong with having two brothers there." So, even though I had two brothers in *Brighton Beach Memoirs* and *Broadway Bound*, the brother was not originally in this play. To some it may have seemed as if I was writing about those same two boys, as if this was an extension of the *Brighton Beach* plays.

BM: I found it interesting that you have Louie, something of a gangster figure, help them develop some survival skills. How did you decide on that mentorship?

NS: They had a father that they loved dearly, but I think they knew there was a weakness in the father. The father was so beaten down by the mother as a boy. He just didn't offer us, the audience and the boys, a sense of strength in his character. And so when they met somebody like Louie, they saw something very colorful about him, something very exotic that they liked. I think that all young kids at that age, twelve, thirteen, fourteen, would be very . . . perhaps not excited, but certainly interested in someone they think is a gangster. Louie was such a small gangster. He carried a gun only because he knew these guys were after him for running off with the money. I remember in my own childhood, I did have an uncle, my aunt's husband and my cousin's father, who was in no way a gangster, and he was the person Louie was based on. He worked for a dress company in the garment industry and just kept the books, but the company apparently was taken over by people who might have been connected with the Mafia. The only part of the story I knew was that he disappeared one day. He was never found again. No one in the family knew the details, but he probably knew more than they wanted anyone to know.

BM: Quite a story!

NS: Well, that's a tragic story, but for a twelve or thirteen year old kid it's kind of a thrilling story. A James Cagney movie. The boys in *Lost in Yonkers* were thrilled with it also. He taught them little things: card tricks or little bits of philosophy . . . how to keep yourself ahead of someone else.

BM: What do you think the magic of *Lost in Yonkers* is?

NS: Well, I think the magic in *Lost in Yonkers* is all to do with Bella. She's the strongest character I've ever written, and interestingly enough, a female character, because sometimes they say I don't write female characters well. I think it's just the opposite. I think the best characters that I've written outside of, let's say *The Odd Couple* or *The Sunshine Boys*, are the female characters. I think that is true of plays like *The Gingerbread Lady*. Bella was so strong because she took on her mother even though she was petrified of her mother. And the mother was so tyrannical, and I think the mother in a sense did a dreadful thing. I think she kept her that way in a sense just to be with her to take care of her in her old age. And I've seen that. It's an enormously selfish thing to do despite the fact that the grandmother thought that she was doing it in Bella's interest. What she taught the children was how to be alive. Happiness had nothing to do with it, because she believed they weren't the kind of people who were going to get any happiness. We see the play through Bella's eyes even though the young boys may be, in a sense, the narrators. It's Bella's courage in the face of everything, and her humor—sometimes unintentional because she couldn't get things quite straight all the time—that make her so loveable.

BM: She does have an appealing combination of vulnerability and strength. You have continued to move in new directions since the

Pulitzer Prize. I found *Laughter on the 23rd Floor* intriguingly inter-woven with the social history of the Cold War period. You got a warm round of applause from your former colleagues on the video of *Caesar's Writers* when the play was mentioned. Were they enthusiastic about your honesty about those days?

NS: Yes, almost all of them. I couldn't say all of them because I did-n't speak to some of them about it, but many of them came to the open-ing night and I saw them later on. And for the most part all agreed that's pretty much the way it was then, and it seemed to them more like a chronicle than a comedy. They were laughing at the memory of what we were all like then, just wild kids writing wonderfully funny things because we had the funniest man in the world to write for. I've recently done a film version of *Laughter on the 23rd Floor*, which will be on Showtime, probably not until next May.

BM: I look forward to it.

NS: In a way it's a much more serious piece. What I've done is to write much more about the Sid Caesar character's real life. There's a darkness to it and yet it's quite funny also. I think it's a richer piece.

BM: Jake's Women seems quite experimental in form.

NS: You know, sometimes critics and audiences get nervous when you experiment. They want you to stay where you were. Ever notice that?

BM: I have.

NS: I remember a woman coming up to me in the aisle after one of the plays opened and she said, "It's not you: it's not Neil Simon." I said "Did you like it or did you not like it"? She said, "Oh, I don't know. I can't tell. It's just not Neil Simon."

They don't want you to change. Sometimes critics, the newer younger critics I guess, when they see a light comedy about a family, they'll refer to it as "a Neil Simon type of play." They'll go back to the earliest works of that ilk. I must say that Ben Brantley of the *New York Times* was very fair with me recently, when he differentiated the second half of my career from the first. He acknowledged that the early plays were more comedic. The second half includes The Brighton Beach Trilogy and *Lost in Yonkers*. I'm glad that he does that, rather than talk-ing about what is a quintessential Neil Simon play.

BM: So you see some truth in that dividing line too.

NS: I think so. I know I'm a much different playwright from what I had been. I know that if *The Odd Couple* had never been written, and I were to sit down and write the play today, it probably would not be as successful because I would have gone much deeper into what the characters were going through. It may have been more interesting but it wouldn't have been as funny. But you write about where your life is at that time when you're writing it.

BM: You have been candid about your personal experience in the plays and in the two memoirs, *Rewrites* and *The Play Goes On.* May I ask about the balance in your life between writing and personal life that you are establishing in your new marriage to Elaine Joyce?

NS: Well, my life is happier now. My writing has always been a constant through the years. I really didn't need a good life or a bad life to write well. The best thing about it is when you are in a good relationship, it's wonderful to share what's happening with your writing, good and bad. When I worked on *The Dinner Party,* which we just did in the Kennedy Center—we're bringing it into New York in October—Elaine was with me almost every day and we talked about it. It was good to have her there watching. So that was great.

BM: Is there anything you would like to reveal about what you're working on now?

NS: Well, I'm sort of taking it easy right now because I've just gotten through what I would call three openings. We did *Hotel Suite* in the Roundabout Theater in New York and I had a lot of rewriting to do because I found that some of the older material didn't hold up and I had to rewrite it a lot. (What I would really like to do is write a third piece to add to the two scenes about Diana and Sidney and make it one complete play.)

So I went into New York for that opening, then went home to California, then went back to Washington where we rehearsed and had our second stop for *The Dinner Party.* Then I came back to New York, where they needed me for *Neil Simon at the Neil Simon,* fourteen of my pieces at the Neil Simon Theater in a benefit for fighting AIDS. That was a lot of work because I fixed some of the scenes. I couldn't just take out eight pages and say, "let's do this," because the audience wouldn't know where they were or why it stopped at that moment. So I did a great deal of writing on that. Then I said, I have to stop for a while now.

BM: You seem entitled to a short breather. Are you pausing in part because of your feeling about Broadway at this time? You have commented recently on the changes you are seeing there at this point in your own long and remarkable career in the theatre.

NS: As a matter of fact, it is very difficult to get a play to Broadway now. By the end of August there will be two plays running, with eight musicals coming in for next season. The owners of the theaters would rather show a musical, because they know it would attract young kids and their families, rather than a play, a serious play. I'm not even talking about my plays, but plays in general. I'm very, very lucky to have been born when I was born, and writing when I was writing.

LESSONS FROM OUR FIRST FRONTIER

Tom Bryant

Into the Cumberland

In 1984, Robert Schenkkan was working as an actor at the Actors Theater of Louisville. He was working on the play *Swap* by Len Jenkin which was part of the Humana Festival for new plays. After a performance, a man in the audience complimented Schenkkan on his performance: he felt it was a very authentic portrayal of a character from eastern Kentucky. The man worked in eastern Kentucky, as it turned out. He was a pediatrician in an outreach program designed to bring emergency medical care for children into rural areas. He wondered if Schenkkan would be interested in taking a trip there. This was the beginning of the process that led Schenkkan to write *The Kentucky Cycle*. Robert Schenkkan describes that trip:

> We drove out of Louisville, past the beautiful horse farms and antebellum mansions and into the hills of the Cumberland. In the mining town of Hazard, scene of some of the bitterest labor struggles in the last decade, we joined up with one of his [the pediatrician's] former nurses and drove with her into "the hollers" as she made house calls on the handful of families she served. The poverty I saw was extraordinary. I remember one family in particular. Their house was situated on what looked like a combination garbage dump and gravel pit. It was a single room "shotgun shack" with a tin roof, a dirt floor and a coal burning stove. The mother, who couldn't have been more than 16 or 17, had two children below the

age of two, one of whom was physically handicapped. The father who was not much older than his wife, was unemployed with little training and few prospects. The smell in that house was what my friend referred to as "the smell of poverty in the mountains"—as though you had taken a corn shuck mattress, soaked it in piss, covered it with garbage and coal and set it on fire.

That evening, we stayed with another friend of his, the owner of a successful coal mining operation who lived in quite different circumstances. I couldn't help talking about the terrible scenes I had witnessed, less than a stone's throw from his palatial mountain top retreat. His reaction was interesting. He wasn't the least bit embarrassed or concerned. If anything, he was indignant. In his opinion, the poverty and the extreme want of his neighbors was their own damn fault, a combination of laziness and stupidity; in any case, it was certainly not his concern. This, despite the fact that his own success was due less to his business acumen than to a freak of international politics, the Arab oil embargo.

There was something profoundly disorienting about these extremes of poverty and wealth existing so close to each other without an acknowledged relationship, without any social contract, without any sense of community. Even the physical landscape seemed to embody this social contradiction. It was, at one and the same time, some of the most beautiful mountain scenery in the country and some of the most devastated. There were lush mountain forests full of oak, flowering dogwood and azaleas and then you'd turn the corner and the other side of the mountain would have been completely strip mined—all vegetation long since bulldozed away. The fertile topsoil buried under a slag heap of crushed rock and mine tailings so heavily sulfurous that they leached a mild form of sulfuric acid when it rained. I was astounded and outraged. What had happened here? (Schenkkan 1921)

Background of the Plays

When Schenkkan returned to his home in New York, he began to read about eastern Kentucky and encountered the work of Harry Caudill. Caudill is one of the most ardent spokesmen for the region and a voice for reform. A lawyer by trade and a former state legislator in Kentucky, Caudill wrote *Night Comes to the Cumberlands* in 1963. The book contains a scathing indictment of strip mining abuses and the terrible poverty in the mountains. It also contains a unique history of the region, noting the economic and social forces that led to the region's problems. At the heart of Caudill's analysis of the region's problems was the attitude toward land:

> The most deadly aspect of American life is the profligacy growing out of the persistent myth of superabundance. In the beginning, there was so much of everything that everything was squandered . . . In the Cumberland, where the frontier lingered for a long generation as a reality and for another century as an unfading folk memory, the myth of super-abundance took deepest root. Even as the land was running out, farmers clung to failing practices rather than shift to regenerative new ones. When mining superceded tillage the myth said that the coal veins were "inexhaustible." (Caudill 1976, 269 & 270)

Caudill's book had a profound effect on the molding of public policy in the 1960s. Both Presidents Johnson and Kennedy made an attempt to bring federal money to the region, and Congress eventually enacted federal strip mining laws, but conditions in the region did not change much. Caudill continued to be a voice for reform publishing almost a dozen more books, including *My Land Is Dying* (1971), an illustrated polemic against strip mining; *The Watches of the Night* (1976), an update on the Cumberland and the effects of the coal boom in the early 1970s; and *Theirs Be the Power: The Moguls of Eastern Kentucky* (1983), a footnoted history of the coal barons in the region.

Although Schenkkan didn't begin work on *The Kentucky Cycle* for almost two years, his experience in Kentucky and his reading of Caudill's work stayed with him. He brooded over it and also over the political landscape of America in the 1980s. Ronald Reagan was then embarked on an ambitious program of rolling back environmental restrictions on business and cutting social programs. There was also the promotion of a nostalgic view of an idealized American history, a view that Schenkkan felt "did not include the sins of our past" (Schenkkan 2000/2001). Schenkkan felt that this was a rollback of the progress that had been achieved in the 1960s and 1970s in terms of social welfare, environmental preservation, and historical awareness, and it galvanized his desire to act. In a sense, his specific readings about Kentucky and his observations about the current political scene became fused in a single vision of a corrupt American mythos leading to environmental and social disaster throughout America's history. As Harry Caudill (1976) put it:

> We see in the Cumberlands microcosm the kind of fate that awaits the
> country when the looming multitudes have exhausted the soil and con-
> sumed the planet's timber and mineral resources. . . . Unless these
> tragedies are understood, they will be repeated elsewhere until one of
> mankind's greatest experiments is needlessly lost. The Kentucky
> Cumberlands are a great many things, but most of all they are a warning.
> (268 & 275)

Schenkkan began his research, both into the history of eastern Kentucky and into American history in general. In the 200 or so years of Kentucky history, Schenkkan began to see many problems that he believed are characteristic of American history as a whole. In his research, he began to trace the underlying corrupt mythos that led to social and environmental disaster.

Joseph Campbell (1968) has written about the importance of myth in guiding culture:

> One function of myth is the enforcement of the moral order: The shaping
> of the individual to the requirements of his geographical and historical
> social group. The instincts have to be governed in the interests of both the
> group and the individual and traditionally it has been the prime function
> of mythology to serve this end. (5)

With an eye toward trying to illuminate the underlying mythos in American culture, and a desire to understand the excesses and corruption that had undermined it as a positive moral force, Schenkkan began writing.

Writing *The Cycle*

In 1985, Schenkkan wrote what is now play six in *The Kentucky Cycle*. This play was called *Tall Tales* and was about the coming of the coal companies to eastern Kentucky in the 1890s. In the play, an itinerant storyteller bilks a farm family, the Rowans, out of the mineral rights to their property and the result is the total devastation of the land.

Soon after, Schenkkan began to consider the idea of a series of short plays that would follow the Rowan family through 200 years of history. Schenkkan (1991) explains:

> At first I saw maybe three plays, four at most. But as I wrote, I discovered that some events made no real sense without the history that preceded them. The Cycle became six, then eight and finally nine plays. Two other families appeared (in addition to the Rowans) and I began to realize that there was, of course, a fourth major character in my story, and that was, of course, the land. The land that these three families had fought over, dreamed about, bought and sold, lost and regained.

This became the basic story that was threaded though the first five plays:

Masters of the Trade, set in 1775. An Irish immigrant, Michael Rowan kills his best friend in order to make a deal with the Indians to get his own land.

The Courtship of Morning Star, set in 1776. Michael Rowan forcibly takes an Indian woman, Morning Star, to be his wife.

The Homecoming, set in 1792. At Morning Star's urging, Patrick Rowan kills his father Michael in an argument over the land. Patrick then kills his mother's lover, James Talbert, when Talbert tries to take him into town for trial.

Ties That Bind, set in 1819. Out of revenge for his father, Jeremiah Talbert tries to foreclose on Patrick's land in court. Patrick sells two slaves, Sallie and Jesse Biggs, to stave off foreclosure, knowing that Jesse was actually Michael Rowan's son and his own brother. Even so, he loses the land and becomes a sharecropper. Patrick's son Ezekial vows revenge.

God's Great Supper, set in 1861. The civil war provides the opportunity for Ezekial Rowan and his son Jed to take revenge on the Talberts and get their land back.

The central dramatic technique in these plays is that one moment of decision in each play changes the lives of the characters forever. These plays are set in the frontier period and Schenkkan felt that an older, more classical style invoked the primal sense of the frontier. Some of the early plays observe the unities of place and time. *Masters of the Trade* and *Ties That Bind* take place in one day, and this focuses the drama down to a single moment of decision on a single day which alters the characters' lives forever. This moment of decision results in unforeseen consequences that re-echo down through time in chains of further consequences. For instance, in *The Homecoming*, when Michael's son Patrick kills his father and then his mother's lover, James Talbert, this sets off the central dramatic conflict in the first five plays, the feud between the Rowans and Talberts over land. In addition, *The Homecoming's* resonances in story to the drama of Orestes, Clytemnestra, and Agamemnon further invoke parallels between the primitive character of the American frontier and the primal character of Greek myth. This taut chain of retribution and revenge befits the historical context of an agrarian lifestyle where individuals fight for possession of land. There is also the issue of race, as the African-American Biggs family tries to claim their place in the Cumberland in the face of racial hatred. The Rowan, Talbert, and Biggs families come to represent the larger issues of class and race that will echo throughout the rest of *The Cycle*.

Writing Part Two

The next four plays, which covered the modern era, posed a new challenge for Schenkkan in the writing of *The Cycle*:

> Once the earlier plays took shape, I began to experiment with the last three plays covering the modern era in terms of tracking the audience's experience: What does the material require in a new century and does that need to be reflected in a new structure? (Schennkan 2000/2001)

The modern era in eastern Kentucky was characterized by the coming of the coal companies and the resulting devastation of the land. The coal industry also brought with it the labor struggles in the mines as workers tried to unionize to secure a better life. But racial divisions divided the workers. In part two of *The Cycle*, Schenkkan began to feel that he needed to use a wider social canvas to represent the complexities of the modern era. Part of his intention was to link the broader thematic ideas in *The Cycle* to the precise social issues that have shaped our lives in the twentieth century. So, the events in these later plays in *The Cycle* echo some of the most important events in labor history in America.

As reflected in *Tall Tales*, the first play of part 2, the coal companies did indeed secure much of the land in eastern Kentucky with the use of itinerant storytellers who traveled from town to town. The weapon they wielded, the "broad form deed," specified in the fine print that, in selling the mineral rights to his land, the farmer was allowing the company the right to completely despoil the land. Much of the coal development was done by enormous coal trusts; John D. Rockefeller owned enormous tracts of land in eastern Kentucky. Through influence in the state legislature, the coal companies arranged to pay almost no taxes while they exported an enormous flow of profit from the state.

The resulting labor struggle also changed the social mores of the region: out of necessity, it brought women to the forefront in the community. In play seven, *Fire in the Hole,* a labor organizer inspires Mary Anne Rowan through tales of legendary labor organizer Mother Jones. Mary Anne becomes just this sort of figure in the struggle against the mine owners in the fictional Howsam County.

The events in play eight, *Which Side Are You On?*, reflect one of the saddest chapters in union history. The switch from coal to oil after World War II created a decline in the demand for coal. The result was that United Mine Workers (UMW) labor hero John L. Lewis was forced to make more and more concessions to the coal companies in order to secure the survival of the union. The resulting compromises on safety, wages, and health benefits preserved the union, but only for a dwindling group of miners, and set the stage for the corruption of the union during Tony Boyle's tenure as president in the 1960s.

Play nine of *The Cycle, The War on Poverty*, concerns one of the most disturbing developments in the history of eastern Kentucky. This was the environmental devastation wrought by strip mining and mountain top removal. By the late 1960s, coal prices had become so low that the most profitable means of mining became those that wrought wholesale destruction on the land. When the oil crisis hit in the early 1970s, a coal boom resulted and vast areas of land were ruined. Sadly, economic pressures on miners being what they were, labor went along with this program of despoilization.

Schenkkan felt that these larger social issues in the later four plays demanded a wider social focus in the writing. The story would have to involve more than just the struggle between the three families and the dramatic challenge lay in connecting the first five plays with the new ones. He decided to show that the same corrupt goals and values in the frontier era, when transposed to the technologically advanced modern era, spelled disaster on a larger social scale. But Schenkkan continued to follow the Biggs, Talbert, and Rowan families through this more complicated social context. The Talberts became representatives of the mine owners, the Rowans became representatives of the mineworkers, and the Biggs family continued to try to secure a future amidst racial and labor strife. This telescoping of the same core moral issues of self-interest from a more personal context to a larger social scale then became the larger dramatic journey in *The Kentucky Cycle*. This journey also accentuated the environmental issues associated with the theme of land in the plays of part two:

Tall Tales, set in 1890. An itinerant storyteller, JT Wells, comes to Jed Rowan's farm and cons him into selling the mineral rights to his land. Total devastation of their land and the impoverishment of the Rowans follows.

Fire in the Hole, set in 1920. A union organizer, Abe Steinman, tries to convince Mary Anne Rowan and her husband Tommy to help unionize the Blue Star Mine owned by Andrew Talbert Winston. Mary Anne plays a key role in helping labor win the struggle.

Which Side Are You On?, set in 1954. Joshua Rowan, the president of the UMW local, decides to look the other way on mine safety issues in order to get a new UMW contract. His son Scott is killed in a mining disaster as a result.

The War On Poverty, set in 1975. Joshua Rowan, James Talbert Winston, and Franklin Biggs are hunting in the woods when they discover an old burial site including the remains of an Indian child. James and Franklin want to sell it but Joshua makes a stand. We see that it is the murdered child of Michael Rowan.

In the modern era plays, there are still critical "moments of decision" that change the characters' fates. But the effects of these moments of decision are seen to be more far reaching and they affect the entire community, not just the three families. In *Fire in the Hole*, Tommy Jackson informs on the labor organizer, which ultimately leads to the break-up of his family and his death. But his act has wider consequences: it almost dooms the union struggle.

Then in *Which Side Are You On?* Joshua Rowan decides to go along with a labor contract that compromises mine safety. This results in a mine disaster in which his own son is one of the victims, but it also kills many other miners and weakens the union as a force for good in the lives of the miners in the area.

The last play of *The Cycle, The War On Poverty*, returns to the more intimate focus of part one: three men sit in the woods, in an area that is now strip-mined, and argue about what has gone wrong in their lives and the region. But the main conflict that arises is very specific: whether to sell the 200-year-old corpse of an Indian baby as an artifact. We understand that the piece of land that the men are on is the original Rowan family homestead. In a sense, the play has come full circle: Joshua Rowan faces a moral decision on the same ground that confronted his ancestor. By returning to this more intimate focus, Schenkkan ties together the more intimate plays we saw in part one with the broader social dramas of part two. The common thematic thread, woven through the entire cycle, is that individual moral decisions, whether in reference to one person or an entire labor union, comprise the collective mythos that guides the fate of our culture.

But *The War On Poverty* is also the one play that breaks this pattern of self-interest. Joshua Rowan makes a decision that heals the previous cycle of retribution. With that act, in effect, he stops the cycle: someone has broken the chain of "expedient" decisions based on self-interest and revenge that have doomed generations. The nature of this cathartic moment in the play is more poetic than literal: All of Joshua's ancestors that we have seen in the plays are "resurrected" on stage. Inside the context of this play, perhaps Joshua senses their presence and perhaps his life will improve, but we have a distinct sense of resolution in poetic terms.

Theatrical Approach

Other aspects of Schenkkan's background informed the work in different ways. Built into the work as a whole are wonderful theatrical conventions, and Schenkkan began to use his experience in the theater to give the work a specific theatrical style. Schenkkan spent thirteen years as a professional actor, and this colored his notions of character:

> I was always appreciative of the challenges that are particularly exciting for an actor such as transformation, playing multiple character roles in one play. I like the idea of taking that craft to the extreme, giving actors a

chance to play multiple characters which are related—give the actors the opportunity to play their own fathers, grandfathers, mothers . . . (Schennkan 2000/2001)

Thus, Schenkkan built a theatrical convention into *The Cycle* that gave a group of actors a unique opportunity to display their craft. Each of the actors had the wonderful challenge of playing a great variety of characters, and the overall sense of the cyclic nature of the story was reinforced. The ritual aspect of the play was also given theatrical expression by Schenkkan's aesthetic taste as an actor: "I had a preference in theater for a more pared down, scenic style—one that emphasizes the actors and the words. I wanted the play to focus on the actors and the words—to give the audience the opportunity to relish that demand on them" (Schennkan 2000/2001).

This emphasis on the actor posed a wonderful technical challenge to the actors, but also underlined the nonnaturalistic character of *The Cycle*. The actor became prominent, not just as a character but as a purveyor of the story itself. In this way, the play's style took on a more primal aspect, hearkening back to one of the earliest traditions in drama, that of storytelling.

Storytelling in Theme and Structure

The idea of storytelling pervades the play in many other ways including narrative style, dramatic device, dialogue, theme, and theatrical presentation. The use of stories as set pieces *within* the plays creates a marvelous use of that art while also weaving into the plays the theme of storytelling itself. During the play *Tall Tales*, JT the storyteller tells several folktales over dinner to the Rowan family. These tales are virtuoso monologues for the actor and we enjoy their performance. But we also see that JT's stories advance the plot: JT is using them to soften up and then fleece the Rowan family. Our enjoyment of them contrasts with our feelings about how the character is using them.

I first used the device of the storyteller in *Tall Tales*. I thought the storyteller was by turns amusing and horrifying. Stories can be completely benign or very destructive. I began to incorporate that idea in other ways in the plays during the workshop process. (Schennkan 2000/2001)

In *Tall Tales*, Schenkkan also has the storyteller JT compare his craft with the writing of history and the practice of business. At the end of this play, he tries to explain to naive Mary Anne Rowan that the lies he told her family to get the mineral rights to their land are the way of the world:

> JT: "*Truth*? Hell woman, there ain't no such thing. All there is are *stories*! . . . Everybody got his stories. Your *daddy* got his stories. Civil War hero, right? Rode with that "gentleman" Quantrill, right? Shit! Quantrill was a thief and a murderer and when he died folks danced in the streets! . . . When they come in here maybe they'll cut the heart out of that old oak tree that you love so much . . . and they'll ship it off to New York where somebody'll cut it into a fine banker's desk and a swivel back chair for Mr. Rockefeller himself! You think when he sits his skinny ass down on that polished surface he gonna be thinkin about some poor hillbilly girl whose heart got broke in the process?! You won't be part of *his story*, Mary Anne! And when I finish my job for him, I won't be part of his story either! See, he'll give some money to a school or something and grateful people will call him a hero, a great man, a real *Christian*! And *that* story is the one that'll survive—he'll see to that. While the other story, the one where he's just a thief, that'll just fade away. That's your "truth." (203–04)

Although the genre format in *Tall Tales* with its plot twists suggests a wonderfully crafted "tale," what JT says about Quantrill and specifically Standard Oil in the play is historically accurate, as Harry Caudill reported in *Night Comes to the Cumberlands*:

> In the summer of 1885, gentlemen arrived in the Cumberland for the purpose of buying up tracts of land. The Eastern and Northern capitalists selected for this mission, men of great guile and charm. They were courteous and pleasant and wonderful storytellers . . . The going price in the early years was fifty cents an acre. The operating companies were able to recover about 5000 tons per acre. For this vast mineral wealth, the mountaineer received a single half dollar. (72)

This blend of historical truth and deliberate dramatic artifice gives a multilayered complexity to the experience of watching *Tall Tales*. One has the feeling that one is watching history told as a simple folk tale, but the use of story telling in *Tall Tales* also comments on the process of writing history. Thus there is simultaneously the enjoyment of the tale as just a tale while one also has a more distanced, ironic awareness of the structural process of historical revision that the playwright has embodied in his construction of it. In this way, the notion of history in the United States as being written by the victorious emerges as both the content *in* the play and the context for our process of viewing it.

Schenkkan's core idea is the ironic association of storytelling with history in the play: the basic form of nine plays spread over a 200-year time span suggests the portrayal of "history," but the plays themselves have the tone and style of fictional "tales" rather than factual accounts. This is intentional; the playwright's goal was not merely to dramatize historical periods or events but rather to show a cyclic process of history in which the same moral transgressions and mistakes are repeated. Specifically, it is the burying of the past in revision and denial that causes generations to repeat the same errors. By the use of storytelling as a "theatrical context," the audience is always aware of the process by which this "history" is being told to them and the agendas that guide this "telling of the story."

The style in which the stories are told is also an extension of this comment on the writing of history. Schenkkan's use of different dramatic genres in each of the plays helps make this theatrical point: "I became conscious of genre in the first plays I wrote in the Cycle and began to play with it as I wrote. It wasn't something I set out to do but happened later after the first three or four plays" (Schennkan 2000/2001).

In the course of the entire cycle, we see a 200-year stretch of history, deliberately told in the context of a variety of fictional formats. But the effect is not to fictionalize history. Rather, it is to make the audience aware of the process by which history is "dramatized." The audience isn't merely sucked into a dramatic rendering but retains a sense of perspective on it. It is precisely because the style of the "stories" changes from play to play that we become acutely aware of the process of choice involved in presentation. This technique, usually associated with postmodernism, involves assembling a collection of different stylistic elements together in the same work to create a sense of relativistic context and ironic comment. The plays in *The Kentucky Cycle* follow the same families over 200 years, but the specific looks at given periods ultimately contrast with each other, subtly giving us a sense of ironic distance. So, *The Homecoming* uses an O'Neill style of classical adaptation to tell a tale of patricide resonant of the Orestia. This is contrasted with *The Ties that Bind*, which uses the format of a courtroom drama to tell the story of a son's use of the legal system to get revenge for his father's death. Then, much later in *The Cycle, Fire in the Hole* uses a 1930s-style epic social drama form to tell the story of the union struggle against the large coal operators in eastern Kentucky.

But the use of storytelling and genre in the play is not merely intended to make a formalistic comment on historical relativism. This comment on history is specifically linked to what is being said in the plays about the history of the United States, particularly in terms of its treatment of Native Americans, African Americans and working people and to show the cycle by which these wrongs are perpetuated. We see different characters, in a variety of plays, repeat the same mistakes in dramatic situations that emphasize the issues of race, class, and family dysfunction, and then try to hide the consequences. We connect this to our understanding of the larger process by which history has been sculpted according to the agendas of the powerful. The audience doesn't perceive this connection immediately. Rather, it dawns on them as the play proceeds and the contrasts between the plays and the repeated content in them becomes apparent.

Perhaps the most subtle use of storytelling within the plays is the way stories about family members are handed down to the next generation. This shows the process of revising history in the most intimate context. Most of the plays are, in a sense, parables of the destructive consequences of attempting to hide moral transgression. Jed, who was horrified by the misdeeds he committed under Quantrill's command during the Civil War sequences in *God's Great Supper*, later becomes an apologist for Quantrill in *Tall Tales* to cover up his own guilt. His daughter Mary Anne thus never really understands her father or learns from his experience. We see the characters engage in a continual process of deceit, disguising family culpability and literally burying the secrets of the past.

The literal example of this involves Michael Rowan murdering his child in play three, *The Homecoming*. Michael's son Patrick never learns the real story of how Michael murdered the child. The result is that Michael's secrets create a climate of suspicion that leads to family disaster. Later in the last play of *The Cycle, The War On Poverty*, Joshua Rowan, James Talbert Winston, and Franklin Biggs discover this child, whom we know to be the long-buried ancestor of Joshua Rowan. In a poetic sense, only when we see this sin from the past unearthed does redemption in the present become possible.

The Design Process

As *The Kentucky Cycle* moved into its production stage, the theatrical aesthetics built into the work took concrete form. Early on in the workshop process, in conferences with Robert Schenkkan, set designer Michael Olich, and director Warner Shook, it was decided that the directorial concept of the play and its setting would emphasize two main concepts: that of "the land" and the process of "storytelling." Set designer Michael Olich (2001) explained how the set emphasizes storytellling via its basic structure:

> A two-story-high frame of scaffolding enfolds the back of the central playing area of the stage. During the play, the scaffolding could transform into different locations and scenes using only lighting, sound and the actor's imagination. The idea was that the process of transformation would be a crucial part of the theatrical experience of viewing a scene, rather than attempting to use literal set and prop elements to create the illusion of reality. The scaffold became at times a coal mine, a river boat, or isolated scenes in other locations.

Related to the idea of storytelling was also the notion of ritual: the actors behave in a formal way when not actively involved as characters in the drama. The ritual aspect of the play was also a key factor in the design, Olich (2001) explained: "The set design also exposes the ensemble as witnesses to the story through the play. They sit on stage and watch and then enter the action. This also heightens the sense of ritual."

At times, the actors, when not in a scene, would be on stage watching the scene in progress. There were chairs, resembling church pews on each side of the stage where actors sat and watched the action. Actors could also watch from the scaffolding above. Actors would then enter the play as "characters" right in front of the audience's eyes. There was no attempt made to conceal this transition of the actor from storyteller to character. In fact, the experience of seeing an actor get up from the side of the stage and then "go into character" and enter the action of a play was marvelously theatrical, and the virtuoso ability of the actor to transform himself in order to tell a story was underlined.

Actors also participated by literally "setting the stage" for scenes: There was an opening ritual at the beginning of *The Cycle,* in which actors came into the middle of the stage and put down the logs for a fire that became the central scenic element in the first play, *Masters of the Trade*. Throughout the rest of the show, actors, in a formal manner, changed scenic elements. These activities performed by actors when not engaged in scenes made them into storytellers, and they created the context that informed the whole production. In this way, the audience was made constantly aware of the process of storytelling while the play unfolded.

The story is actually a theatrical ritual in which the ensemble presents all the characters but one: the land. The land, as theatrically embodied in the set design, was the other key element in the design. Olich (2001) explained:

> I thought of the set as a ritual space in which the character of the land was represented and modified through the actors' rituals. The erasing of the land was shown by the covering of the stage floor with wooden floor plugs as the story progressed. The progressively changing house of the Rowan family represented the interaction of the characters modifying the land and the character's urbanization of it. Finally the characters returning to the original plot of land in play nine created a sense of reconfronting the original issues with a new viewpoint.

The main idea is that the empty space of the stage, representing nature, was transformed by settlement during the play. Having theater space with a thrust stage for the first productions at the Intiman Theater and the Mark Taper Forum provided a wonderful opportunity to utilize the floor as a way of showing this progress. The first play of *The Cycle,* which takes place in the wilderness around 1750, was performed on a bare stage with just a few logs to designate a campfire in the woods. In next play, *The Courtship of Morningstar*, some planking covered the stage and a few pieces of furniture denoted a cabin. With each succeeding play in *The Cycle,* more of the stage floor became covered with wooden planking and the set piece elements designating the outlines of houses became larger. Michael Olich's main idea was to use the floor to show the encroachment, and, finally, domination of nature by settlement. At the end of part one, set around 1865, the final remaining part of bare floor was covered with a piece of planking during the funeral of a murdered child.

This set the stage for the second part of *The Kentucky Cycle,* which deals with the coming of coal mining and industrialization to the region. Throughout part one, in addition to the floor, which was a metaphor for "the land," there was also a large cyclorama-type screen serving as a sky. Lighting effects on it highlighted locations and mood. But this screen was then transformed in part two. At the very end of play six, Mary Anne Rowan mourns the loss of her family's land and its despoilization by the coal company: "They came a couple of years later, just like he said they would, and they cut down all the trees including my oak. I was right about it holding up the sky cause when they chopped it down, everything fell in: moon, stars and all."

At the end of this monologue, there was a major scenic transition: the entire backdrop of the sky, hinged in the middle and tipped forward, crashing down on the stage and becoming a large, raked platform. The effect was indeed like the sky falling and the transformation of the space from the natural setting to an industrial one. The last three plays in *The Cycle* were performed in this setting, representing the modern era.

The common link between these two elements of storytelling and the land was the idea of transformation. Ultimately, events in *The Kentucky Cycle* combined with the actors telling the story transformed the space. Costumes became a crucial part of this effect of transformation and had to mirror the role of the actor in that process. Costumes represented a big challenge, as costume designer Frances Kenny (2001) explained:

> The actor's rapid changes of costume and the need to show a continuity of theme through the plays demanded that the costumes have a continuity throughout the plays in spite of specific changes of period. The solution lay in having very minimal basic silhouette that spanned 200 years and then suggestive pieces being added that took us to a specific time, that is,

adding a miner's cap during that era. Or a soldier's cap during the Civil War era. Thus basic garments took on a different cast and period look without obscuring the continuity from play to play.

Thus the basic idea of transformation as an extension of "story-telling" and "the land" was shown as the unifying context that gave thematic cohesiveness to the cycle.

The Evolution of the Play in the Rehearsal Process

The Kentucky Cycle has a unique and elegant structure that makes great virtue out of theatrical necessity. The length posed special problems in terms of the realities of production and thematic coherence, and the play evolved during the process of workshops leading to its first production at the Intiman Theater in Seattle in June 1991 and in later rehearsal processes leading to its Broadway premier in November 1993. Obviously, a play that covers 200 years of Kentucky history and consists of nine separate plays lasting a total of six and a half hours cannot be enjoyed in one sitting. Early on, different strategies were explored for the presentation of the material. Most crucial was the demarcation of act breaks and intermissions as a way of supplying a major dramatic arc to the sweep of history.

Up until the second workshop at the Mark Taper Forum in 1990, Robert Schenkkan had seen *The Kentucky Cycle* as a work in three, not two main parts: the idea was to see it in one day with a lunch and a dinner break or on three successive evenings. This divided the drama into very natural and logical historical groups: The early plays (plays one through three) focused on the early frontier days and the encroachment on the Native Americans' land by frontiersmen. The mid-period plays (plays four, five, and six) roughly covering the 1800s, mainly focused on the battle over land among the Talbert, Rowan, and Biggs families and the attendant issues of class and race. The final plays (plays seven, eight, and nine) were set in the modern era and involved the coming of coal mining to Kentucky and the union struggle.

During the second workshop of *The Kentucky Cycle* in the New Works Festival at the Mark Taper Forum in 1990, Robert Egan, then associate director at the Mark Taper Forum, suggested that practical economic realities precluded this division of the material: three successive evening performances would leave only three possible performances of the entire cycle per week, whereas a two-part format would allow four.

So, a two-part format was decided on. This made the experience of the flow of history different but equally interesting. In part one, plays one through five formed a look at the era in which personal battles over the land were the central issue. The focus at first was on the battle between Native Americans and early settlers and then shifted at intermission to the Rowan and Talbert families' battle over the land. Although these plays in part one involved larger issues of class and race, the focus was intimate, using very few characters to dramatize the larger issues and conflicts. But the end of part one foreshadows the new era that is coming: the last play in part one, *God's Great Supper*, deals with the coming of the Civil War to the region, and the expansion of the conflict in the region from a more personal domain to a wider social scale. Form following content, *God's Great Supper* uses, for the first time in the cycle, a much larger cast of actors and a much wider sweep of time. Thus, *God's Great Supper* serves as a foreshadowing of the wider social struggle that will occur in the coal mining era in part two. The plays in part one, with the exception of play two and play five, all adhered to the unities of a single time and place, using few actors.

Conversely, the plays in part two (particularly plays seven and eight) utilize a much larger cast in plays that telescope over time and many events and has the feeling of broader social drama. Part two opens with a reference back to the intimate family context we have seen in part one, but with an elegant twist: in play six, *Tall Tales*, an itinerant storyteller comes to the Rowan family and cheats them out of their mineral rights. The unmasking of this figure of folksy traditional culture as an agent working for large eastern coal companies serves as a brilliant dramatic segue from the intimate family context of the earlier plays to the modern context of the later plays, which feature the coming of coal mining to the area. The storyteller is a Trojan horse that the Rowan family welcomes into their hearth, mistaking him as one of their own, and he lays waste to the intimate agrarian life that people in the region have known for generations. The issues in the region then become collective social issues, brought on by this wave on industrialization.

What became the main writing focus in part two was the emotional tracking of the Rowan, Talbert, and Biggs families in this larger social context. In play seven, *Fire in the Hole,* the larger issue was the struggle to found the miners union. Earlier drafts of this play tended towards broader social drama, which focused on the collective issues and the miners as a whole. The Rowan family tended to recede into the larger social fabric. In rehearsal in Seattle for the 1991 world premier, the need for balance was the main issue in rewrites. Eventually, balance was achieved by placing a greater focus on how the union divided the Rowan family in particular and how their conflicts typified the struggle in the region as a whole. Much of the middle of *Fire in the Hole* became a series of more intimate scenes in which the labor organizer's education of Mary Ann Rowan represents the larger change in consciousness in the whole region. Thus there was a more specific tie-in to play six, *Tall Tales*, as we see Mary Ann grow beyond her shattered innocence. The key to this change of consciousness in Mary Ann Rowan was the union organizer's stories about Mother Jones, who provided a real role model for her. In this way, the broader theme of storytelling in *The Cycle* was woven through *Fire in the Hole* via the more distinct idea of class consciousness. The focus in this play then shifts in the later scenes to feature mass strike scenes with a large cast of characters and with Mary Ann as the leader. The result of this structural change in later drafts was that the mass movement was seen to grow out of the more intimate changes in consciousness in specific people. In this way, the larger social issue of the union became connected more precisely to the specific themes in *The Cycle* and the more personal journey of the characters.

A similar balance had to be found in the last two plays of *The Cycle*. In *Which Side Are You On?* the collusion of union leadership with management on safety issues forms the larger conflict. The original drafts again focused more on the larger social context. But eventually, the placing of Joshua Rowan's son Scott in direct opposition to his father on the issue of miner safety brought the family drama more to the fore in later drafts.

The last play of *The Cycle, The War on Poverty*, had always evoked a sense of the first play in *The Cycle, Masters of the Trade*: three men are alone in the woods at night. In the first play, the events that follow grow out of self-interest and deal making pushed to a horrifying point. But the tone in the last play, in spite of the similarities, was vastly different as originally written. As the last play was examined in the rewriting process, this point of difference was explored, deepened, and brought out: Franklin Biggs, James Talbert Winston, and Joshua Rowan are all old men who have had their fill of corrupt deals. In marked contrast to the men in the first play, these later three men stumble through their attempts to perpetuate the cycle of greed, but their reflection on their past misdeeds dampens the fires of their self-interest to exploit the corpse they have found. In a poetic sense, the murdered baby is equated with the murdering of the land in which these men have actually participated. One sees the larger poetic transformation at the end of play nine grow out of Joshua's success in forcing the other men to understand their lives and so not perpetuate the cycle. On one level, the central action of this play concerns the decision to not desecrate the baby's grave, but in terms of character journey, it is the reflections of the men on their lives that form the main shift and change in the action. Thus the action of self-interest in play one gives way to the action of self-reflection in play nine.

The telescoping from the more personal scale to the larger social scale then becomes the dramatic journey linking the two parts in *The Kentucky Cycle*. This approach also accentuates the environmental issues associated with the theme of land in the play. The structure of *The Kentucky Cycle* reinforces this understanding by showing how the same sort of moral decisions, based on the same flawed values, telescoped from a personal context of land feuds into a larger context that includes the entire ecosystem. The common thematic thread that is woven through the whole cycle is that individual decisions, whether in reference to one person or an entire labor union, are the key to fate. But the tragedy lies in the inability to escape from the forces that create the context for our choices. Robert Schenkkan (1992) explains:

> Even as the play began to acquire a life of its own, and to expand in ways I had never envisioned, it became clear that the original questions I had tried to answer for myself were also expanding. The problems of the Cumberland are not simply political, or economic or social; they lie somewhere in a bewildering maelstrom of corrupting legacies that has trapped the people and the region in recurring cycles of poverty that are as much spiritual as physical.

Although *The Kentucky Cycle* is particular to the Cumberland region in terms of the material it uses for its stories, it is universal in terms of the broader issues it presents. Audiences in New York, Los Angeles, and Seattle as well as other regions have responded to the essential issues of class, race, and environmental devastation that are addressed in the play. *The Kentucky Cycle* also speaks to American culture as a whole in terms of our collective need to redress the sins in the American past. The experience of *The Kentucky Cycle* is similar to, and fulfills many of the same social functions of cultural myth making and historical revision that are inherent in medieval mystery cycles, Shakespearean history plays, and Greek tragedies: The dramatic journey through a multigenerational time span gives one a broader sense of historical perspective and helps elucidate the key forces that shape our lives, no matter what time period or place.

Note

Caudill was a state legislator in the Kentucky House of Representatives from 1954 to 1962. He has written nine books on the region, fiction and nonfiction, all of which consider the relationship between "progress" and its impact on the natural environment.

Works Cited

Campbell, Joseph. 1968. *The Masks of God: Creative Mythology.* New York: Viking Press.

Caudill, Harry M. 1963. *Night Comes to the Cumberlands.* Boston: Little Brown.

———. 1976. *Watches in the Night.* Boston: Little Brown.

Kenny, Frances. 2001. Interview conducted by the author, January.

Olich, Michael. 2001. Interview conducted by the author, January.

Schenkkan, Robert. 1992. "Into the Cumberland." Performing Arts Music Center of Los Angeles County. January, 26.1: 6–7.

———. 1993. *The Kentucky Cycle.* New York: Penguin.

———. 2000/2001. Interviews by author, tape recordings, December–February.

INTERVIEW WITH ROBERT SCHENKKAN

Interview conducted by Tom Bryant
in February 2001

Tom Bryant: Why did you start writing plays?

Robert Schenkkan: It was so lucrative. [laughter] I always saw myself as a writer. I was always interested in theater. It was a fairly natural direction to take. At the time I was supporting myself as an actor. But I always saw myself as a writer and actor and eventually as a director.

TB: What do you identify as particular obstacles or rewards that one faces in writing for the stage?

RS: There's very little meaningful support for new work. It's extremely difficult to get a play produced. If it does not go brilliantly in its first incarnation, the chances of a second are diminished further. To a playwright, the importance of journalistic criticism to the success of a play is crucial. In fact the playwright is very vulnerable to dramatic criticism. It definitely can impact the success of a play, whereas the same is not true of a film, which has a wide opening and as often as not doesn't really depend on critical success in order to have commercial success. It's also very difficult, even if you are very successful, to make enough of an income on a regular basis to support yourself and a family, which means that most writers are forced into a second career of some sort, like teaching. It's a fairly discouraging business that requires a fairly strong stomach.

TB: What do you think about the current state of theater?

RS: Given the practical commercial aspects of the industry that I've just lined out, I think there's an odd dichotomy: There's so many playwrights writing. In fact, I think that there's never been such high numbers of playwrights writing at such a relatively high level of ability.

TB: Do you really think that? As opposed to a period like the 1940s?

RS: I think there's as many good writers writing, although there may not be as many great writers writing. Of course, it's a little hard to judge; sometimes you have to step back ten or twenty years to really be able to assay a judgment about that. But I think that, by and large, there are lots of good writers writing out there and probably more so than at any other time.

TB: What are some examples of the playwrights out there that you like?

RS: Oh all the usual suspects. I like Paula Vogel, Tony Kushner, Eric Overmeyer.

TB: What do you think of the status of the playwright now as opposed to in the past?

RS: You know I can't see that there's a huge improvement in the status accorded the playwright. If anything, it seems very similar. To read the journals of writers in the 30s and 40s who toiled as playwrights to make a living, it's very similar to what I hear today: their most fervent wish seems to be that they can sell the rights of their plays to the movies for a large enough sum to support their playwriting habit for a couple of years.

TB: So the challenges and the status remain the same?

RS: I think at the very least, I can't say that it's improved.

TB: How do you think regional theater has affected the situation for the playwright, as opposed to a previous era where theater in America was more centered in New York?

RS: I think it's a positive thing. When there was just one locus of theater in New York, it meant you had just one benchmark of theatrical opinion against which every work had to be judged. It meant that some genres, some writers, were overlooked or not encouraged, simply because they weren't fashionable according to the dictates of a very narrow view. The fact that there's a better network of regional theater out there encourages regional writing, which I think is a good thing. I do think that that's a healthy change.

TB: How do you think your regional background has influenced your work? You grew up in Texas, didn't you?

RS: I think that my background has been a powerful influence on my work, although it took me a long time to realize it. I come from a part of the country where storytellers and storytelling is popular and accepted. In my own family, the idea of storytelling, inventing stories and yarns, is something that my father did for pleasure and was quite good at. So, I grew up with a deep appreciation of the ability to spin a yarn and to hold an audience. And I don't think that has ever really changed. On some level, that is really what I see myself as: a storyteller. That's what I do. You can gussy it up and call it what you want, but that's what I do and that's what I enjoy. I guess that it goes all the way back to that guy at the bazaar who for a couple of copper coins will tell you a golden tale.

TB: What do you think about politics and how that's reflected in theater as a means of that debate? Do you see much good stuff happening?

RS: I find that, in contrast to the European theater, the American theater has always been more uncomfortable with the idea of politically pointed drama. We seem to be more comfortable with comedy rather than drama in this regard, but even there, there's not the same kind of support or pleasure that you find in the European theater for a really potent political debate within the context of the dramatic work. It's a much rarer creature here in this country. It tends to be couched in much more acceptable social issues, such as the politics of discrimination against race.

TB: Why do you think there is not as much focus on politics?

RS: I'm not really sure there is a good answer for that. Maybe because theater in this country is regarded by the majority of people as an entertainment?

TB: As opposed to an art form?

RS: As opposed to something that's a bit more challenging in terms of its aesthetic, that requires more from the audience in terms of their participation. Perhaps it's something along those lines. I don't know. I do know that this is not the case in England and it's not the case in France. Political and philosophical debate are not only acceptable but anticipated aspects of the theatrical experience. Perhaps part of the problem in America is that theaters function on an almost totally commercial basis here, with little federal government financial support, and this creates a nervousness on the part of producers. This results in a kind of pandering to the lowest common denominator.

TB: What do you think of the lack of government support for the arts in the U.S.?

RS: It's pathetic, of course. If you look at the amount of money that the United States spends on the arts with its tax dollars and you compare that percentage of our resources with the amount spent by European countries, we're so far down the list that it's pathetic. I think it reflects an interesting ambivalence on the part of Americans towards the theater and art in general: Should art be supported? Is it supposed to support itself? If it is supported, are we then invested in it and then does that give us the right to set parameters on what it may or may not do and may or may not discuss? These are issues that just don't really seem to be pertinent across the ocean and I think they have really hamstrung theater in this country, particularly in the commercial realm. But this is also an issue that every regional theater faces. Almost no theater in the country (in fact I can't think of even one) can operate solely on the basis of what it takes in at the box office. All theaters have to fundraise, and they all have to seek grants. This situation doesn't tend to make theaters more likely to put themselves on the line with what they try and produce. I think it makes for a much more commercial, much safer, hedge-your-bets type of mentality. The result is that you see less controversial work, less experimental work.

TB: How much of an influence has avant-garde or experimental theater had on you? One sees this influence in aspects of *Kentucky Cycle* in the use of nonnaturalistic modes of presentation and narrative style.

RS: I think there is clearly an influence on my work, but I think it is mainly an influence that comes from my reading of other writer's plays and from a few seminal theoretical works like Peter Brook's *The Empty Space* and Artaud's *The Theater and Its Double*. In other words, my exposure to new ideas and a wider range of aesthetic philosophies mostly comes through my reading of work as opposed to an actual exposure to avant-garde theater groups, of which there were very few in Austin, Texas in 1965 when I was growing up. Although there were one or two groups in Austin, mainly doing political work like street theater or Guerilla Theater in response to the Vietnam war.

TB: When you were working as an actor, was that an influence on your work?

RS: Oh undoubtedly. Not only was acting in general an influence, but I was an actor whose career was spent mostly, somewhat to my surprise, doing contemporary works and in developing new plays. I did a lot of premiers of plays. And I worked in a lot of places that were devoted to the development of new plays and emerging playwrights like the O'Neill, the New York Shakespeare Festival, the Ensemble Studio Theater, and the Actor's Theater in Louisville. I was constantly working as an actor to develop new work, so I was exposed to much of what was cutting edge during that time.

TB: Can you give specific examples of certain plays you were in and what impression those plays made on you?

RS: Swap by Len Jenkin, *A Full Length Portrait of America, New Jerusalem* at the New York Shakespeare Festival.

TB: So you first experienced the process of playwriting from the point of view of an actor working on new plays?

RS: Yes. I found that to be very influential and a very positive influence. I think it has helped me in a number of ways. I think I know, on a gut level, what kind of writing gives an actor something that is playable and I think that always grounds my work in a concrete way. On a technical side, I can speak an actor's language when I'm in rehearsal on the play, unlike some writers, who are intimidated or just don't know how to talk to actors.

TB: Any more thoughts on contemporary theater?

RS: It's interesting to see the changes that New York Theater has undergone in the last 15 years. It went through a period where there was simply no product at all compared to, say, 30 years ago when you had so many more new plays. There's a bit more life right now, although a continuing and alarming dearth of new plays being premiered on Broadway. What you see are a whole lot of variety shows of one kind or another and the occasional British import. Or transfers of an American play from an off-Broadway venue. At one time several years ago, off Broadway had taken over as the breeding ground for American new work but has relinquished that role in recent years to off-off-Broadway and regional theater where the bulk of new plays are being produced.

TB: What have you been working on recently?

RS: I've written a children's play called *The Dream Thief* that had its world premier in Milwaukee and I have a new adult drama called

Handler, which had a workshop production in Atlanta and which will have a full production at the Oregon Shakespeare festival in 2002. I've also been commissioned to write a play for the Pioneer Theater in Salt Lake City, which will be a departure for me in that it will be something of a comedy. I continue to do workshops and give speeches around the country, usually in connection with a production of *The Kentucky Cycle*.

TB: Are there any particular playwrights you have been influenced by?

RS: I'm very influenced by O'Neill. I had an encounter with *Long Day's Journey into Night* at an early age and it just knocked me over. I devoured the rest of his canon and was so impressed with the way he kept experimenting throughout his life. I was also influenced by Arthur Miller and Peter Weiss for their tackling of social and political issues. I have also had a real appreciation for writers who are not afraid of poetry, to be bold with language, ranging from Tennessee Williams to Sam Shepard.

TB: Are there any topics you'd like to address?

RS: I have to say that I've spent so little time reflecting on the state of theater because I'm just out there working, trying to get the next play done. On the page and on to the stage.

KUSHNER'S ARCADES: "THE BORDERS ARE FULL OF HOLES"

Framji Minwalla

Tradition is a matter of much wider significance. It cannot be inherited, and if you want it you must obtain it by great labour. It involves, in the first place, the historical sense, which we may call nearly indispensable to anyone who would continue to be a poet beyond his twenty-fifth year; and the historical sense involves a perception, not only of the pastness of the past, but of its presence; the historical sense compels a man to write not merely with his own generation in his bones, but with a feeling that the whole of the literature of Europe from Homer and within it the whole of the literature of his own country has a simultaneous existence and composes a simultaneous order. This historical sense, which is a sense of the timeless as well as of the temporal and of the timeless and of the temporal together, is what makes a writer traditional. And it is at the same time what makes a writer most acutely conscious of his place in time, of his contemporaneity.

—T. S. Eliot, "Tradition and the Individual Talent"

Writing about influences that drive a writer's work is often unsatisfying. The assumption behind any such project holds that particular formative pressures help articulate the shape, syntax, aesthetic strategies, even meaning of individual works. But meaning is never so simply accessed, and rarely admits an easy heritage. Contradictory impulses, desires, obsessions, all subjective, all political, push writers to the work they cre-

ate, often unconsciously embedding in their texts the hidden traces of a
barely recognizable history. Tony Kushner is no exception, and the influences on his work, already dissected in numerous essays,[1] reveal little
about what his plays do, why he writes them, why they're useful, or how
they intervene in and refashion our cultural maps.

In every interview or talk he gives, almost every essay he writes, and
in the prefaces to his published plays, he thanks people who have helped
him—teachers, mentors, directors, dramaturgs, actors, other writers,
audience members—not least as an honorable gesture for their individual labor on his behalf. This constant thanking perhaps indicates a need
to deflect questions about who or what shapes his imagination, a point
most wittily made in his rejoinder to "The Proust Questionnaire," sent
to him by a dramaturgy intern at Center Stage for inclusion in a study
guide to accompany a production of *Slavs!*.

> *My favorite writers in prose*: Herman Melville, Doestoevsky, Virginia
> Woolf, Abraham Lincoln, Anton Chekhov, Tennessee Williams, Zora
> Neale Hurston, Raymond Williams, Ernest Block, Martin Luther King Jr.,
> Bertolt Brecht, Emerson, Alfred Doblin, Italo Calvino, C. L. R. James,
> Trollope, Dickens, Wodehouse, Lewis Carroll, Trotsky, Marx, Freud,
> Benjamin, Marguerite Yourcenar, etc.
>
> *My favorite writers in verse*: Shakespeare, Brecht, Wallace Stevens,
> Whitman, W. C. Williams, Pound, Robert Duncan, Mandelshtam,
> Akhmatova, Tsvetayeva, Adrienne Rich, Audre Lord, Stanley Kunitz,
> Elizabeth Bishop, Marianne Moore, Thom Gunn, Thomas McGrath, Li-
> Young Lee, Wordsworth, Dickinson, Charles Olson, etc. (Vorlicky 1998,
> 120)

Those splendid etceteras, a deliberate refusal to complete his catalogue, marks Kushner as both more than, and separate from, the sum of
his discernable parts. He understands, as so many writers do not, that
making an aesthetic object, especially a theatrical one, is always a communal act. Kushner writes as much with as for this community—a community that contains both living and dead audiences—negotiating how
a varied literary and political tradition together with contemporary ideological pressures mold his investigations.

The true picture of the past flits by. The past can be seized only as an image which flashes up at the instant it can be recognized and is never seen again. . . . Every image of the past that is not recognized by the present as one of its own concerns threatens to disappear irretrievably.

To articulate the past historically does not mean to recognize it "the way it really was" (Ranke). It means to seize hold of a memory as it flashes up at a moment of danger. Historical materialism wishes to retain that image of the past which unexpectedly appears to man singled out by history at a moment of danger. The danger affects both the content of the tradition and its receivers. The same threat hangs over both: that of becoming a tool of the ruling classes. In every era the attempt must be made to wrest tradition away from conformism that is about to overpower it. The Messiah comes not only as the redeemer, he comes as the subduer of the Antichrist. Only that historian will have the gift of fanning the spark of hope in the past who is firmly convinced that even the dead will not be safe from the enemy if he wins. And this enemy has not ceased to be victorious.

—Walter Benjamin, "Theses on the Philosophy of History"

Kushner, with Benjamin (and many contemporary post-structuralist historians), distinguishes between an unknowable past and the comprehensible forms we give it in historiographical narrative, between history as fiction and fiction as a peculiar kind of history. History for Kushner consists precisely in the conjuring of Benjaminian images—Ethel Rosenberg's ghost reciting *kaddish* over Roy Cohn's corpse in *Angels in America*; Die Alte, the spirit of Germany's imperial past, in *A Bright Room Called Day*; the pickled human brains preserved for future study in the Pan-Soviet Archives for the Study of Cerebro-Cephalognomical Historico-Biological Materialism in *Slavs!*—images that become recognizable the instant they "flash" on stage. What this far from exhaustive list should suggest is that history here appears in many different guises—as received knowledge, as spectral visitation, as preserved artifact. The very multiplicity of these citations suggests a radical reformulation of the now, a Benjaminian sensibility which constructs a knowledge of the past, and its lived presence in contemporary experience, as that crucial investigation through which tradition can serve as both subduer and redeemer, as that messianic force that emancipates the present by disclosing and confronting ancient shibboleths.

Kushner's work isn't concerned just with revising how we understand the events that have shaped us, but also in using geographically and historically specific narratives through which to reveal the ways we negotiate our social identities, and to point toward the ever shifting potential through which we, as individual human agents, can effect change. The impulse here is clearly Brechtian, but where Brecht's dramaturgical techniques measure history through a mostly dialectical lens, one that produces a mutual defamiliarization through the juxtaposition of opposites. Kushner shapes history as queer, as a narrative odd and plural. The very idea of history, and the particular ways his characters articulate this idea—the ways they construct the historical analyses they use to make sense of their worlds—announces the central trope of each play: history is an unstable coming together of vastly different angles of vision; its images flee even as we try to capture them; all individuals represent their own idiosyncratic versions of what happened, versions which only sometimes overlap, and these versions articulate a future by revealing the psycho-ideological biases of the present. Over and over, his characters ask fundamental questions about their relation to the past, questions that push Kushner and hopefully his audiences to engage the complex, problematic, pleasurable, and often ruinous ways in which we embody, and figure forth, the future.

History itself, then, in its various messy formulations provides the formal and substantive context for Kushner's investigations, the impetus for his imagination, and serves as the arbiter of the efficacy of his political interventions. The Kushner who emerges from the evidence of his writing, more than any of his characters, is like Klee's famous angel, the one Benjamin describes in "Theses on the Philosophy of History": "His face is turned toward the past. Where we perceive a chain of events, he sees one single catastrophe which keeps piling wreckage upon wreckage and hurls it in front of his feet" (Benjamin 1968, 257). But unlike Benjamin's angel, propelled by the postlapsarian storm blowing from Paradise, Kushner uses his writing to stop, survey the wreckage, and propose ways to move forward.

All I have is a voice
To undo the folded lie,
The romantic lie in the brain
Of the sensual man-in-the-street
And the lie of Authority
Whose buildings grope the sky:
There is no such thing as the State
And no one exists alone;
Hunger allows no choice
To the citizen or the police;
We must love one another or die.

— W.H. Auden, "September 1, 1939"

The argument is the architecture. Without Zillah, the syntax of the play erodes to a politics of sentimental nostalgia. Zillah's bodily presence centers the anger, the ethical force, of the argument, by refusing dramaturgical closure. Without Zillah, there is no play because there is no narrative resistance, no dialectic. Without Zillah there is politics but no anger, performance but no theater.

The play, of course, is *A Bright Room Called Day*, Kushner's first professionally produced work. The narrative, set in the same apartment, though fifty years apart, alternates between a group of friends living in Berlin in 1932–33, and monologues spoken by Zillah Katz, a thirty-year-old American Jew visiting Germany, monologues which rage about the social injustices perpetrated by the U.S. Republicans in the 1980s and 1990s.

The title, Kushner reports, came from a chance encounter with an exhibition at New York City's Lincoln Center:

A videotape was on display showing Agnes de Mille at work on a new dance she was choreographing . . . for the Joffrey ballet. . . . I thought I heard the venerable Ms. de Mille tell her interviewer that the title of the new dance was "A Bright Room Called Day." That sounded like fun and solace, so I went over to the videotape only to discover that the title of the piece was actually "A Bridegroom called Death." From a bright room called day to a bridegroom called death: The metamorphosis was emblematic of the times. (*Bright Room* 1994, 174)

"The times" he refers to are the darkening days of the conservative ascendancy in U.S. politics. Ronald Reagan had just been elected for a second term. Influenced by the death of a relative, a car accident involving a close friend, the impending departure from New York of his mentor, and the bankruptcy of his fledgling theater company, it's no surprise that the work is bleak and uncompromising. As he reports, "With a grim relentlessness that now seems almost magical, every day brought news of either global failure or some intimate loss" (*Bright Room* 1994, 173). The bright room called day, then, is the space before calamity arrives, the space that opens to revolutionary possibility before, as one character sys, "the sky and the ground slam shut" (*Bright Room* 1994, 151).

The play charts the overwhelming of the German left and, through Zillah, of the American left, by the charismatic onslaught of two fascists, Hitler and Reagan. While many, especially critics who saw the first production, chastised Kushner for remarkable naiveté,[1] in hindsight his comparative analysis doesn't appear so far amiss. The proto-fascist Reagan revolution's legislative assault on individual freedoms and civil liberties has bequeathed a frightening legacy of reactionary governance to the Bush-Cheney junta.

To think through the play today is to ask again the questions Kushner asked while writing it: "The play is intended as a warning signal, not a prediction, but I often ask myself: Is it politically effective? Will it galvanize an audience to action, or, less ambitiously, will it make an audience think, argue, examine the present through the argument of the past" (*Bright Room* 1994, 180)? An answer doesn't come easily, especially not outside a production, but the question is worth asking if only because it opens to a larger assessment of the efficacy of a particular theatrical strategy, one imbedded in a dramaturgy greatly influenced by Bertolt Brecht—can the representation of a historical event, one rooted in its own peculiar temporal and physical location, shift the way we reconstitute the present? Would a production of *Bright Room* today provoke the ethical and critical force necessary to halt, or even correct, injustice and oppression?

In twenty-five scenes, eight "interruptions" (Zillah's monologues), a prologue, and an epilogue, the play charts how and why the left in Germany failed, and by comparison, how in many ways the same conflicting drives and needs pull the left apart today. To make this failure concrete, the play performs the dissolution of a group of friends—two actors, a communist graphic designer, a filmmaker, and a homosexual (all artists and outsiders)—even as they try to articulate an effective response to National Socialism. Kushner's strategy here measures the particular failures of each of his characters against the larger ideological tensions that prevailed among the various communist, socialist, and liberal parties in Germany whose inability to form crucial alliances ultimately brought the Nazis to power. As he notes, "In a way the play is the story of the failure of these four people who are Agnes's friends, within the context of an entire social movement failing [Agnes is the play's focal character, and the owner of the apartment in which the early Berlin scenes are set.]. . . . The collapse of Agnes's little coterie is in no way removable from the collapse of the German Communist Party, or the entire progressive movement for that matter" (Vorlicky 1998, 13–14). Each scene stages this collapse incrementally, demonstrating how the rise of the Nazi party—to borrow a phrase from Brecht—ultimately was resistible.

Brecht's influence is everywhere present here: scene titles, the allegorization of a historical event, a self-reflexive theatricality, the development of character from the social rather than the psychological, a Marxian dialectic embedded in the fabric of an episodic narrative. In an interview with his mentor, Carl Webber, Kushner comments, "I took a Brecht play that I have very little respect for, which is *Fear and Misery in the Third Reich*, and attempted when I started out to write *Bright Room* to do a sort of Reagan era version of it" (Vorlicky 1998, 111). Kushner experiments with Brecht's episodic form, constructing a sequence of scenes representing quotidian details—meals, squabbles— scenes which begin somewhat separate from the political maelstrom outside Agnes's apartment, but then proceed to show the world cracking in, scenes which depict the daily lives of his characters as they negotiate their own relationships when these become increasingly complicated, especially once the violence on the streets bleeds into their lives.

Kushner uses Zillah's interruptions, and toward the end of the play scenes where the past and the present converge, to produce a narrative self-consciously aware of its own historicity. While Agnes[3] provides the hub around whom other characters revolve, she also folds back to the previous occupant of her apartment, Die Alte (the old one), and forward to Zillah. The three women serve as alter egos, different and yet the same, each specific to her own historical location and yet confronting a similar moment of crisis: as Die Alte tells Agnes, "Time is all that separates you and me" (*Bright Room* 1994, 122). Kushner's dramaturgy effectively compresses three distinct time periods to reveal how each emerges from and informs the others.

One pattern positions that Die Alte, whom Kushner describes as "somewhere between 70 and dead-for-20–years" (*Bright Room* 1994, viii), as both the specter of Germany's imperial past and the voice of the ordinary citizen, the one who looked away while those in power disemboweled her world: "I wasn't here/didn't know/didn't want to know/never pulled a trigger/never pulled a switch/feel nothing for these beds/of sleepers, deep asleep/but only/look at how thin they are" (*Bright Room* 151). Zillah, on the other hand, gestures toward the possibility of future resistance. She, as Kushner states, "goes to Berlin to reconnect with history in as visceral a way as possible at the very time the Right is claiming that history is over" (Vorlicky 1998, 15). Agnes, then, connects the two. Her life is a story of failure, trapped between a future we already know and by a history she cannot affect. She remains, alone of all her friends, in Germany to play her small part opposing Hitler by allowing escaping communists to use her apartment as a safe-house. And dies there, probably, as Zillah tells us, "Not in the camps, and not in the war, but at home, in front of a cozy fire . . . , of a broken heart" (*Bright Room* 1994, 118).

The final scene stages alternating monologues delivered by the three women. Their keening voices weave an impressionistic shroud for Germany.

> Agnes: I live in a modern flat.
> On one side lives nightmare,
> on the other despair.
> Above me, exhaustion,
> below me, a man
> with the pale face
> and red hands of a strangler.
>
> Die Alte: The planes came back
> every day

to bomb the craters they'd created
only the day before.
The water was oily
and full of typhus.
Everyone was patchy,
delirious, diseased,
and waiting for the end . . .

Agnes: I fear the end
I fear the way
I fear the wind
Will make me stray
Much further than
I want to stray
Far from my home
Bright room called day;
Past where deliverance or hope
can find me.

Zillah: Now.
Before the sky and the ground slam shut.
The borders are full of holes.
(*Bright Room* 1994, 148–151)

Images of death, disease, destruction, a history of fear and betrayal, resonate through these attempts to define the relation between an interior and exterior, between desperation and the pressure of inexorable fact. Die Alte sees and doesn't see her world, scrounging for food to keep herself alive while ignoring the slaughter around her; Agnes sits trapped in her room, "past where deliverance or hope can find" her. Only Zillah asserts the need for immediate action, but with characteristic reticence, Kushner refuses to define the precise action she should take.

The education of Zillah, like the education of the audience, becomes one of the primary lessons of the play, both in how to watch and how to think dialectically. In this sense, Zillah is perhaps the most Brechtian of Kushner's characters—contemporary, recognizable, most easily accessed, but also (because of her dissonant hectoring, her habit of lecturing her audience) distanced, strange, an irritant just itchy enough to keep people awake. Kushner writes in his production notes to the play, "The impulse to interrupt the Weimar-era play with Zillah Katz's editorializing . . . came from a curiosity about the necessity of metaphorizing political content in theater. Why . . . shouldn't audiences hear an unapologetically didactic presentational voice, as well as representational scenes" (*Bright Room* 1994, x)? Zillah forces us to confront contemporary politics just as much as the scenes set in the past displace the way we have assimilated the fascism of the thirties. The deliberate equation of Reagan and Hitler, while certainly exaggerated, might deliver exactly the critical jolt an audience needs to scuttle its sedimented complacency.

At the end of the play, Zillah chooses to go back to the United States. As Kushner says, "It's a kind of reverse exile, a decision to reengage" (Vorlicky 1998, 15). There is both closure and renewal here, a recognition that keeping the space between earth and sky, the space of possibility, propped open requires vigilant resistance.

History moves through human subjectivity and its objective forces have to be conveyed in subjective forms: we live and create our contemporary history—it isn't something that is "done to us." Objective forces in history create subjective forms, and these have their own existential value. . . . In fact human subjectivity . . . is incorporated into the determining forces of history, not as an independent will . . . but . . . as a genuine free will, since human beings can make their own situations within history. . . . History isn't isolated events whose consequences we have to bear or utilize—it is a continuous process and makes no distinction (formally) between shipwreck and shipbuilding. . . . That is why we have art, to understand ourselves as shipmakers and shipwreckers, as agents of history: we are creators who make plans and maps of our activities, but we also need plans and maps of ourselves so that we understand ourselves and the consequences of our actions. . . . Human . . . subjectivity is the way we participate in history—which we do as inevitably as a fish swims in water. And so if our subjectivity is our relationship to history, our subjectivity has a political form—it is created and expresses itself through political gestures.

—Edward Bond, Letter to Sharon Cooper

Kushner interrogates history in his work not as something done to us, but as something we make, consciously or not. The plays demonstrate that the less conscious we are of the way we participate in history, the less able we will be to create effective and lasting change. All Kushner's work explores the consequences of the failure to negotiate complexly the relation between history and the present, manifest specifically in the ways his characters are condemned to repeat past errors or submit to ideological forces that shape them as citizens and subjects. The work demands an active engagement with the world, an engagement which compels new ways to think about it and remake it by acting in it.

While *Angels* explores the many possible ways individuals work to survive in an oppressive, homophobic society, *Slavs!* interrogates the relation between theory—the how-to-think part—and history. Kushner comments,

> The road that theory is supposed to lay down for us is that in the place of blind religious faith, theory gives us the belief that there is a way of understanding history, so that the steps we take have a certain direction and a certain design. When a very great theory, and Marxism is a very great theory, suffers the outrages of history, as it has—as well as causing a few outrages of history—then we're left reexamining what that was, why that happened, and what we're going to do now. (Kusher, quoted in Vorlicky 1998, 150)

Theory here provides the frame through which we can both interpret and create history—a grand ordering of thought which figures forth action. *Slavs!*, in many ways, examines what happens when theory falls prey to the manipulations of the powerful.

A theory for the way forward, if too inflexible, risks breaking either the people it intends to help or itself on the implacable rock of necessity. A theory too malleable melts into a generalized wash of often noble, but sentimental abstractions which bring no progressive results. Where the characters in *Bright Room* fail because of the latter, those in *Slavs!* suffer because of the former. In the interview in this volume, Kushner states that his view of theory conforms most closely with Hannah Pitt's, expressed at the end of *Perestroika*. "You need an idea of the world to go out into the world. But it's the going into that makes the idea. You can't wait for a theory, but you have to have a theory" (*Perestroika* 1992, 147).

*The past is of no importance. The present is of no importance. It is
with the future that we have to deal. For the past is what man should
not have been. The present is what man ought not to be. The future is
what artists are.*

—Oscar Wilde, "The Soul of Man under Socialism"

"What is to be done?" The question, asked repeatedly at the end of *Slavs!*,
finds no resolution. This is the dark answer to Prior's utopian vision at the
end of *Angels*. It is the question Kushner poses in order to force the play
beyond the limits of the performance space and into the world we inhabit.
There is no comfort in being forced against a difficult question. And yet,
there is immense political satisfaction. "What is to be done?"

Slavs! begins where *Angels* ends: it stages a nation on the brink of
rethinking itself, the Soviet Union immediately before and immediately
after the collapse of historical communism. The play represents a cross-
section of Russian society—politicians, the poor, party workers, peas-
ants, the middle class. But where the end of the second part of *Angels*
optimistically attempts to carve out a new, queer world, one that
embraces difference, *Slavs!* maps the dissolution of this promise, the
drowning of revolutionary possibility by unenlightened self-interest and
opportunism.

Kushner says he wrote each of the four scenes that make up the first
act of *Slavs!* as curtain-raisers for the first four acts of *Perestroika*, each
Russian scene, then, providing a lens and an opposition to the American
narrative. The two systems, both imploding, place in relief the necessary
theoretical flipside to the politics of the other. But when *Perestroika* was
shortened from seven to three and a half hours, these scenes—except for
one speech—were the first to be cut. Jon Jory at the Actors Theatre of
Louisville then commissioned Kushner to take these scenes and construct an entirely separate play.

Slavs! then began as a dialectical argument with the way capitalist
power reaffirms an unjust status quo, represented in the earlier play by
Roy Cohn and the Angel of America. But its new context demanded an
entirely different tack. Kushner writes:

I wanted in this play to get away from the Cold War model of analysis
which mandates that, as an antidote to Western propaganda, every criti-

cism of the Soviet system must be balanced with a criticism of the West. . . . I wanted to make a critique of the failure of the Soviet system from a socialist left standpoint. . . .

And I assume that it is clear that *Slavs!* is in every sense a play by an American, in part about America; it is as much about the territory Russia and the Soviet Union occupy in this American's imagination, as it is about anything historical and real. (Kushner, in Smith 1994a, 177)

The shape Kushner gives *Slavs!* is entirely different from either *Bright Room* or *Angels*. While the scenes proceed episodically, each of the three acts, the prologue, and the epilogue compose self-contained wholes—the first revolving around Aleksii Antedeluvianovich Prelapsarianov's speech on theory before the Politburo debating the way forward after Chernenko's death (the only part of *Slavs!* that Kushner retained from *Perestroika*); the second focused on a love triangle among two lesbians, Katherina and Bonfila, and Katherina's somtime suitor, the Politburo *apparatchik*, Popolitipov; the third set in remote Siberia where one of the lesbians, Bonfila, a pediatric oncologist, has been transferred to treat children exposed to high doses of nuclear radiation. There is no obvious narrative connection among the play's three parts, no plot that unfolds as the play proceeds, only the displacing of characters from one act to the next (Popolitipov appears in Acts I and II; Bonfila and Katherina in Acts II and III; Rodent, a party worker in Acts I and III; Prelapsarianov and Upgobkin in Act I and the epilogue. Vodya, a chid suffering from radiation poisoning, in Act III and the epilogue.) There are, however, layered thematic connections and, more important, a carefully built dialectical argument interrogating the position of socialism in Russia after the collapse.

The play frames a debate about the efficacy of Marxism in an age in which Marx's ideological program, as an alternative to capitalism, appears to have lost its political force. Kushner chooses yet another of those crucial historical moments, when the potential for sweeping change momentarily holds imaginative sway, and then dramatizes the national effects of the demise of socialism, the demise both of the idea and the practice. In this sense, then, the weight of Soviet history—its national emergence in 1917 as a global beacon for justice and equality measured against the quick collapse into Stalin's totalitarian terror—

defines the particular parameters within which the characters attempt to create a new order.

The answer to the question, "What is to be done?" hangs as a specter, then, over the entire play. And the debate this produces constitutes the focus of the play's action. As Kushner (1995a) notes in his short introduction:

> The action of much of the first act [and, I would add, the entire play] is *to think*—about the long standing problems of virtue and happiness—a lively, active, vigorous, passionate thinking, not introspective brooding, *but thinking hard, discussing*. . . . These are all people who speak their thoughts, rather than people who think and then speak. There is no need for pausing to arrive at an idea or an articulation—rhetorical grandeur is second nature for them. (94–95)

As such, it is a difficult play for American audiences nurtured on a theater where psychology is almost wholly separated from the social circumstances which generate it. Kushner's characters are determined by their social location, and the psychologies they perform match the ideologies that drive them. These characters embody their history, and it is history itself that we see taken apart and reformulated through the particular debates in which they engage.

The play is framed by a prologue in which two babushkas sweep snow off the steps in front of the Kremlin while debating the relative merits of Gradualism versus a vanguard-driven revolution. When Upgobkin and Smukov, two high-ranking members of the Politburo, interrupt their argument, the two turn into "sweet, toothless old ladies, head-bobbing, forelock-tugging mumblers" (*Slavs!* 1995, 100). The two men mostly ignore them—certainly they don't see that these ordinary citizens are as supple at dialectical reasoning as any of their colleagues. But aside from the laughter these juxtapositions evoke, the sequence illustrates a serious point: part of the difficulty confronting the Soviet government is too little faith in its citizens. These women know enough, can debate with intellectual agility, display an acute sense of irony honed by many years of bitter oppression, and provide a perspective crucial to the argument which forms the substance of the first act. That they're ignored epitomizes the attitude the Soviet state takes towards the people it governs, and this, ultimately, signifies perhaps Kushner's main point:

one solution to "the longstanding problem of virtue and happiness" is the coupling of a socialist sensibility to the vibrant and vital, yet always fragile, institution of pluralist democracy. His critique in *Angels* revolves around the co-opting of democracy by White, straight men; in *Slavs!* he explores the betrayal of socialism first by Stalin and totalitarianism, and then by a rapacious, global corporatism.

The debate in the first act, between conservatism and progress, between the heart and the head, between Popolitipov (who claims that the heart rules the body, and that the heart is not progressive) and Upgobkin (who affirms the necessity of a rational vision), frames the central opposition of the play. And if, as he suggests, Prelapsarianov represents a third term, a crude historical synthesis of reason and passion that hasn't worked, then the key to a successful staging of the play would deliberately modulate this pattern—thesis, antithesis, synthesis—through the other two acts.

The progressive love in the second act, represented by the two lesbians, Katherina and Bonfila, and celebrated in the Pan-Soviet Archives for the Study of Cerebro-Cephalognomical Historico-Biological Materialism (the dead brain library), where Katherina works as a night guard, suggests that the systemic failure of Soviet communism is in fact exactly the opposite of what Popolitipov asserts. The heart is in fact progressive. The dead brains, stored in the unlikely event that scientists will one day be able to extract their great wisdom, evoke with gruesome accuracy the moribund state of the Communist Party, an institution "floating in some sort of lime-green sudsy mummifying juice" (*Slavs!* 1995, 130) promulgating stale ideas in order to sustain what Katherina calls "the Great Grey Age of Boredom" (130).

The third act sees the two lovers together and, though in remote, radioactive Siberia, working to help people live better lives. Bonfila tells Rodent, the *apparatchik* we met in the first act now come to gather information for Yeltsin, "Why didn't I go back? Because I thought I could do some good here" (1995, 174). Where the first act shows the possibility of change, the last articulates the undermining of this—the drift into a situation that mostly still prevails today. Russia lies ravaged by greedy businessmen who plundered the country the moment the safeguards erected by socialism had crumbled. Perhaps most indicative of this is Rodent's admission that the Russian government plans to process and store, for money of course, radioactive materials for foreign countries even while its own nuclear waste oozes into the ecosystem—the literal fallout from the cold war.

Kushner personifies his condemnation of the future the old party bosses have made in Vodya Domik, an eight-year-old mutant child, product of radioactive decay, malnutrition, and national neglect. Where Katherina declares facetiously, "I have no history" (*Slavs!* 1995, 142), here we face a child who has no future. So it is fitting that she, in an epilogue set in the afterlife, confronts the two oldest Bolsheviks we saw in the first act, Prelapsarianov and Upgobkin. She speaks now for the first time, chastising the two men even while placing Russia's economic, social and cultural predicament in historical context.

> The socialist experiment in the Soviet Union has failed, grandfathers. . . .
>
> And what sense are we to make of the wreckage?
>
> Perhaps the principals were always wrong. Perhaps it is true that social justice, economic justice, equality, community, an end to master and slave, the withering away of the state. These are desirable, but not realizable on the earth. (*little pause*)
>
> Perhaps the failure of socialism in the East speaks only of the inadequacy and criminal folly of any attempt to organize more equitably and rationally the production and distribution of the wealth of nations. And chaos, market fluctuations, rich and poor, colonialism and war are all that we shall ever see. (*little pause*)
>
> Perhaps, even the wreckage that became the Union of Soviet Socialist Republics is so dreadful to contemplate that the histories of Red October, indeed of hundreds of years of communitarian, millenarian and socialist struggle, will come to seem mere prelude to Stalin, to gulags, the death of free thought, dignity and human decency, and "socialist" become a foul epithet; and to the ravages of Capital there will be no conceivable alternative. . . .
>
> I am inexpressibly sad, grandfather. (*Slavs!* 1995, 183–84)

This long, complicated, splendidly rhetorical speech, immediately made slightly odd in that it's spoken by a child, should affect us in the same way as Zillah's call to action does in *Bright Room*. While Vodya's audience resignedly mumbles, "It is bitter," we should recognize simultaneously the reasons for this defeatism, perhaps even empathize with this despair, but also be moved to do something. The play's critique of the left today, its inability to organize against the rampant despoilation of our planet resonates back through *Angels* and *Bright Room*. The three arguments against socialism Vodya articulates—the religious, the capitalist, defeatist acceptance—all lead only to further despondency, not to change. Kushner's work aims to refute all three. The play's final line—"What is to be done?"—echoes and opposes Prior's utopian optimism in *Perestroika,* where he turns to the audience and exclaims, "You are fabulous creatures; each and every one. And I bless you: *More Life.* The Great Work begins" (*Perestroika* 1994, 148). Here, instead, Kushner forces the play beyond the limits of the performance space and into the world we inhabit. The warning seems clear: without collective action now, there will be no future, at least no future worth living.

The rest is up to us.

We live our lives; we tell our stories. The dead continue to live by way of the resurrection we give them in telling their stories. The past becomes part of our present and thereby part of our future. We act individually and collectively in a process over time which builds the human enterprise and tries to give it meaning. Being human means thinking and feeling; it means reflecting on the past and visioning into the future. We experience; we give voice to that experience; others reflect on it and give it new form. That new form, in its turn, influences and shapes the way the next generations experience their lives.

That is why history matters.

—Gerda Lerner, *Why History Matters*

Notes

1. See Savran, David, *Take it Like a Man, White Masculinity, Masochism and Contemporary American Culture.* Princeton: Princeton University Press, 1998; Bigsby, C. W. *Contemporary American Playwrights.* Cambridge, UK: Cambridge University Press, 1999; and the many interviews collected in Vorlicky, Robert, ed., *Tony Kushner in Conversations,* especially "The Proust Questionnaire" and "I Always Go Back to Brecht."
2. See Bigsby, note 1.
3. Kushner states that he chose this name to acknowledge the title he took from Agnes de Mille, but it also resonates biblically—Agnes as the lamb of god.

Works Cited

Auden, W. H. 1989. September 1, 1939. In *Selected Poems*, ed. Edward Mendelson. New York: Vintage.

Benjamin, Walter. 1998. Theses on the Philosophy of History. In *Illuminations*, ed. Hannah Arendt. New York: Schocken Books. 253–264.

Bond, Edward. 1997. Letter to Sharon Cooper, 4 March 1986. *Letters III*, ed. Ian Stuart. New York: Harwood Academic Publishers. 3–4.

Eliot, T. S. Tradition and the Individual Talent. In *Selected Essays*. Faber and Faber: London. 3–11.

Lerner, Gerda. 1997. *Why History Matters*. Oxford and New York: Oxford University Press.

Kushner, Tony. 1994a. Afterword. In *Humana Festival '94: The Complete Plays,* ed. Marisa Smith. Lyme, New Hampshire: Smith and Kraus.

———. 1994b. *Angels in America Part Two: Perestroika*. New York: Theatre Communications Group.

———. 1994c. *A Bright Room Called Day*. New York: Theatre Communications Group.

———. 1995a. Author's notes. *Thinking About the Longstanding Problems of Virtue and Happiness*. New York: Theatre Communications Group.

———. 1995b. *Slavs!* In *Thinking About the Longstanding Problems of Virtue and Happiness*. New York: Theatre Communications Group.

Vorlicky, Robert, ed. 1998. *Tony Kushner in Conversation*. Ann Arbor: University of Michigan Press.

Wilde, Oscar. 1954. The Soul of Man Under Socialism. In *De Profundis and Other Essays*. London and New York: Penguin. pp. 16–53.

INTERVIEW WITH TONY KUSHNER

Interview conducted by Framji Minwalla
in April 2001

Tony Kushner: It's hard to do interviews, so I'll do the best I can.

Framji Minwalla: You're a very good interviewee, actually.

TK: It depends on what is happening at the moment. This is a hard time. I think I told you, when I'm really in the middle of writing, I get very fuzzy-headed and it's really hard to get back into that offering of opinions because everything that I say I immediately think of 25—I mean I do that anyway—you just kind of get into an endless dialectical frame of mind and I tend to stay far away from panel discussions and things when I'm in the middle of writing a play because I get really anti-social and abstract.

FM: I know this is a question you don't particularly like, but I'm going to ask it anyway. In other interviews, you talk a lot about Brecht and Williams, and in "The Proust Questionnaire" you mention all your favorite writers, but which specifically have influenced your use of language?

TK: God, who hasn't? Let me think for a second. . . . I really feel there are so many people that I feel indebted to stylistically. I think certainly the first and most powerful influence probably was Brecht, although I've gone far away from Brecht. I think more in his poems than in his plays. But that sort of sparse and extremely rational, unadorned, quotable, epigrammatic style . . . the inversions, the paradoxes, those things really had a great impact. And I still find myself very much drawn to poets like Brecht.

I just went to a town hall meeting, the big celebration for Stanley Kunitz's 96th birthday. And thirteen poets each read a poem by Stanley and then he got up and read three himself—he's had a tremendous influence on my writing. It's a kind of writing that I don't actually know that I do, but it's a sort of a gold standard, it's an ideal to strive for. It's writing that seems to be completely not artificial, it seems to be incredibly direct and simple and have the kind of vatic quality of biblical statement—not King James biblical—but you know, really kind of the word of god sort of thing. Czeslaw Milosz also writes like this, and actually writes about writing like this.

Translations of Horace, really good translations of Horace who is a poet I love. And actually a lot of translations from Latin. I know very little Latin, but a good translation always gets that kind of apparently unadorned, uncomplicated kind of statement that is of course, in point of fact, highly artificial and contains immense complexity. Those wonderful poems of Stanley's late period, all about his garden, that really contain just shattering ideas about life and longevity and what is achievable in the course of a lifetime and what isn't and facing death. There's something sort of Roman about it, as well as Jewish. Very powerful stuff.

Probably the person that I think, well two people that I think are the most liberating—sort of the other side of it—the people without whom I wouldn't have written, but also because I've never actually been able to write like them, only on very rare occasions, are Melville and Wallace Stevens. Beckett I would also put in that camp. It's a kind of articulation that doesn't come easily to me. I think that it requires a certain degree of toughness and courage that I find myself lacking. And I think that Melville and Wallace Stevens, and to an extent Whitman and the Americans, who really give you permission to be excessive, to write your way to an idea even if it means that what you are creating is inexcusably long and full of all sorts of distractions and discursions. Well that would certainly be what Melville gives you permission to do. Everything that Melville wrote . . . and he's probably the only writer of whom I've read everything that I know of. There may be things that we don't know about but I've been pretty diligent, obsessively tracking everything down. He's a great liberator. It's a very radical kind of writing. It's a rejection of the idea of norms and rules. Whitman is similar.

Stevens I think just gives the freedom to not make sense in the name of trying to find a kind of sense that's very hard to articulate. And just in a sort of astonishing richness of expression and also he's a very dialectical poet. He's probably the first really difficult poet that I managed to understand so it gave me a whole new relationship to the idea of difficulty in writing which is a problematic and complicated thing for playwrights because it's hard to be difficult in the theatre. But I think it's really important for playwrights to wrestle with difficulty, so Stevens has been useful. And I've used him a lot in teaching. Stevens and Kant, because I think that it's good for playwrights to recognize, to deal with writing that only yields up its meaning with incredible effort. Just so we don't get lazy.

Heiner Mueller. I just did the introduction to this Heiner Mueller reader and he certainly has had a more recent but profound effect.

Among playwrights, Mamet had, with me and everybody else, a huge impact. John Guare. The first playwright that I sort of consciously thought, "Oh, I want to write like this," was probably Guare. When I was a college student and I read *House of Blue Leaves* and I thought that this is how you would write poetry onstage so that it doesn't sound like T. S. Eliot.

And Fornes. She had a huge impact. Churchill certainly had a tremendous impact.

FM: So when you were writing *Hydriotaphia* . . .

TK: Monty Python.

FM: Were many of these writers—certainly the excessiveness of Melville and Whitman . . .

TK: And Thomas Browne, who had a huge impact on Melville through [Thomas] de Quincy, especially "The Confessions of an English Opium Eater." I started out just wanting to take Steven Spinella, this was in 1987, and have him do the essay, "Hydriotaphia." We read it a little bit and I thought, this isn't exactly what I want, and then various things happened. An uncle of mine died of cancer of the bowels and the play sort of emerged from that. But definitely Melville, and—I think I say this in the introduction to the book—"Krazy Kat" by George Herman, which had just been published. I had never heard of it before. The summer before I wrote, I finally took a deep breath and I read *Ulysses* from cover to cover. You can't even describe it as an influence;

it just changes the way your brain processes language. It makes you recognize the plasticity and dynamism of language.

I just did this tiny little introduction for—I'm Mister Introducer now—Wayne Koestbaum's book, the Heiner Mueller thing, and I've been writing introductions all spring. The last one was this little thing for Charles Ludlum's . . . the big collected plays is now out of print so TCG is bringing back just five or six of the most famous plays. And I was reading it to write this little one-page thing for the book. I saw lots and lots of Ludlum when I was a college student in the eighties, but I never thought of him much as a writer because the performances were so marvelous. But he's an absolutely astonishing writer, an undiscovered great. I really came to this feeling that when enough time has passed so that that way of doing these plays is gone, somebody can come and take these things, the early bizarre ones and rethink them.

Dickens—every time I'm stuck I either read Wallace Stevens or Dickens and it unsticks me. Especially if I'm working on plot, I like Dickens. And again, it's sort of this protean sense of how language is cobbled. And then Shakespeare. I was just reading this book, *Conversations with Goethe,* about this guy who followed Goethe for years, and it's page after page of great things that Goethe threw over his shoulder to this guy, and he tells him you should only read Shakespeare once a year if you have a creative mind. He's really severe: "Don't read more than one play once a year because you'll stop writing." And it's really true. It's hugely depressing. Beckett to an extent had that effect. Some of the Beckett makes me think I have no idea how he did this; it doesn't seem possible.

FM: In your intro to *Hydriotaphia,* you say the play is about "the treachery of words, about writing." You also suggest that in fact it is the "swooniness" of Browne's writing which attracted you to the character in the first place. Is there a connection between "swooniness" and "treachery"? And what do you find treacherous about language?

TK: Oh, you know, nothing especially surprising, only that words are elusive, slippery, unreliable, all we have if we want to make meaning, and everyone wants that, but the meanings we make are so full of ambiguity and contradiction because we are always saying or writing more than we mean to, or not what we mean to, or what we mean to but don't realize we intend. The "swoon" in Browne's writing, and Melville's and others—Proust!—is . . . what? Well I suppose an intoxication with language, and an intoxication with its dangers, with the urge to specify, specify, elaborate, clarify, trying to pin down meaning, and of course, in the process, words proliferate and the meanings do as well; thoughts become clearer and far more cloudy, both at once. Legal writing is also wonderfully tricky in this way.

FM: Those characters who are in some sense activists—either progressive activists or even reactionary activists—have the permission in your plays to use that kind of excessive language; Belize on the one hand and Roy Cohn on the other [in *Angels in America*], Zillah on one hand and Die Alte on the other [in *A Bright Room Called Day*], and Browne and the Ranters [in *Hydriotaphia*]. Is that conscious, do you think?

TK: I have this materialism/idealism split, and I have to give that up to a certain extent, but I absolutely believe in ideology. I believe that the world is constructed of words and that words have tremendous power and effect. I am drawn to characters like Thomas Browne or Roy Cohn who invent a world that they then inhabit, and that world is invented by words. What Roy says in *Perestroika* about this is something I believe very deeply, that this county is completely made by lawyers out of words. I mean it didn't exist, and the Constitution . . . a handful of genius, gentleman farmer lawyers, Madison and Jefferson, created it and changed everything.

I'm very interested in legal language. I keep thinking that I should go to law school. I'm really interested in legal articulations. A play that I'm working on now [*It's an Undoing World, or Why Should It Be Easy When It Can Be Hard?*], that I'm fiddling with, has as one of its characters Benjamin Mason Cardozo, a Jewish [Supreme Court] justice who wrote incredibly strange legal documents, who changed the way decisions were written because he wrote this sort of weird, pretentious, incredibly-difficult-to-decipher prose. He was politically conservative, at least in terms of corporate responsibility. He created a whole bad precedent in terms of jurisprudence, giving corporations more immunity from responsibility than individuals. And frequently, unlike Brandeis who was a great, luminous, progressive jurist, somebody who really took the most powerful progressive strains of Judaism and brought them to the

Supreme Court, Cardozo is a reactionary. But his writing is so weird that it creates immense confusion, and in the confusion all sorts of interpretations. It's Talmudism brought to the law. So I'm really interested in him.

Something like the fourteenth amendment, which is an incredibly simple statement, but [that] has transformed America, and of course there's a lot of blood behind that transformation, it's not all just words, but the right wording clearly can make all the difference.

FM: Do you see your use of language in some ways as a synthesis of Brecht's dialectical, epigrammatic style and Melville's and Whitman's hyperbole? Is this partly also where you see the materialist/idealist enlightenment split in your own work?

TK: I'd be very happy if I managed to achieve such a synthesis—sounds great! In a way, the ruthless demands of stage-time, of modern attention spans, forces all us playwrights towards the epigrammatic and terse, towards a classical severity; right now I'm hacking page after page off *Homebody*.[1] It's not possible to be really garrulous. But are Melville and Whitman idealists? Not really—they're both so grounded in both the material world—did either one believe in God?—and in the materiality of writing itself, the bookiness of books, the action of writing. Neither had a grand theory; well, Whitman had democracy but that was more a love affair than a considered ideology, and Melville had none, I think, while Brecht sort of did—so in a way, isn't *he* the more idealist, the more theory-bound and abstract?

FM: You mentioned you need to get away from this dialectic? Why? Do you think it might have outlived its political efficacy? So much of your work, and so much postwar political theater, is built on this, on the gap between ideals and facts, that it almost sounds like you're looking for a new, formal way to write.

TK: The recrudescence of various kinds of premodern vicious theologies and fanaticisms, doing appalling damage to the world, and the new sentimentality even progressive people feel towards religious faith, makes the old privileging of materialism really appealing sometimes—though I feel that I have been guilty of and have benefited from that sentimentality—well we *had* to reconsider the absolute rejection of religious faith. But we have also gotten very goopy about it—and surely if there is a God, smart people at least are expected to be agnostics or at least agnostically inclined. And then there's the question of the "idealism" implicit in any metatheory. Of course I'm thrashing about in this, we all are, I would think. I worry that my attachment to the dialectical model, and to this dialectic in particular, is sentimental. I think it would be ideal if one could manage to reinvent oneself as a writer each time, or almost each time one wrote. Every subject brings with it its own specific formal requirements, and every good subject should throw ideological certainties into a tizzy, so each new play should make a playwright start at the beginning. A "style" is not something I want, I don't want to be trapped by that, though I know what I write will sound like I've written it. I think it's probably the case that new philosophical models will have to be proposed to inspire us writers, rather than the invention of new philosophies coming from us. We may grope our way blindly towards a new way of understanding the world—that's our job—and then people with a talent for rigorously abstracting, explicating and parsing the nuances of new vision will have to make theory out of it—that's their job. Marx and Heine, for instance, are a good example of what I'm talking about. Benjamin and Brecht.

FM: Getting back to difficulty, in your essay "On Pretentiousness," you speak about a connection between posing large political questions and pretentious writing. Do you see a connection between pretentiousness and difficulty? Is there an audience for work that isn't easy? If there is, it probably isn't a big one. Is there a link between difficulty and the "matzoh" playwright, Beckett?

TK: Beckett is supremely difficult, in that he creates texts that are resistant to interpretation, lacking in ordinary comforts, demanding of an audience, requiring concentration, quickness, and critical and imaginative faculties far greater than many people have or are accustomed to using. Over-reaching writing can certainly also make for difficult work, sometimes by making its audience work hard, sometimes just because it's tiresome. *Homebody*, the Afghanistan play, starts with an hour-long monologue that's rather hard work. And then there are two more acts to follow. I try to entertain, but it isn't easy-easy. Is there an audience? Small, like you said. But one can't write down to one's audience, that's disgusting; if difficult work is what you like, it's what you've got to try to write. We could create a bigger audience for hard work if we had decent free public education. If we taught people how to read.

FM: Would you like to talk about the new play at all?

TK: Sure, if you want to ask anything specific.

FM: Do you see the play as an allegory about ethnic conflict and sectarian violence?

TK: The play addresses to an extent the nature of the ethnic and sectarian violence in the country, and also the origins in the violence in modern times in colonial adventure and its aftermath, the cold war, the great game. Afghanistan is a fantastically complex place in every sense, and it's in absolutely cataclysmic shape, and I think the way the world helps it rebuild, to the extent that the world does help it rebuild, must be governed by as much of an understanding of that complexity as possible; and no blunt easy solutions, boycotts, bombs, exploitation by Unocal—none of these will do anything other than worsen what is already as bad as it gets.

FM: Does it deal with the aftermath of the civil war?

TK: It's set in '98, in August, about a week and a half after Clinton bombed looking for Osama bin Laden's missiles. It's set in Kabul, after the Taliban have been there for about two and a half years—a situation which holds at this moment [April 2001], except that since I wrote the play [rebel commander Ahmed Shah], Masood has been invited to Pakistan, and he's been invited to speak at the E.U., which makes me very unhappy. And, of course, all the stuff with the Bamiyan Buddhas doesn't really alter the situation much.

It's a situation in which it's simply not possible to know what should be done. As Oscar Eustis, a dramaturg, said to me, "confronting Afghanistan's history, especially what's happened in the last twenty years, is a hubris-defeating exercise." And I'm angry at a reaction in America that seems to play into the hands of the worst people, into the hands of Republicans, and people in Clinton's administration too, who really are interested in Afghanistan only insofar as it concerns oil pipelines and gas pipelines. The idea that one can simply apply as a blanket solution to every country economic sanctions and boycotts, with an occasional missile strike—the idea that a country like Afghanistan should be sanctioned economically—is an ugly, ugly joke. It's very supremacist, it's anti-internationalist. It's very much about keeping the third world, the developing world, in debtor condition, in colonized condition, and guaranteeing that unequal development becomes a permanent state of affairs.

I'm also interested in the whole feminist, multiculturalist debate—whether or not progressive, first-world, Western politics have any bearing on Afghani history. In very practical terms, the response that liberal feminists have made to the horrible situation confronting women in Afghanistan is legitimate, but in its rhetoric also helps make the case for economic sanctions, which is insane. Or throwing all of our weight behind Masood and the Northern Alliance, which is also insane and isn't going to work, clearly. I was just talking to a guy who had been there, and we were laughing because we wound up making some of the arguments which were made, of course, for fascism in the thirties. "They came in and took over so at least someone was running things."

It's horrifying, what happened in Afghanistan, just horrifying. I don't know what to do with it. I guess in a way we're all in a huge crisis of theory right now, and those of us who organize our understanding of the world around certain features of Marxist and socialist theory are now rummaging through what's left of that to see what's salvageable and what isn't.

FM: That makes you sound like Prelapsarianov.[2]

TK: I agree with him in a certain sense. He's right and he's wrong. Glasnost and Perestroika failed, to a certain extent, because it didn't have a theory. It opened Russia up to complete predation by gangsters from within and economic exploitation from without because no one could articulate a theory of some kind of new economic policy. And I think the best people, like Andrei Sakharov, were those who retained socialism with democracy. Not being allowed to do that by the International Monetary Fund and the World Bank and forces within Russia has helped to lead them into a quagmire. God knows what's going to happen there.

At the end of the play [*Perestroika*], what Hannah says is what's closest to my sense of it. You *can't* have a great metatheory but you also have to have one. I don't believe that if the rest of politics is completely and totally rooted in the practical, it is ultimately going to be enough, because I think that we're anarchic mostly. I'm sort of hoping that before I get too old for it to matter, I'll be able to see the *mizrach* arrive.

FM: Do you see this as one of those moments, as Agnes says in *Bright Room*, before the sky and the ground. . . .

TK: Before it all closes up?

FM: . . . snaps shut.

TK: Well, in a way yes, and in a way no. I mean the only thing that I see really snapping shut, the legitimate doomsday scenario, is that we're simply going to fail over the next thirty years to do anything about global warming, and we're going to be faced with a planet that becomes increasingly unlivable. The end of the world. We don't have political leaders in this country who really begin to articulate an international vision for the future of American democracy, not a colonialist or an imperialist vision, but a notion of the interdependency of the environmental, the ecological . . . a political ecology of the world.

I think that the world could really come to an end. I didn't used to believe that, and it seems to me now we're clearly going to be deeply fucked in the next fifty years. There will be death on a holocaustal scale, from changes in storm patterns and rising seas and droughts. People will probably endure, like people in the thirteenth century endured the black plague—speaking of plagues, AIDS in Africa. In a way this is a moment where it's possible to engage in activist opposition to what's going on. And it *is* there, those kids protesting the World Bank wherever those depraved idiots, criminals, gangsters are meeting, it's remarkable. In some ways it's objectively harder for these kids to do what they're doing than it was to go downtown and march against Vietnam, which was heroic and did a lot of good, but a lot of people were doing it then. These kids clearly have no money and are getting themselves to Zurich and places like this, risking serious mistreatment by the authorities, and long jail terms, it's very heroic. And those kids at Harvard sleeping in the president's office. *It's still there.* Perhaps old crusty people like me should be participating as well. And maybe there's a way of turning things around.

FM: Do you think there's a reason why the progressive left has not seized the moment?

TK: There have to be lots of reasons. I mean I have my own complaints about us, about people who voted for Nader, people that say there's no difference between Bush and Gore, or that there's no difference between Ariel Sharon and Barak. It seems to me that revolution has proved to be very problematic. And it really has been since 1789, 1791. Well, as a dream, as a road to utopia it's an enormously powerful thing. In actuality, it seems very, very problematic, and the violence of it seems to produce monstrous regimes. I say that still feeling what I believed since I was young, that the violence of a revolution has to be seen in the context of the secret violence of an economic order like ours. But, it's really hard to look back on the history of the twentieth century, and the ninteenth century for that matter, and have great faith in the power of revolution. Certainly you can't be a Marxist-Leninist anymore, you can't be a Bolshevik anymore. You can't believe in a vanguard. That just hasn't worked. I think that's inarguable.

People's appetite and capacity for sudden transformation is limited. So often what Lenin said is true, and one of the things he said was, "politics really begins in millions." I believe that, but if you can say that then you also have to recognize that among the millions, 850,000 are people who are really not going to be able to handle a rapid, sudden transformation of their world. They can handle some rapid change, they can go from living in the segregated south to knowing a year later that you now have to sit next to a Black person. It's hard and people will die as a result of asking you to do that. It's going to be a bloody, ugly business, but it can happen and sometimes it should. Those types of revolutions should happen, but those are revolutions within the context of a functioning democracy. I just hear in the left so much left over from the sixties, left over from the thirties—it's an aroma mixed from many sources, this kind of absolute rejection of American democracy as being about anything other than selling out to corporations and making a good environment for profit maximization. It isn't that, and it's stupid to think that, and I think that we are fucking ourselves. There's a great deal of truth in the idea that we have willed ourselves into irrelevance because we can't organize anything. Because we really do say Clinton was so compromising and awful we'll just keep our hands clean and vote for Ralph fucking Nader. Even in Florida, in a close election. It's just so dumb. And you know you have surrendered agency. I think that that's the problem.

FM: Edward Bond says at the end of his preface to *Lear* something like, "we don't need a vision for the future, we need a method of change," and in a sense really we need both. But a method of change, that's what we don't have.

TK: A method of change I think can be agreed upon. But utopia is incredibly important. I think that's the real function of theater. Utopia is the unreachable paradise and you don't have to create it within a generation or two, but it gives you a sense of where you're aiming at. And a few steps short of utopia there's the notion of a just, ordered society within a just, ordered world. I think there are things to debate, like can one have a centrally planned economy. That to me is still a very interesting question which still hasn't been answered. Had Lenin had microchips and the Pentium processor, wouldn't that have made a difference? E. H. Carr says they really fucked up with the number crunching. If this information technology was used in any kind of progressive way, was actually used to coordinate, then is there any way to plan an economy that doesn't destroy freedom and democracy, and doesn't create some sort of techno-fascist state? I don't know the answer to that. But it's a really interesting question. But of course we're not even remotely asking that, just believing that a market economy makes sense, and it clearly doesn't. I would agree with Bond except what worries me is that that kind of statement, . . . is that the original preface to *Lear*?

FM: Yes, but he has moved away from that considerably. That was in the seventies.

TK: Because a lot of people have moved right there, I mean a lot of people are saying, "I don't know what we're heading toward but I know this sucks. What's happening in my kids' schools sucks, what's happening with GE and the PCBs in the Hudson sucks, what happened in Florida sucks; so I'm going to focus on that." And that is completely legitimate, but . . . I certainly learned from the struggle with the NEA around the question of arts funding and freedom of expression. I feel that we really missed the boat by not having a more international, global vision, a solidarity-based vision about connecting what was happening to us and being done to us with the struggles of other oppressed communities around the country and around the world. The best fights that we waged were still pretty insular.

FM: Issues of activism are central to your plays. There's that scene in *Bright Room* where Baz is in Munich sitting alone in a dark theater with a loaded gun when Hitler and his SS walk in and sit a few rows in front of him, and he doesn't shoot. It's a moral issue, and today a very pertinent moral issue. For Baz, living seems more important than taking the moment, seizing the moment, in an activist way, whatever the consequences of that activism. And in many ways *Bright Room* is about people who do or do not take stands in relation to the Nazis. Those issues are complicated and discussed and argued and confronted, whereas today we don't seem to confront them at all, we don't even seem to discuss them.

TK: What Baz does in a way is inarguably bad, I mean he had the opportunity to kill Adolf Hitler, he could've changed everything. But on the other hand, you can argue that the ability to sacrifice one's life . . . People are doing it all the time, people in Turkey who are on hunger strikes, the Zapatistas from Chiapas who marched all over Mexico, people all over the world are putting their lives at risk, and losing their lives. What's sad about what Baz does in a way is that he's already been dragged into an SS office and threatened, told about the camps, but he believes that he can save himself. And he does, in a way: he ends up leaving Germany. And that's the shame, because so many of these people left. I mean, you have nothing to lose but your chains, that moment is the revolutionary moment, that's the moment when you sacrifice, when you literally have nothing but your enslavement, and you've moved so far down that you really have nowhere else to go, and death is not that much worse in a way than continuing to live. We're like Baz. There's that great Buddhist parable about the burning house. Buddha sees these people in the house and the roof is on fire. He begs them to leave and says, "Your roof is on fire." And they say, "Where will we sleep if we leave this house, is there a better house?" And Buddha says, "You will have to burn to death before you understand."

And it isn't discussed. One of the reasons is that the Soviet Union has fallen apart, eliminating not only a geopolitical space, but also an ideational space of opposition to this. There was a sense of a world with two systems in it. You know, it's Marcuse, we need to have a sense that even if you don't subscribe to the choices you are being offered, you have to have the idea that the world is dialectical, not one dimensional. He was right, and we've sailed into a one dimensional universe. There is no oppositional space. And I think that's just infecting all of us terribly.

FM: Where do you think American theater is heading? And in what direction do you need it to go for theater to become a politically useful tool?

TK: It will always be politically useful, it really shouldn't aspire to be a "tool." Art has purposes which speak directly to the political moment and also other purposes; though all human activity has a political valence, dimension, meaning, I believe there is probably some distinction to be made between interior and exterior life, between public and private—separate realms with porous borders. American theater will be glorious and dreadful always, and more or less multicultural depending on how extensively it is subsidized. I think the form needs cash, and if it comes from ticket prices, too many are excluded. There are forms of theater that don't require obsessive devotion, but I think great theater probably comes from that sort of devotion, at least as the world is presently constituted. I think it should be possible for people to survive with dignity, remunerated, in theater. I think the slo-mo destruction of the NEA is intended to make theater White and irrelevant again. We'll see.

Notes

1. Kushner's most recent play, *Homebody/Kabul*, produced by New York Theater Workshop in November 2001.
2. Aleksii Antedelluvianovich Prelapsarianov, a character in *Perestroika* and *Slavs!*.

"A'S" LAST MEMORY: CONTEXTUALIZING ALBEE'S *THREE TALL WOMEN*

Thomas P. Adler

Three Tall Women (Vienna, 1991; New York, 1994), which won Edward Albee his third Pulitzer Prize for Drama, marked a critical and popular renascence for a major American writer. Even commentators largely dismissive of the playwright's works since the mid-1960s championed it: John Simon (1994) in *New York* magazine remarked that he "hardly believed [his] eyes and ears" about "how good" it was, singling out especially "the canniness and multivalence of Albee's construction" (118), while Robert Brustein (1994), writing in *The New Republic*, reported he was "happy to join other former detractors in saluting Albee's accomplishment," concluding that "His late career is beginning to resemble O'Neill's, another dramatist who wrote his greatest plays after having been rejected and abandoned by the culture" (26, 28).

Recently, Margo Jefferson (2000) has noted "that what distinguishes American art in all its variety is idiosyncrasy, improvisation and a willingness, even at the cost of imperfection, to break old forms and try new ones" (B2). Albee has, of course, from the days of his earliest one-acters in the late 1950s, been an experimental dramatist, although he prefers to severely restrict the formal categories within which his dramas are discussed, distinguishing only among levels or degrees of naturalism:

All of my plays are stylized, to one extent or another, but all drama is artifice. Within those parameters, all of my plays are absolutely naturalistic. Some are less what the audience expects than others, which is my definition of stylization. (Albee 1994, 38)

And yet, his stylistic experimentation assumes many different forms, from surrealism (*The Sandbox*) to absurdism (*The American Dream*) to allegory (*Tiny Alice*); from symbolism *(The Zoo Story)* to the quasi-metaphysical drawing room play (*A Delicate Balance*) to the fable or parable (*Seascape*); from the picaresque journey *(Malcolm)* to the dramatized lecture (*The Man Who Had Three Arms*); from scenes linked by cinematic techniques (*The Death of Bessie Smith*) to a series of vaudeville sketches or turns (*Counting the Ways*) to monodrama for a disembodied voice (*Box*).

In the Introduction to *Box and Quotations from Chairman Mao Tse-Tung* (1968), his most radical departure from traditional realism thus far, Albee (1970) comments on the dual obligation of any playwright to "attempt change" by "mak[ing] some statement about the condition of 'man'" and by "mak[ing] some statement about the nature of the art form with which he is working"; in order to accomplish the second aim and keep art from "wither[ing]," "the playwright must try to alter the forms within which his precursors have had to work" (9). So his subject becomes, at least in part, the modernist concern with the difficulty of making art. Remarking effusively upon the dramatist's ability to incorporate and yet somehow go beyond what has come before, August Staub (1997) regarded Albee's latest award-winning play as a *fin de siècle* artistic statement and achievement:

> In its structure, it is . . . so contemporary, in fact that it might well be called one of the great summation moments of 20th century theatre. *Three Tall Women* could not have been written before . . . Realism, nor before the breakthrough of the Expressionists into the inner vision of consciousness. . . . Nor could [it] have been written before Einstein's concept of relativity, nor before Quantum Mechanics, nor before the fluidity of cinema, nor even before the outrageous manipulation of time in the theatre by such postmoderns as Caryl Churchill. [It is] a completely original work . . . of the theatre of its times and a work of seeing and public art. (153)

What is thrilling new about *Three Tall Women* is the *coup de théatre* in Act Two (somewhat spoiled in the reading) when the ninety-one- (or it may be ninety-two-) year-old woman named A, whom we think we see upstage in bed dying from a stroke, suddenly enters elegantly dressed and begins talking with correspondingly costumed characters B and C. Characters who possessed separate identities, respectively, of paid companion and representative of a law firm in Act One have now become representations of A at earlier stages of her life: B at age fifty-two, C at twenty-six. Fluid shifts in pronouns in their dialogue, "you" becoming "me," "we" becoming "I," confirm that they are indeed one person at different times. As John Lahr (1994) noted in *The New Yorker* in one of the most provocative comments about the play, "What we get is a kind of Cubist stage picture, where the characters are fragments of a single self" (104). Albee is, as is well known, a great connoisseur and collector of modern art; back in 1980, for example, he even wrote the introduction to the catalogue accompanying a retrospective exhibit of Louise Nevelson's works at the Whitney Museum of American Art, claiming for her body of work something that could also be said of his own: "all her pieces, have been one enormous sculptural idea—or world, if you will," and praising her for "transform[ing the viewer] from spectator to participant," making—again, as is true of his plays—"art . . . instructive and . . . an act of aggression against the familiar and the 'easy'" (Albee 1980c, 100–1). And Cubism, what Guillaume Apollinaire (1972) defined as "the art of painting new compositions using formal elements borrowed, not from visual, but from conceptual reality" (268), might be an especially appropriate context here. For what Albee produces in *Three Tall Women* can perhaps be seen as analagous to Cubist paintings such as Marcel Duchamp's *Nude Descending a Staircase*, whose geometrical patterning suggests transformation through time and space as she, in X. J. Kennedy's felicitous phrase, "Collects her motions into shape"; or to Robert Delauney's *The City of Paris* (also 1912), with its layerings of past over present to create the impression of a single moment that, in Apollinaire's words, "evok[es] all the colors of the prism at once" (270); or to the Cubist-inspired totemic sculptures in Nevelson's *Dawn's Wedding Feast* (1959).

Nevelson had first encountered the Cubist movement—"one of the greatest awarenesses that the human mind has ever come to"—when she studied in Germany in the early 1930s, claiming that it revealed "order in a visual sense" and "gave [her] definition for the rest of [her] life about the world." As she explained,

Now, according to metaphysics, thinking is circular. The circle is the
mechanics of the mind. It is a mind that turns and turns. It doesn't solve
anything really. But when you square the circle, you are in the place of
wisdom. There you are enlightened. . . . Cubism gives you a *block* of
space for light. A *block* of space for shadow. Light and shade are in the
universe, but the cube transcends and translates nature into a structure.
(quoted in Albee 1980b, 23)

Albee, in fact, put a huge cube on stage as the setting for *Box*, and
from it emanates the play's disembodied voice. He was particularly
entranced upon entering the environment created by Nevelson's archi-
tectural assemblage of sculptures in "Mrs. N's Palace" (1964–77),
whose structure, like that of his own *Box*, he equated with a musical
composition by Bach. Moreover, and more generally in the theatre, what
is the room upon the stage if not a lighted cube (or rectangle) that an
audience must enter, an initially empty spatial world where experience is
ordered visually by the dramatist?

Act Two of *Three Tall Women* actually contains a second striking
instance of that visual (re)ordering of figures in space in the one moment
that the dramatist himself claims "came as a complete surprise . . . when
the boy came onstage. I remember stopping and saying, 'Well, isn't *that*
interesting? How did you ever figure *that out*'" (Albee 1994, 38). The
boy's unexpected appearance leads directly into a consideration of the
work as both an (auto)biographical play and a memory play. As Albee
himself makes clear in his introduction to the printed text of the play,
and as Mel Gussow further detailed in chapters 17 and 18 of his 1999
book, *Edward Albee: A Singular Journey, a Biography*, in *Three Tall
Women* the dramatist stages his adoptive mother and the conflicted
response she sparked in him. Although no longer harboring any "ill-will
toward her," he could still "not move much beyond . . . grudging
respect": "it is true I did not like her much, could not abide her preju-
dices, her loathings, her paranoias, but I did admire her pride, her sense
of self. . . . I was touched by the survivor, the figure clinging to the
wreckage only partly of her own making, refusing to go under" (n.p.).
But if he refashions his mother, he also stages himself as a young gay
male, though he wishes to be seen as "a playwright who's gay [rather
than as] a professionally gay playwright" for whom "being gay [is an]

overriding preoccupation" that would lead him to "concentrate on writing gay themes in [his] plays" (Albee 1997, 8).

Albee's first, and still his only, explicit rendering of a gay male relationship comes in *Finding the Sun* (1991), a luminous one-act play in twenty-one short scenes involving a mother and her teenage son and three other male/female couples interlinked by filial or marriage relationships. Actually, there is yet a fourth "couple," since Benjamin, now wed to Abigail, and Daniel, now married to Cordelia, were once lovers and are still intensely attracted to one another. Daniel, for instance, admits to possessing "a very roomy heart" (24). The work's title, repeated a half-dozen times in the brief opening scene as the eight characters arrive on the beach one "bright" August day, plays on the pun sun/son, as did the endings of Henrik Ibsen's *Ghosts* and Sam Shepard's *Buried Child*. The sun is consistently associated with life, and its absence behind the clouds with death; for this play, like *Sandbox* of twenty-five years earlier, is another deathwatch on the beach: the grandfatherly Henden, who as early as his thirties had arrived at an awareness of death as something that would happen to him personally but who still feels frightened, slips off in his sleep; while the distraught Abigail, who desires an apocalyptic end with the sun "burn[ing] out" and turning cold, attempts suicide by drowning. Though the sun may be life-giving, it can just as easily have a corrosive rather than creative effect, causing skin to weather and age and cancer to grow.

The "bright and beautiful" sixteen-year-old Fergus journeys from innocence to experience, being introduced to the existence of gay sexuality and apparently feeling simpatico with it as he sees the sheer "fun" and teasing banter that Daniel and Benjamin share when they are together. When Fergus's turn comes to address the audience, he speaks of the need for embracing and exploring "options" to arrive at maturity. As the sun in all its "glory" shines at play's end, the boy, however, is prominently missing from the beach. But Henden's wife Gertrude reassures Fergus's mother—who fears that he will turn out to be "less than he promises," or be "tarnish[ed]," or even "die young" (35)—that "He'll come back . . . they do" (43). What she might consider a fall from grace may, for him, be an opening out, even a coming out. So the work's conclusion presages the return of the son after a period of growth, though possibly one involving estrangement. This gentle play might be seen, then, as Albee's own wish fulfillment or fantasy of a mother's desiring the return of the son, willing him to come back and ready to welcome and accept him for what he is. The prodigal son's/playwright's homecoming, both in life and in *Three Tall Women*, where he remains symbolically silenced and mute, will, in reality, be quite other.

Watching the son in *Three Tall Women* (1995) appear after B and then A say, in sequence, "We have one; we have a boy. . . . Yes, we do. I have a son" (89) helps crystallize the possibility that what the audience sees is occurring in the mind of the dying woman, with the son being a projection that materializes onstage. The boy enters preppily dressed as he was when B threw him out of her house at twenty-three for being gay; now he again sits silently by the bed of the dying mother, as he had when, after twenty years away, he first returned to A when she was sick. An "enraged" B calls him "Filthy little . . ." and orders him to "Get out of my house!" A more tolerant A responds, "He never loved us, but he came back. Let him alone" (90). But there would always be a gulf between them, as A recalls of his earlier return: "And there are no apologies, no recriminations, no tears, no hugs; dry lips on my dry cheeks; yes that. And we never discuss it? Never go into why? Never go beyond where we are? We're strangers; we're curious about each other; we leave it at that" (91). As Albee himself says of the something unspoken between his own mother and himself: "She would never come to terms with my nature, my sexuality, wouldn't think of discussing it with me. We never reconciled" (quoted in Richards 1994, B6).

To read *Three Tall Women* in the context of other well-known memory plays—such as Tennessee Williams's *Glass Menagerie* with its neo-Brechtian legends and images projected on a screen and its narrative frame and interludes, or Arthur Miller's *Death of a Salesman* with its "mobile concurrency" of past and present and its acted-out interior monologues, some of them hallucinatory in nature—is to understand anew how words and images can replicate the way in which memory works by association; how, in the mind, all time, past and present, exists simultaneously as, in the words of the Israeli poet Yehuda Amichai, "entirely relative, relational . . . imaginatively comparative and continuous"; how memory, with the passage of time, becomes selective, or even a process of imaginative (re)creation and fictionalizing; how perception and perspective shape experience and reality. It also prompts one to investigate and probe the nature of interiority, the construction of identity, and the limits of human control and choice.

As Brustein (1994, 26) and Gussow (1999, 368) have both noted, the memory play that may well have been the most influential and instructive for the composition of *Three Tall Women* is Beckett's *Krapp's Last Tape* (1960), which, in fact, appeared in 1960 [note: the New York performance was 1960, although the play dates from 1958] together with *Zoo Story* on the double-bill off-Broadway that first introduced Albee to New York audiences. In *Women*, Albee even pays homage to Beckett through a direct verbal echo of the line in which Krapp designates as the "Happiest moment" his reveling in the memory of saying the lovely word "Spooool!" (25). Although we see Krapp on stage only as an alienated, nearsighted old man of sixty-nine who sings that "Night is drawing nighigh" (17), two earlier selves are present through his tapes from old times: Krapp on his thirty-ninth birthday, around the point of his mother's death when he felt himself to be "intellectually . . . at the (*hesitates*) . . . crest of the wave" and "less alone" (14–15); and Krapp in his late twenties, either twenty-seven or twenty-nine, when he was at the end of an affair and knew that "his youth [was] over." Now, in old age, he rejects the temptation to "Be again, be again" that would be made possible by remembering "All that old misery" (26) and recording it over again on tape. Instead, he listens to the old tape whose words he mouths soundlessly in a kind of reverie, but he hears only a record of diminishment and loss: "Perhaps my best years are gone. When there was a chance of happiness. But I wouldn't want them back" (28). If memory allows one to "be" over and over "again," then the loss of the possibility for change as well as the stoppage of memory—whether sought after or unwanted—would signal death (as it does for the poet Hirst in Harold Pinter's *No Man's Land*).

Although Brustein (1994) claimed for Albee "a great spiritual debt" to Beckett in "evok[ing] the same kind of existential poignance" (26), both the tenor of the two plays and the place at which they arrive are quite distinct. First, A reaches, as we will see, a level of understanding and acceptance that seems lost on Krapp. Second, whereas Krapp chooses to leave the self fragmented and deconstructed, A reincorporates and reassembles those fragments into a unified whole. And finally, if Krapp considers his earlier selves well lost, A welcomes her earlier selves as well found.

The affinity between the two plays might also provide a point of departure for a consideration of postmodernism in drama. In the same way that *Krapp's Last Tape*, with its texts dissolving into other texts, might be called postmodern in its focus on the fragmented self or split consciousness, so, too, does *Three Tall Women* display some of the characteristics of postmodernist theatre, with its emphasis on intersubjectivity and a multiplicity or plurality of viewpoints to demonstrate how perspective can skew perception; with its disruption of a strictly linear narrative; and with its avowed exploitation of an active rather than passive spectator's role in the construction of the text through such nonrealistic devices as characters addressing the audience. In its rejection of a grand or metanarrative or a unitary, holistic self, "postmodern drama," as Deborah Geis (1995) claimed, "reinvents subjectivity (and the ideology of the subject) as multilayered texts reflect polyvocal, nonunified subject positions" (169). If Act Two of *Three Tall Women* is considered a monologue of the dying A (re)connecting with her younger selves, then, again to borrow Geis's terms, "the dialogue is actually a manifestation of [the] splitting, doubling, and multiplication on the part of the single consciousness" (20), accomplishing through words what the Cubists achieved through images.

Yet if *Three Tall Women* (1995) is memory, it is also, for B and most particularly for C, somewhat akin to flashforward in cinema, to premonition and prophecy as they see the women they will become. And C, in her youthful naivete, does not like what she sees, protesting, "I will not become '*that*'," and even, "I DENY YOU" (69). So is to know the future something ordinarily closed off to us, to make it any less frightening and unwelcome? Later, C's lament will become a less defensive, more rueful, "How did we change?" (92) as she is forced to recognize that the achievement in reality often falls far short of one's lofty ideals.

One of Albee's persistent thematic motifs has always had to do with the tension between clinging to the safe status quo and accepting or embracing change: the opportunity, even the necessity to change; the fear of change and of venturing into the unknown; and the diminishing possibility for constructive change that comes with the passage of time. The opportunity for change in Albee often comes through a character who presents a test, challenging another to leave behind a death-in-life existence and become more fully human, as happens when Jerry accosts

Peter on a bench in Central Park (*Zoo Story*) or when the renowned black blues singer arrives dying at a Southern hospital (*Bessie Smith*), or when Harry and Edna arrive at the home of their dearest friends Agnes and Tobias (*Delicate Balance*), or when the lizards Leslie and Sarah emerge out of the sea (*Seascape*). To fail to meet the challenge, as happens, for example, in *Delicate Balance* (Pulitzer Prize, 1967), is to resist the opportunity for salvation and settle once again into the comfortable condition of stasis; to meet it, as Nancy and Charlie do in *Seascape* (Pulitzer Prize, 1975), is to open oneself up to all the possibilities for progress and growth, to, in the play's final word, "Begin."

The fear of change, and yet the absolute necessity to embrace it, is perhaps seen nowhere better in the Albee canon than at the end of *Who's Afraid of Virginia Woolf?* (1962). It is early Sunday morning, and George has just intoned the mass for the dead for his and Martha's illusory child, leaving her frightened of living without illusion. His only reassurance is that "It will be better . . . maybe" (*Who's Afraid* 1962, 240), for the unknown—along with the uncharted territory of death, contemporary man's only certainty—needs to be faced without any knowledge of what is to come. To not make the choice is to risk losing the ability to choose, as happens most emphatically in all of Albee's plays in *Delicate Balance* (1966), where, as Agnes wistfully says, "Time happens" and it becomes "too late" (169). Nor can one know at the time what the decisive choice is that will establish the pattern of one's life, that moment when character becomes fate and "one's true self"— the phrase is Mary Tyrone's from O'Neill's *Long Day's Journey into Night*—is either lost and abandoned or brought to fruition and fulfilled. For in Albee (and this seems to be a take on the interplay between freedom and determinism peculiar to the American sensibility), life is a matter of diminishing possibilities: to choose option A over option B is not just to embrace A but is also to forever cut oneself off from what might have followed if B had been chosen. So each choice effectively halves all future choices as well; "the road not taken" can never be traversed.

The characters A, B, and C, as women at three ages when varying degrees of possibility seemed open to them, have quite different recollections of the same event, such as, for instance, their initiation into physical sexuality: B claims it "was wonderful," while A counters that "It hurt." And their varying responses to the question of what is "the happiest moment" of one's life reflect the degrees of experience and levels of insight that come with age. For C, still of limited experience, the happiest moment must be yet "to come"; for B, settled into a middle age in which she hopes the worst and most bitter has been safely left behind and she can seize what's left, it must be "now." For A, however, it is the kind of detachment only possible with the impending surcease of life: "Coming to the end of it, I think, when all the waves cause the greatest woes to subside, leaving breathing space, time to concentrate on the greatest woe of all—that blessed one—the end of it" (*Three Tall Women* 1995, 109).

Addressing the audience directly, more with a kind of Beckettian relief than with resignation and with no promise of anything more to come, A reaffirms: "So. There it is. You asked after all. That's the happiest moment. When it's all done. When we stop. When we can stop" (*Three Tall Women* 1995, 110). The insistent "you" moves the audience from "passive spectator" to engaged participant, forcing us to jettison all those habits of thought and systems of belief that, to borrow O'Neill's words, we traditionally draw upon "to comfort our fear of death with," leaving us disquieted, bereft of comforting illusion. As Albee himself explains, "a good play is an act of aggression against the status quo—the psychological, philosophical, moral, or political status quo. A play is there to shake us up a little bit, to make us consider the possibility of thinking differently about things" (Albee 1997, 9). What *Three Tall Women* demands we think "differently about" is death, discussion of which frames this play: what closes with A's "we can stop" virtually opens with B's "You start . . . and then you stop." She goes on to say, much to C's horror: "I'd like to see children learn it —have a six-year-old boy say, I'm dying and I know what it means. Make 'em aware they're dying from the moment they're alive" (13–14).

Although radically different in emphasis from the medieval "coming of death" plays with their religious orientation and awareness of salvation in an afterlife, *Three Tall Women* is only the most recent of several works in the Albee canon that might be called "deathwatch" plays. The first of these is *The Sandbox* (1959), featuring another feisty dying woman, in this case one the dramatist admired unwaveringly, his maternal Grandma Cotter, to whom the play is affectionately dedicated. What begins as a highly self-conscious and surrealistic send-up of a cartoon-like Mommy and Daddy seemingly out of Ionesco attains an unexpected level of poignancy as Grandma breaks through their platitudinous inanities to experience genuine emotion. In a ritual stripped of meaning and replete with ready-made dialogue of the greeting card variety, a dominating Mommy and an emasculated Daddy indecorously dump Grandma into a sandbox on the beach and then wait for her to die. As she shovels sand over herself against the minimalist backdrop of the archetypal sea, a young actor of heightened physique in a bathing suit— waiting for Hollywood to give him a name and thus an identity, however commodified—attracts her gaze (and the audience's) by doing calisthenics that mimic the flapping of wings; for he is, after all, the Angel of Death. In this child's space, with plastic shovel and pail, Grandma as stage manager orchestrates her own end. What begins, however, as a game, as *playing at dying*, becomes the reality of death to be accepted. In the instant that Grandma becomes aware that she can no longer move, she can only resign herself to death. Such acceptance provides a measure of dignity and control, so that she can "go gently" and with tranquility, while the young man, too, becomes strangely affecting in the realization that his role has become reality.

Like *Three Tall Women*, Albee's 1971 play, *All Over*, takes place in an elegantly appointed bedroom, but in this case the one dying, a man of some celebrity in the public eye, is never seen but lies hidden behind a screen. The focus remains, then, on the family and friends who will survive and on the largely wasted lives of "quiet desperation," of "living but partly living" that they lead. Self-absorbed, "think[ing] about [them]selves," "lov[ing] to *be* loved" (*All Over* 1971, 126–27), they fall back on prescribed customs and protective rituals, on proper form as a way of denying whatever they can and of coping with what they must. In this "sad and shabby time we live in" (56)—here, a Beckettian "go[ing] on" in the face of selfishness and unhappiness—The Wife and The Mistress each recall what apparently was for them their one Edenic moment: The Wife, who sees her role as providing "stability," remembers retreating contentedly into the orderly (that is, controlled and passionless) formal garden; whereas The Mistress, who prides herself on being a "refuge" for the dissatisfied and needy husband, remembers her own sexual initiation with a beautiful young boy. Much of their discussion centers on death (which, as the droll Nurse says, "gets us where we live" [89]) and on a dying that "can [be] suffered with" as well as upon the difference between being aware of death in the abstract and as a personal experience.

For as A remarks near the end of *Three Tall Women* (1995), "There's a difference between knowing you're going to *die* and *knowing* you're going to die. The second is better; it moves away from the theoretical" (109). In a postproduction interview after the opening of *All Over*, the playwright attributed some of the critics' negativity to the work's intention of "mak[ing] us aware of our mortality. It's about us, because it's about death, and you can't fob off death." He went on to say:

> I had an awareness of death when I was 15, but when I turned 36 or 37 I became aware that *I,* Edward Albee, was going to die. The realization did not fill me with dread. I simply became aware of the fact that this is the only time around for me. I'm going to be alive for a certain time, and then I won't exist anymore. (Albee 1988, 105)

Likewise, when The Wife inquires of The Best Friend at what age he "became aware of death"—a realization he equates with becoming a philosopher—he first responds "fifteen"; when, however, she clarifies that what she really meant to ask was "when [he was] aware of it for [him]self," he replies "thirty-eight" (*All Over* 1971, 106–07).

In *All Over*, the self-obsessed characters concern themselves less with the dying man and his death than with their at times petty, at other times meaningful disagreements—which perhaps accounts for why the deathbed remains unseen, hidden behind a screen. On the other hand, in Albee's *The Lady from Dubuque* (1980), the focus rests clearly both on Jo (dying from an unspecified illness that has all the symptoms of cancer) as well as on how her dying and her death affect her husband, Sam, who must continue to suffer on alone after her suffering has ceased. As the widowed Long-Winded Lady in *Box and Quotations* (1970) plaintively laments: "But what about me! . . . I . . . am left . . . his dying is all over, all gone, but his death stays . . . he had only his dying. I have both" (88–89). In *The Lady from Dubuque* (1980), the summoners who come to assist Jo in her realization that she must welcome death are Elizabeth, a stranger who claims to be her mother, and her black traveling companion, Oscar, who, "*Arms wide, beatific,*" reminds us of the Angel of

Death from *Sandbox* (153). Although Jo initially vents her pain and bitterness on the friends who gather round her, she knows that she must not succumb to self-pity, but also that she cannot go it alone and so must depend on her husband to have the necessary greater strength to see her through her last agony until "the day will come when [she] won't need a soul. And then, of course, the day won't come" when she finally joins "The very dead; who hear nothing; who remember nothing; who are nothing" (47, 138). But as Jo "diminishes. . . . To bone? To air? To dust?" (61), Sam's own need to "hold on to the object we're losing" threatens to make him impotent in aiding her. Perhaps understandably, though surely self-indulgently, he resents any intrusion from others who might help him shoulder his burden, for he egocentrically "needs" to be the only sufferer.

If, as Elisabeth Kübler-Ross posited in *On Death and Dying* (1969), the survivor must pass through the same stages as the victim in arriving at an acceptance of the inevitable end of life, then Sam is as yet unable to make the leap to necessary detachment that requires responding no longer selfishly but selflessly; he even claims, "I'm dying." His hesitancy in recognizing Elizabeth as Jo's mother is a denial that death is the mother of us all. Since he does not "know who [he is]," he cannot "possibly know who" (*The Lady from Dubuque* 1980, 152) this woman—Elizabeth/the Lady from Dubuque/Death—is. And because Sam insists on trying to fight back and forestall Jo's embrace of death, Elizabeth and Oscar must assume the role that more rightfully should belong to him. Despite Elizabeth's assurances that there is "No time to be afraid" and that "Everything [is] done before you know it" (160–1), Sam remains skeptical. Although the living, as Elizabeth admits, can never really "know what [dying] is," Albee tries to move his audience ever closer to that knowledge in *Three Tall Women*.

Yet while attempting this, Albee refuses to in any way sentimentalize dying and death despite the concluding image of the three fragmentary beings, against the background of the dying (dead?) mother and the silent son, joining hands stage front, signifying a kind of reintegration. If Act One of *Three Tall Women* concerns the physical diminishment or shrinking (the once-tall A bemoans, "I've shrunk") that comes with age and approaching death, Act Two focuses squarely on moral shrinkage or slippage: the realization, like Krapp's, that in the process of living, accommodations, compromises, bad choices, and decisions have been made. While C tries to deny that she will one day become A, A near the point of death must accept that she was once B, and before that C, with all their/her flaws and imperfections, yet also with their/her options and missed opportunities for change. As Albee (1997) responded when he was asked to "pinpoint" the play's theme:

> I think we have to be terribly careful as we go through our lives to stay right on top of ourselves so that we don't end up as the lady does in *Three Tall Women*, filled with anger and rage and regret. She gets trapped into getting by, making do. Everybody has to make choices. Some of them turn out to be terrible compromises, of course. (8)

In order to face death with a measure of equanimity, A must refuse to excuse, and indeed must even admit regret for having done those things she should not have done, and for having left undone those things she should have done. To arrive at the more expansive wisdom implied by the play's ending, she must acknowledge the deficiencies and limitations of herself at earlier ages, including C's debilitating romanticization that things would always remain the same, as well as B's bitter renunciations and retaliations. In a passage tinged with rebelliousness against a smug and self-satisfied establishment that suppresses the possibility for growth and change, however painful these may be, B warns C:

> They *lie* to you. . . . Never tell how it is—how it's *going* to be—when a half-truth can be got in there. Never give the alternatives to the "pleasing prospects," the "what you have to look forward to." . . . Parents, teachers, all the others. You *lie* to us. You don't tell us things change—that Prince Charming has the morals of a sewer rat, that you're supposed to *live* with that . . . *and* like it, or give the appearance of liking it. (*Three Tall Women*, 93–94)

But though others may fail us by setting up and fostering false expectations that will never be fulfilled, Albee distributes the blame, placing some of it squarely on the person herself.

In his treatise *Three Uses of the Knife: On the Nature and Purpose of Drama*, David Mamet (1998) proposed that "Most great drama is about betrayal of one sort or another" (67). And this is certainly true of *Three Tall Women*, where A must live with and die with regret over having betrayed others. Not only is there B's betrayal of husband and son by committing adultery with the groom, but there is also B's rejection of the gay son for being sexually Other. This is played off against yet another instance of sexual desire perceived as being "different" or "abnormal," with the revulsion followed by a leaving—a rupture in a relationship what will never be repaired. When A remembers her husband coming to her with a beautiful diamond bracelet hanging from his erect penis, she is unable to respond by fellating him and instead rejects him:

> No! I can't *do* that! You *know* I can't *do* that! And I couldn't, I could never do that, and I said, No! I can't do that! . . . and the bracelet slid off, and it fell into my lap. I was naked; deep into my lap. Keep it, he said, and he turned and he walked out of my dressing room. (*Three Tall Women* 1995, 56)

Unlike Hannah in Tennessee Williams's *The Night of the Iguana*, who can consider it a "love act" and not something "dirty" to respond nonjudgmentally to the request of the underwear fetishist for a piece of her clothing because she has never seen such loneliness before, A is unable to act from such a magnanimous ethic as "Nothing human disgusts me unless it's unkind, violent" (Williams 1976, 117). A's memory is followed by a "*Long silence; finally she weeps, slowly, conclusively.*" There will be no such cleansing tears over the parallel rejection of the son. And so, while the mother may be exorcised in *Three Tall Women*, the son is "found" to exist only in a continuing silence. Albee's decision to keep the boy literally silent, as well as his writing of the play itself, might both be seen, finally, as acts of resistance from a dramatist in whom a compassionate moralism has always existed beneath an elegant surface and alongside a deeply subversive impulse.

Works Cited

Albee, Edward. 1962. *Who's Afraid of Virginia Woolf?* New York: Atheneum.

———. 1967. *A Delicate Balance.* New York: Pocket Books.

———. 1970. *Box and Quotations from Chairman Mao Tse-Tung.* New York: Pocket Books.

———. 1971. *All Over.* New York: Pocket Books.

———. 1973. *The Sandbox and The Death of Bessie Smith.* New York: Signet.

———. 1975. *Seascape.* New York: Atheneum.

———. 1980a. *The Lady from Dubuque.* New York: Atheneum.

———. 1980b. Louise Nevelson: The Sum and the Parts. Intro. to *Louise Nevelson: atmosphere and environments.* New York: Potter, pp. 12–30.

———. 1980c. The World is Beginning to Resemble Her Art. *Art News,* 79.5 (May), 99–101.

———. 1988. Edward Albee Fights Back. In *Conversations with Edward Albee,* ed. Philip C. Kolin. Jackson: University Press of Mississippi, pp. 101–5.

———. 1991. Finding the Sun. *Antaeus* 66 (Spring): 15–43.

———. 1994. Yes is Better than No. *American Theatre,* September, 38.

———. 1995. *Three Tall Women.* New York: Plume Penguin.

———. 1997. Aggressing Against the Status Quo. *Harvard Gay and Lesbian Review,* 4.1, 8–9.

Apollinaire, Guillaume. 1972. Modern Painting. In *Apollinaire on Art: Essays and Reviews, 1902–1918,* trans. Susan Suleiman. New York: Viking, pp. 267–71.

Beckett, Samuel. 1960. *Krapp's Last Tape and Other Dramatic Pieces.* New York: Grove.

Brustein, Robert. 1994. The Rehabilitation of Edward Albee. *The New Republic,* 4 (April), 26–28.

Geis, Deborah. 1995. *Postmodern Theatric[k]s: Monologue in Contemporary American Drama.* Ann Arbor: University of Michigan Press.

Gussow, Mel. 1999. *Edward Albee: A Singular Journey, a Biography.* New York: Simon & Schuster.

Jefferson, Margo. 2000. Critics Judge, and Are Judged, across the Centuries. *The New York Times,* 11 August, B2.

Lahr, John. 1994. Sons and Mothers. *The New Yorker,* 16 May, 102–5.

Kübler-Ross, Elizabeth. 1969. *On Death and Dying.* New York: Macmillam.

Mamet, David. 1998. *Three Uses of the Knife: On the Nature and Purpose of Drama.* New York: Columbia University Press, 1998.

Richards, David. 1994. Critical Winds Shift for Albee, a Master of the Steady Course. *The New York Times,* 13 April, B1, B6.

Simon, John. 1994. Trifurcating Mom. *New York,* 28 February, 118.

Staub, August W. 1997. Public and Private Thought: The Enthymeme of Death in Edward Albee's *Three Tall Women. Journal of Dramatic Theory and Criticism* 12.1 (Fall): 149–57.

Williams, Tennessee. 1976. *The Night of the Iguana.* In *Three by Tennessee.* New York: Signet.

INTERVIEW WITH EDWARD ALBEE

Interview conducted by Joan Herrington
in January 2001

Joan Herrington: What inspired you to write your first play?

Edward Albee: When I was quite young, my family went into New York City to see lots of musicals and things like that —when I was five and six years old. And even though I wrote my first play, a three-act sex farce, nine minutes long the whole thing, when I was twelve or thirteen, I really worked on novels, poems, and short stories all through my teens and early twenties. I made a couple of half-assed attempts at plays. And nothing was working. All my prose and poetry I thought was pretty terrible and one day I decided to write another play and it turned out to be *The Zoo Story,* which was so different and so much better, even though I say it myself, than anything I'd written before and was also a lot better than the stuff I was seeing, that something miraculous happened in my head and it was now time for me to become a playwright.

I write plays because I'm a playwright. I think like a playwright, I walk like a playwright, I smell like a playwright, and I write like a playwright.

JH: Have you returned since to writing in any other form?

EA: No. I stuck with what I know how to do reasonably well. Of course, I was seeing a lot of plays when I moved to Greenwich Village in the middle 1940s and in the 1950s, Beckett, Genet, Ionesco and all of those people. I was being engulfed by the avant garde and I was very interested in that.

JH: What do you consider to be the particular rewards of writing plays as opposed to writing in other forms?

EA: Simply that I do it better.

JH: Do you believe that writing a play is inherently more difficult than writing in other forms?

EA: No, I've never found writing a play difficult. I've always found it a joyous experience. Sometimes it takes a while to get the play out of my head and onto the page but I've never been troubled by it, never anguished. It's what I do. It's my job. And I seem to do it fairly naturally.

JH: What is the most challenging part of the process for you?

EA: The most challenging part is knowing when it's time to start writing it down—when it is time to move it from what is going on in the mind—when it's time to commit it to the page. Waiting long enough so that that can happen naturally.

JH: Is there a certain period of time that your plays usually sit in your head?

EA: Here's the trick. I don't know how long I've been thinking about a play until I'm aware that I'm thinking about it. I could have been thinking about a play for two years before my mind told me that I was thinking about it. Because there is the unconscious, you see. And by the time I'm aware of the fact that I'm thinking about it, oh it could have been anywhere from two or three weeks to two or three years until is it ready to be written down. I always have more than one play in some kind of construction in my head.

JH: Does that ever become confusing?

EA: Not at all. I can go from one to the other. It's like going from one room to another. I can do that without too much confusion.

JH: How long does it take you to get a play out of your head and onto the page?

EA: I don't know. It varies. I don't think once I've started to put a play on paper it's ever taken any longer than six months to get it finished.

JH: What is the most rewarding part of actually writing it?

EA: The experience of watching and hearing the play as I write it.

JH: How much do your plays change from the time you write them to the time they first appear on the stage?

EA: Not very much. I don't do many revisions.

JH: Do you do revisions once you've seen a play up on the stage?

EA: I see it when I am writing it. I see it and hear it as a performed play as I am writing it. But when I watch the actors do it if I think, "Oh this scene is a little too long," or "I forgot to do something there," I'll tinker a little bit, but no major tinkering.

JH: Has your approach to playwriting changed over the years?

EA: No, I think it's the same kind of procedure.

JH: Has your relationship with the theater-at-large changed over the course of your playwriting career?

EA: Oh, sure. I was the fair-haired boy for a number of years and then condemned for a number of years, and then back in fashion. But that's all superficial stuff. One musn't pay any attention to it. I think I know my craft a little bit better now.

JH: Do you think that the relationship of the new playwright to the American theater has changed over the course of your career?

EA: Unfortunately it has. They're trying to turn playwrights into the same kind of employees that they've turned movie script writers into— at the beck and call of the director and actors and the producer to alter things if they think that will be more commercial. That's one of the awful things that's happening to playwrights. Even though we have the protection of the Dramatists Guild in our contract, playwrights are still being urged and pushed to compromise, to simplify, to overclarify, to make plays pleasant rather than unpleasant, to use Shaw's phrase.

JH: Do you think this is a product of the interest in "play development" which has been generated in the American theater over the past 25 years?

EA: It's not play development, it's play destruction. It's much more play compromise as I see it. There are some playwrights who don't know how to write a play until other people tell them. But mostly, these "play developers" are there not to clarify the play but to make it safer. And that's very troubling.

JH: Do you think there are sufficient opportunities for new playwrights to have their work done in the theater?

EA: It depends on what you mean by theater. There are so many small theater groups that a playwright can pretty generally, if a play is any good or if it's bad enough, get it produced somewhere fairly quickly. But plays open and they close before I get a chance to see them in these small theaters. They get interesting reviews but if I'm away for two weeks, when I come back, the play's gone. They can't develop an audience. But some of the regional theaters and some of the off-off-off-Broadway theaters around the country and even in New York are doing a responsible job. Broadway's a wasteland. Let's not even talk about it.

JH: Do you think that there is any way to remedy the circumstance wherein plays are destroyed by their production in the American theater?

EA: Create an audience that wants to see plays that are not destroyed by commerce.

JH: Is that a chicken and egg problem, then?

EA: Yes, exactly.

JH: So, how do you develop that audience?

EA: You have to have critics who urge people to see plays that matter. You have to have brave producers who want to do the play that the playwright wrote. You have to have actors who are more interested in the work rather than themselves. You need a whole bunch of changes that I'm not holding my breath about.

JH: Do you think the next generation of playwrights will survive to see that?

EA: Oh, playwrights will always survive. We're a tough breed. Some are going to compromise. Some are going to get killed by the theater, but generally speaking, we go right on. Take a wonderful playwright like Jack Gelber, for example. He and I began around the same time, he with *The Connection.* He's been writing plays for forty years and I read them and I see them occasionally, and they're first-rate plays. But most people don't know who Jack Gelber is anymore, which is a great shame. But he goes right on because he is a tough and courageous and honest playwright.

JH: Do you think the theater can compete for young writers against the media industries?

EA: Well, it depends on the reason the writer went into the racket in the first place. If you're there to make a bunch of money, then go write movies or television. If you're there because you've got stuff that's important that you want to say, and you're tough enough to insist, "No, you do it my way," then stick in the theater. Otherwise, leave it quickly.

JH: Do you think that given play "development/destruction" and the playwright's relationship to the audience, that the rewards of writing for a public forum still exist for the playwright?

EA: If people put on the play that the playwright wrote, without trying to compromise it for commercial purposes, yes, then there is a rewarding forum. But unfortunately, people aren't getting, as often as they used to, to see the play that the playwright wrote. "Oh come on, shift and change it, they'll like it better." And that creates a lazy audience.

JH: Is that pressure still applied when your plays are in production?

EA: No. Well, there are pressures but I don't give in to them. Here's an interesting example. *Three Tall Women* opened at the Vineyard Theater and got all of those extraordinary reviews and everything. My producer Liz McCann wanted to move it to another theater and she asked two or three of the Broadway managements and they were interested. "The play's too dark," they said. So we found a wonderful off-Broadway theater where it ran for two and a half years. It was probably happier, by the way, when it got to its 500-seat off-Broadway theater than it would have been on Broadway.

We don't have proper size theaters in New York. We should have a lot of 500-seat theaters. Apparently they are going to be building three or four of them on West 42nd Street, which will be nice. Right now to move to a bigger theater you have to have a particular kind of audience and a particular kind of commercial review. It can't be one of these thoughtful reviews that says, "This is an extraordinary, interesting, and difficult play," because people stay away. You've got to get a "money review" to be able to move. And a money review is not necessarily an intelligent one, it's merely an enthusiastic one.

JH: So you aren't very optimistic about there being a change which will make the theater most hospitable to playwrights?

EA: I don't think it's going to change unless we have an economic collapse, which we might possibly have under the Bush administration. Then maybe things would get better. Right now audiences are pleased with themselves and don't want the boat rocked too much. And that creates problems for serious playwrights, because our job is to rock the boat.

HORTON FOOTE: MYSTIC OF THE AMERICAN THEATRE

Crystal Brian

Almost seventy years ago Horton Foote began an artistic odyssey that has brought him in contact with some of the most important artistic visionaries of the modern era. Always seeking what he has called his "comforts," the playwright instinctively sought to create a style that could accurately convey his understanding of human existence. His journey led him to artists diverse in mission and method yet sharing a common belief in the spiritual component of great art and its ability to transcend human limitation. After training in New York with the artists of Stanislavski's Moscow Art Theater, Foote became involved with the great modern dance pioneers of the 1930s and 1940s. He studied Pound, Eliot, Larkin, Bishop, Moore, and other poets of the modernist movement, seeking new ways to capture the universal. Finally, he found an artistic soulmate in the iconoclastic American genuis, Charles Ives, who called for "new ears" with which to apprehend the human experience. Ultimately, Foote was able to combine all of these influences in forging a style uniquely capable of embodying the ineffable: a transcendental style.

Quietly yet persistently, through years of experimentation and reflection, Texas playwright Horton Foote has manipulated contemporary audience expectations in an attempt to evoke the transcendent. In a twentieth-century context in which the theatre has been most often preoccupied with social and political themes, such an aesthetic goal is unusual. With the great exception of Chekhov, no European or American playwright has been credited with manipulating theatrical means to these ends. But Foote has created in his dramatic works clear evidence of the effectiveness of transcendental style in the theatre. His choice of material and stylistic technique combine, on the deepest level, to mold reality in such a way that audiences will look with new eyes at the world around them. The unique nature and power of Foote's writing is not found in its subject matter, but in its style—a style that transcends the limitations of seemingly ordinary people and events.

Foote (1993) insists that much of his creative process is "unconscious," and the evolution of his unique style was a matter of "instinctual seeking out of the forms which would best allow me to tell my stories." The elements of Foote's distinctive style that enable him to use the most specific particularities of time, place, and character in achieving the archetypal can best be described as the gift of communicating that for which there are no words. Foote is a playwright whose medium is not primarily text, but a unique integration of words, movement, and music. Thus, it has been to poets, dancers, and composers that the Texas playwright has consistently turned for inspiration. Again and again, the playwright has, in a seemingly haphazard manner, found himself in the midst of artistic pioneers who share his view of art as spiritually potent. Foote describes his creative process as "meditation," the process through which he discovers the extraordinary within the ordinary and then shares his revelation with readers and audiences who are otherwise too enmeshed in the chaos of material reality to be able to see the patterns he discerns or hear the music he hears.

Acknowledging that the seeming simplicity of Foote's work has caused him to be overlooked by many contemporary critics, Reynolds Price (1987) has written:

> Where is there a genuinely illuminating discussion of Blake's "Tyger," Gluck's "Dance of the Blessed Spirits," or Joan Baez's traversals of the Child ballads—one that helps us understand how and, above all, why such complex but supremely satisfactory ends are achieved in such small and evidently transparent vehicles? As readers' minds are most engaged, in narrative fiction, by wicked or at least devious characters, so the mechanistic methods of modern critics require complexity of means before their intricate gears can begin to grind. (ix–x)

Paul Schrader (1972) went so far as to call the critical method futile when applied to transcendental art:

Like transcendental art, the criticism of transcendental art is a self-destructive process. It continually deals in contradictions, verbalizations of the ineffable. The concept of transcendental expression in religion or in art necessarily implies a contradiction. Transcendental expression in religion and art attempts to bring man as close to the ineffable, invisible and unknowable as words, images and ideas can take him. Like the artist, the critic knows that his task is futile, and that his most eloquent statements can only lead to silence. The critical inquiry, Roger Fry stated, ends at the gulf of mysticism. (8)

In a career spanning more than sixty years, Horton Foote has won a Pulitzer Prize, two Academy Awards, and multiple lifetime achievement awards. He was one of the best-known writers of television's "Golden Age" and his plays have appeared in major Broadway and regional theatres, as well as in small showcase spaces in New York and Los Angeles. He has been called a southern regionalist, a kitchen-sink realist, and a gentler (or, to some tastes, blander) version of Tennessee Williams. Indeed, his settings (Gulf Coast Texas) and themes (variously characterized as the search for roots in an increasingly rootless society, the dignity of the human spirit, or the healing power of love and faith) have consistently drawn the focus of critics. But, too often critics—and viewers—have based their perceptions of Horton Foote's work on surface trappings such as period and regional settings or family-related material, rather than penetrating to the radical thematic and stylistic issues with which the playwright was often concerned. The most unusual aspect of this prolific writer's work is not his use of regional material nor his exploration of the human condition—for what twentieth century American playwright has not dealt with similar preoccupations, but his structure. Foote is a stylist, and one so subtle, so seemingly artless, that his most unique achievement has been the one most overlooked in the critical arena.

Superficial appraisals of Foote's plays have sometimes contributed to the skewed image of the playwright being firmly entrenched in conservatism and the genre of realism. A lack of immediately apparent and easy-to-label political or topical themes have led some readers and viewers to assume that Foote's work is "nostalgic," "heart-warming," and a comfortable reaffirmation of conventional values. Yet, the playwright has, throughout his career, shown great passion and commitment in advocating for change in art and society on the most profound levels. As long as critics continue to treat Foote as a regional realist, or judge him by the standards of an aesthetic that the playwright long ago rejected, his work will continue to be misunderstood.

In his introduction to Volume II of the collected plays of Horton Foote, Robert Ellerman (1996) wrote of the spiritual aesthetic in Foote's work:

> Horton Foote is an artist of spiritual transcendence. His characters are the conflicts of the soul struggling for inner peace. At the center of his plays is loneliness, loss, grief, courage and love: the existential state of our common humanity. The elemental through-action of Horton Foote's world is Beckett's "I can't go on . . . I will go on." The conflicts between characters in a Foote play are rarely motivated by the egotism we label "success" and "failure." His creations are on a path of action which inspires all of the world's great religions. These men and women are seeking the experience we call God. To be englightened, they are willing to face the divine nothingness of reality and the 'infinite within' of the human spirit. . . . The theatre of the soul's imagination is the place to experience Horton Foote's transcendental art. To borrow from Eva LeGallienne's tribute to Eleonora Duse, Horton Foote is our "mystic in the theatre." (vi)

Horton Foote's first "calling" as an artist was to become an actor. But even at the age of sixteen, Foote was driven by an instinctive need to escape the conventional limitations of the American theatre of the time. For two years he studied at the Pasadena Playhouse in Southern California, but was disenchanted with the old-fashioned, superficial approach to the craft taught at the school. Foote was a novice in every respect, yet a deep, perhaps unconscious, yearning to discover a more profound approach to his craft took him to New York City. What he discovered there would indelibly influence the young artist, first in his then-chosen path as an actor, but eventually in what would become his true passion, playwriting.

Arriving in Manhattan in the mid-1930s, Foote became a student at Daykarhanova's School for the Stage. The faculty for the School for the Stage, Tamara Daykarhanova, Vera Soloviova, and Andrius Jilinsky, had been involved with some of the great innovators, theorists, and artists of late nineteenth- and early twentieth-century theatre. These students of Konstantin Stanislavski's Moscow Art Theater had participated in the experimental studies from which Stanislavski developed his acting "system" and had worked with the innovative methods of Michael Chekhov. From these teachers, Foote would absorb a profound conviction that acting without a sense of truth at its center was not art at all and that the same assessment should be applied to the work of the theatre in all of its manifestations.

The importance that Stanislavski and his pupils allocated to the human soul as the primary impetus and guide for artistic creation must have deeply influenced the young actor and soon-to-be playwright. For these first-generation students of the great Russian director, work was holy and not to be undertaken without a full understanding of the enormous spiritual commitment required from those who chose to spend their lives as artists of the theatre. Foote could not have devoted himself to a goal more antithetical to his original boyish dream of becoming a movie star, nor could he have found himself in an atmosphere further removed from the heady and transient unrealities of Hollywood.

> It was a sobering time. Our teachers said that the American Theater was moribund and decadent and that most of the acting and writing was old-fashioned and cliché-ridden. That the precepts taught by Stanislavski practiced at the Art Theater were the ideal and the basis for the theater of the future. We students were deeply impressed and thought, at last, we had found the way to true theatrical art. That when we learned this way of working, our search would be over, and a new world would miraculously be established. (Foote 1989, 14)

Equally influential for Foote was the way in which one of his Russian teachers instilled in the future playwright a musical understanding of dramatic structure so deep that it was forever to permeate his work. Musical perceptions and structure underlay all of Jilinsky's classroom work; many of his acting exercises "had to do with thinking of work in the theater as having a musical construction" (Wolf 1991). Believing that all plays were structured musically, and that, until the actor could discern and respond to a playwright's particular music, he would not be able to capture the playwright's vision, Jilinsky hoped to train actors in their ability to carry a musical framework subjectively into physical action.

Foote was enormously impressionable during these early days of his training, and Jilinsky's use of music as a way of understanding a dramatic script must have made a deep—albeit apparently unconscious—impression on him. Jilinsky's passionate commitment as an artist, his conviction that there could be no calling higher than that of a life in the theatre and the inspired nature of his teaching also indelibly marked the young Foote.

Jilinsky (1990) eloquently described his own theatre aesthetic for the "living" theater.

> I am afraid only of the theater which deals with shallowness, in small things, in the superficial manifestations of everyday life—the theater which is preoccupied with thoughts and feelings that are common, political or petit-bourgeois. And I am afraid of the so-called "radical" theater. Just as art without a "why" is nothing, so the theater without a problem is nothing; but while there may be radical words and sometimes radical thoughts on the stage, the human heart cannot be described as either conservative or radical—it is first and foremost human, and always ready to react to truth and beauty, wherever they exist. Life is the sufferings of human beings, and art is about them. (6–7)
>
> If you want to create truth on the stage, you must be acquainted with your own truth, and the truth of your life. It is something that belongs not only to the tradition of acting, but to the moral content of the theater. Here lies the secret of the living theater, which gives an inexhaustible source of creative power and makes the theater a constructive force in life. (7–10)

The training Foote received from the artists of Stanislavski's First Studio had a powerful and long-lasting impact on Foote's development as a writer. When asked many years later what influence had first made him aware of the unlimited possibilities of his chosen artistic medium, the playwright would unhesitatingly reply, "The Russians" (Foote 1992).

As a member of the American Actors' Company, Foote began to write plays in the late 1930s. Through his work with the company as an actor, Foote had become quite familiar with the work of such playwrights as Paul Green, E. P. Conkle, and Lynn Riggs. The "folk plays" of these writers seemed appropriate material for the new company, allowing for the type of regional exploration that was one of the stated goals of the ensemble. Foote's own early plays—including *Wharton Dance, Texas Town, and Out of My House*—were very much in this vein; however, the playwright soon grew dissatisfied.

Early on—I think because I was exposed to so many plays that were called at that time, with great pride, folk plays, often merely sentimental reworkings of Synge or Yeats, striving for quaintness, eager to show in a most literal way how different they are in speech and dress from other parts of our country and the world—I became impatient with this kind of writing, as I felt it was very limited, and I had no desire to be known as a regional or a folk playwright. So I turned away from my earlier play forms; and through my friendships with dancers, choreographers and musicians, I attempted to find a more abstract style. (Foote, Fairleigh-Dickinson Lecture, 1987)

The ideals of the former artists of the Moscow Art Theater were reflected in Foote's frustration with a genre that seemed to preclude rather than foster a universally significant art.

Foote's work with the American Actors' Company brought him in contact with a group of dancers and choreographers that included Jerome Robbins, Agnes DeMille, Katherine Litz, and Sybyl Shearer—artists who would have a profound impact upon his development. The playwright attended rehearsals and watched the dancers work, his interest excited by a form and process new and foreign to him. The American Actors Company shared a theatre with Doris Humphrey and Charles Weidman, and Foote was fascinated by the work of these pioneering dancers and choreographers. In the company of such American artistic innovators, Foote had found a group as idealistic and committed to their craft as were his Russian teachers. He was as drawn to what he perceived as their "seriousness of purpose" as he was drawn to the passion and poetic starkness of their aesthetic.

Many of the dancers used poetic material as bases for their dance, having the poems narrated as a background accompaniment for the performance. This work, with its marriage of text, music, and dance, fired Foote's creative imagination; when Valerie Bettis asked him to collaborate on a solo concert, he eagerly agreed.

The dancer and the playwright had long talks about the relationships between dance, music, and words. Bettis was interested in nonrealistic forms that would combine elements of dance, theatre, and music in a bold and innovative new way. Although their collaboration, *Daisy Lee*, employed familiar material and themes, Lois Balcom's (1944) review of the dance play revealed that Foote was beginning to experiment with structure and style and noted Foote's unconventional use of offstage "voices" as a way of structuring character and plot. Balcom characterized Foote's work as "original to the point of deserving the term 'daring'" (15, 20).

Other avant-garde artists of the time also inspired Foote. Evenings spent with Merce Cunningham, John Cage, Martha Graham, Louis Horst, Martha's composer and advisor, Tamiris, Hanya Holm, Sibyl Shearer, and Harry Holtzman (Mondrian's disciple and controller of his estate) focused on new concepts of art and approaches to radical changes in the art of the time. Such arguments and discussions, sometimes continuing until three or four in the morning, must have been eye-opening for a playwright whose first plays had been rather solidly in the realistic mode.

In the winter of 1944, Foote began writing for *Dance Observer*, the most important dance magazine of the period. His articles reveal the way in which the playwright's approach to his craft—and his overall view of the theater he wished to create—was being transformed by his association with modern dancers:

> Under the influx of war money, the Theater is showing signs of great material prosperity, but for the serious worker in the Theater the problems are still very much the same. The managers and the producers are on the lookout for the tried, the true and the obvious. They are suspicious of anything new, experimental, or really bold and serious in content. This is not a new condition and there is no point in decrying it. The writers who are out to search for new meanings of content and expression have always had to fight ingeniously and hard for the chance to exhibit their findings.
>
> The Theater can't compete realistically, neither with the enormously high budgets, nor the dull naturalism of the screen—nor can we promise always the enormous returns and the safety of subject matter Broadway demands of its investments. The writer, of a certain type, who is constantly frozen out of these mediums, has to find a new means of expression. It seems to me the dance is one way. (Foote 1944, 7)

Foote's passionate involvment with the avant-garde theater of his day at this early stage in his artistic development predicts the enduring pattern of the playwright's career, for this unconventional writer would be forced to seek out "new means of expression," as he was repeatedly "frozen out" of the commercial mainstream. Inspired by the potential for artistic exploration which had so strongly attracted him to the world of dance, he was prescient in describing the path of his own aesthetic growth over the next thirty years:

> Each individual writer will come up against his own set of problems and will find solutions that only working at a thing can bring. I am sure that if he really tackles the problems seriously, he will find great rewards. . . . He will find ways of vaulting over the four walls the Theater has so arbitrarily put up, and he will be able to escape with complete freedom the restrictions of our realistic and naturalistic Theater. (Foote 1944, 7)

Foote was drawn to the modern dance in part because of its poetic potential—its ability to convey multiple levels of significance through image and composition and to imbue ordinary situations and characters with the evocative and complex significations of the poetic. Much of Foote's development in the melding of the specific with the universal can be attributed to his work with the founder of modern dance, Martha Graham.

In 1944, Foote was commissioned by the Neighborhood Playhouse to write a one-act play for the graduating students. The piece was to combine dance, acting, and music—the different disciplines taught at the school. Foote was to direct and Martha Graham, head of the school's dance department, would choreograph. Foote's collaboration with Graham took place approximately three years after the American Actors Company production of his first full-length play, *Texas Town,* and it affected him profoundly. "It was one of the great learning experiences of my life. She took my play and my direction, and through her great imaginative powers transformed it into something quite undreamed of by me" (Foote, Spalding Lecture, 1987). In later years, when asked what he had learned from his tremendously influential collaboration with Martha Graham, Foote (1995) replied, "Martha taught me what can be said without words." This resonated deeply with Foote, who shared Graham's belief in the powerful spiritual component of art. Graham's experiments in dance provided Foote with a vision of what theatre could be when lifted from the realm of the material. As a playwright committed to an aesthetic that stresses the common spirituality of all mankind and downplays the differences between individuals, Horton Foote was also drawn to Graham's fascination with Jung and his theories of the "collective unconscious." Graham and other modern dancers of the period were experimenting with forms that would resonate on the deepest levels of emotion and human response.

It was the universality of the dance form that drew Foote to incorporate movement with spoken word. Once again he was working toward a distinctive style for conveying his vision. These experiments with modern dancers would have a strong influence on the plays Foote was to write in the 1970s and after. The culmination of stylistic innovation in the melding of music, movement, and text is most strikingly apparent in such plays as *Courtship, Convicts, The Widow Claire, Lily Dale, Valentine's Day,* and *1918* of *The Orphans' Home* cycle, as well as individual plays such as *Night Seasons, Laura Dennis,* and *Talking Pictures.*

In the fall of 1945, having absorbed the influences of his Russian mentors, of the regional experiments of the American Actors' Company, and of the burgeoning modern dance movement, Foote sought the freedom to experiment and develop his vision as an artist. With his new wife, the playwright made the first of a series of retreats from New York and Hollywood, the citadels of commercial drama. Foote's years in Washington, D.C. (1945–1949) were an intense period of growth for the writer. Foote returned to New York in 1949 and saw productions of his plays on Broadway. He became a successful writer in the then-new genre of live television. And he began a career as a screen writer which would eventually win him two Academy Awards. But Foote was driven to continue his search for the new forms necessary to embody his vision.

In the late 1950s, the playwright moved his growing family away from New York City, to the suburb of Nyack, New York. He hoped to find more time for artistic experimentation, but Nyack did not provide the isolation he instinctively knew he needed as an artist. In 1967 he moved his family to New Boston, New Hampshire. It was a move that further isolated him from the commercial mainstream, but Foote found solace in family and in a solitude rich in artistic possibility.

> My wife and I found a wonderful old house in New Hampshire, and we decided to live there and raise our family. I lived in the woods on a dirt road, and I had plenty of time to write. If my phone rang, it was to offer me a book to adapt for the screen, and I undertook three (never produced) to put bread on the table, as they say.

In the silence of those woods, I began work on my nine-play cycle, *The Orphans' Home*, and wrote three full-length plays, *Pilgrims, The Night Seasons* and *In a Coffin in Egypt*. In due time, they were all sent out by my agent to Broadway and off-Broadway theaters and rejected. (Foote McDermott Lecture, 1986)

In the New Hampshire woods, far from the theatrical and film worlds of New York and Los Angeles and despite his pessimism, Foote was beginning another intense period of artistic experimentation that would ultimately produce the most distinctive and unique works of his career. Here Foote found the freedom to continue an artistic odyssey that would take him even further afield from the contemporary theatre. The material and themes that drew him most strongly seemed clear; he had explored them repeatedly in his plays of the 1940s and 1950s and in his numerous teleplays such as *The Travelling Lady, The Trip To Bountiful, The Old Man, The Tears Of My Sister, Flight, The Night of the Storm, The Midnight Caller,* and *A Member of the Family*. What remained elusive was the method, the style, which would most truly communicate his perceptions. Live television had provided some opportunity for structural experimentation and had allowed the playwright to begin to fuse the feeling for mythic, universal theme to which he had been drawn during his involvement with modern dance and in his experimental work in Washington with the realism and specificity of time and place often associated with regionalism. Experimentations with the techniques available in live television, such as the subjective camera angle, and his refusal to follow conventional dramatic structure in his teleplays had allowed him to imbue what were primarily realistic, regional settings and characters with the heightened pathos and power of poetry. Yet the blend of universal truth without self-consciousness or pretension, and the specificity of time and place without sentimentality, was harder to create in the theatrical medium. In film, or even television, the camera offered many possibilities for creating the sense of mystery and poetic resonance that Foote sought. In theatre, the goal was more difficult to achieve without resorting to obviously heightened language or situation. And Foote sought to avoid any trace of artificiality; one of his primary goals was to disguise as completely as possible the shaping hand of the playwright and to create works which seemed to possess a reality independent of their creator. As he continued to balance work on adaptations and occasional trips to the west coast with the growing demands of rearing four children, Foote intensified a private search for inspiration and clarification of his talent. At a time when all outward signs seemed to indicate he was at a crossroads and needed to look away from the theatre as a livelihood, the playwright began what was the most inward-focused and committed quest of his career for a way in which to forge a style consistent with his vision. In his third floor study, locked away from the distractions of daily life, he began a rigorous study of the poets whose work he loved most: the modernists.

Foote had long been interested in poetry, even attempting to write poems of his own during the period when he and his family lived in New York City. Years before, Mary Hunter had suggested he look to poetry as a way of elevating his work from the realm of the superrealistic and lending it a more evocative, universal quality. Recognizing that one of the things he loved about the work of certain poets was their ability to take extremely personal, seemingly ordinary material and infuse it with profundity, Foote began to explore in greater depth the ways in which these artists achieved their impact.

Three features generally accepted as characteristic of modernism are important characteristics of Horton Foote's singular dramatic style: fragmentation, or the sense that individual experience is composed of loosely or even unconnected multiple perspectives; an emphasis on discontinuity with the past combined with the appropriation of historic and cultural materials within nontraditional contexts; and experimentation with new conventions of poetic and prose structure in an effort to revitalize moribund forms and forge a more vital audience–artist relationship.

Foote's use of fragmentation in his plays springs from an organic base. In lectures and interviews, Foote has often alluded to the way in which the stories he heard as a child eventually influenced him as a playwright. He has used the characters and particulars of these stories in myriad ways in his later works, and the way in which the stories would be altered and transformed by a particular teller—or the time and place in which it was related—made a lasting impression on the young Foote. One of the most characteristic elements of Foote's writing, his practice of examining material from multiple viewpoints, may be traced back to his early contact with Southern storytellers.

Southerners have a great oral tradition, and they love to tell you details. They go on for hours about what this one said and that one said and what kind of a day it was and what they were wearing. That really is where I got it, and I got it from four or five different points of view. (Foote, AFI Symposium Lecture 1986)

They wandered in and out of the store, remembering the past, telling the news of the day. These stories of the past were fascinating to me. The men often told essentially the same story, but each teller, I soon observed, had his own embellishments. It was like a theme with variations in music. (Foote, Spalding Lecture, 1987)

The multiplicity of viewpoint in Foote's work creates a strong sense of fragmentation and of the unverifiable ambiguity of reality—the futility of attempting to know anything with certainty. Each varying point of view reinforces the chaotic, constantly fluctuating nature of human experience. Yet Foote—true to the Modernist aesthetic—will not accept the finality of futility or despair. Rather, he reaches beyond the despair to a hope of personal and social communion, although the salvation he offers is never directly suggested or even hinted at. This almost subliminal offertory, too, is in the modernist tradition.

Foote's work is also true to the discontinuity of modernism. His material is drawn from the past—from his family's history and the history of the area in which he was reared. Yet Foote is no apologist for the past or purveyor of nostalgia, although he has been labelled so by some critics. When utilizing an historic event such as the flu epidemic of 1918 or Armistice Day at the end of World War I, Foote always treats the material with an ironic twist, never failing to layer period values and perceptions with contemporary ones. Just as Eliot and Pound appropriated the great Western myths to provide structure for their view of the chaos of contemporary civilization, Foote has utilized American myth and American history for his own aesthetic/philosophical agenda.

Although the philosophical conclusions to which Foote's plays may guide their audience are not those of many of the modernist poets, the techniques those writers developed in an attempt to define a chaotic world seemingly spun free of its moorings had great influence in the evolution of Foote's style. The courage of Eliot in daring to ignore reader expectations while searching for adequate means to express his own vision resonates deeply in Foote's adherence to what he calls "truth." Foote's determination to avoid traditional structure and surefire audience appeal was the beginning of his attempts to forge a style that would ultimately enable him to create dramatic works with the feeling of independent reality, of objectivity—plays in which, increasingly, the author's controlling hand was not perceived. Foote's developing technique allowed the playwright to permeate his fiction with a powerful sense of truth, a quality that would continue to constitute his work's most powerful claim on an audience's attention. Once a Foote play established credibility as independent reality, then the playwright could explore his themes and preoccupations with greater effect.

The thread of William Carlos Williams's "doctrine of perception"— his insistence that all art be based on "the real"—may be traced throughout Foote's creative process. Elizabeth Bishop's invocation of the particular in achieving the universal and her genius for the devastatingly powerful understatement is everywhere evident in the plays of *The Orphans' Home* cycle. Marianne Moore's use of found material—her penchant for esoteric "quoting"—coupled with her lifelong struggle to balance a strong faith with the ironic sensibility of the modernist, make her work peculiarly compatible with Foote's own sensibility. Randall Jarrell, the "master of the heartbreak of everyday," offered yet another rich inspiration for Foote in his construction of a "moral and social history of a particular time and place" (Foote 1990). And Philip Larkin's evocations of death, oblivion, and the ultimate meaning of human existence had a profound influence on the playwright and his work during the intensely productive and ground-breaking period of the 1970s.

But the playwright's search for a style that could take him beyond the limitations of conventional theatre would continue, finally leading him to the work of an American artist as unconventional and determinedly "transcendental," as Foote himself.

In the New Hampshire woods, Foote began to listen obsessively to the music of Charles Ives. At long last, the playwright had found the "comfort" for which he had searched. In Ives's music, the aesthetic, and the philosophy, were merged with the various facets of Foote's long, artistic quest.

I think playwrights can learn from all the arts: painting, sculpture, music—particularly music. Often when I was resting from working on the nine plays in *The Orphans' Home* cycle, I would listen over and over to the music of Charles Ives. I got to know the symphonies, the songs, the sonatas, the concertos, the piano pieces—all of it—intimately. Not just passively listening, but questioning. Why this choice? Why this quote from a hymn, from a march? Why this structure? (Foote, Spalding Lecture, 1987)

It's his own order . . . it uses found things and dissonance in order to create order. . . . The earlier conventions of music were to find principles of harmony. And Ives was out to break all that up. And to create a new kind of synthesis. I think all harmony finally exists somewhere in nature, don't you? I mean, that's mystical, and I don't know that you could prove that . . . he was rebellious, and he wanted to say, "Look, what you think is ugly, isn't really ugly; you put it together, and you make something quite beautiful." I think to teach people to look at things in a different way—that's more his synthesis, his principle. And to listen. And to find beauty in what many people would think was not beautiful. (Foote 1993)

To understand the strong attraction which that most iconoclastic of American modernist composers held for Foote, one must look beyond Ives's unique musical structures and aesthetic theory to the philosophical, religious, and personal influences that guided Ives's own development. For contained within Ives's great love of the New England transcendentalist writers and thinkers are the seeds of Horton Foote's unique style and vision.

Ives's career as a composer was as extraordinary as his music. He published his own scores, refusing royalties and copyrights, did not fraternize with professional musicians, and seldom went to concerts; yet the New England eccentric was years ahead of the musical mainstream. Ives anticipated the atonality of Schoenberg and the polytonality of Stravinsky and Milhaud; he experimented with quartertones, disjunct melodies, jazz and ragtime elements, and asymmetrical rhythms long before anyone else (Rossiter 1975, 191–192). His shyness and self-imposed isolation contributed to his lack of professional recognition. As is often the case with a genius, Ives was so far ahead of his time that it took years for the musical establishment to grasp the true significance of his accomplishment. It was not until the 1970s that Ives, after years of complete obscurity, became generally acknowledged as America's greatest composer (Rossiter 1975, 309).

Two of Ives's most persistently pursued artistic goals were the representation in music of human experience and the creation of a distinctively American music, imbued with American idealism. These two aesthetic tenets were inseparable. Authenticity was vital in true artistic creation; a real artist must represent human experience with profundity. "When the people's music is brought into a composition, the spiritual and emotional meanings of the music must come along as well" (Burkholder 1985, 15).

When he first heard Ives's work, Horton Foote felt an immediate shock of recognition. "I guess I'd always been looking for a kind of kindred spirit. And I stumbled on Ives; and, the minute I heard him, I knew this was my boy" (Foote 1993).

Reasons for his instinctive response to Ives's work became clearer as Foote launched an intensive study of the New England composer's technique.

> As I began to know Ives, I began maybe to understand why I did it. It's one way of defining a sense of place.
>
> I remember, as a boy, sitting on my porch at night, or on the gallery, and down in the flats I could hear black music, or once in a while in the distance you could hear a little Mexican band, or I could hear a child practicing, or Sunday nights you could hear a choir in the distance. So it was part of it, part of life. All you know now is that inevitable radio or television; but it's not only the music, it's also the sounds. And, particularly in small towns, I think you're very conscious of it.
>
> I have a great dislike of manipulative music. You'll notice, in my films, I fight like crazy to keep any kind of interpretative score out, because I don't like it at all. I really like found music, you know, which I think is the most helpful, because it tells you about the place and about the people, because they listen to the kind of music they like. I mean, in my plays, you don't often hear them listening to Bach. (Foote 1990)

Horton Foote's parents died in the early 1970s, barely a year apart, and the loss acted as a catalyst, precipitating a period of creative growth during which all of the influences—the Russians, dancers, poets, and Foote's own memories—came together in the culmination of an artistic apprenticeship that had lasted over thirty years. It was not coincidental that Ives's music became a significant inspiration during this period, for Ives had taken a similar journey in his own mission to make the past universally significant through his art.

Indeed, long before Foote began his intense study of Charles Ives's music, the playwright had unconsciously emulated Ives's revolutionary techniques. In *The Trip to Bountiful*, written in the early 1950s, Foote had used hymns to evoke associations in the audience on multiple levels. His practice of using "found" music in his plays dated back to his earliest works from the late 1930s and early 1940s. But the playwright's discovery of Ives helped Foote analyze his instincts as a writer.

Ives appropriates familiar material such as hymns, popular songs of an earlier era, and ragtime melodies and then uses this material in a completely unconventional—and decidedly unsentimental—manner, clearly separating himself from other American composers who often draw from the same sources but with quite different results. In a technique that has had a profound influence on Foote, Ives uses the old melodies allusively, never quoting them as a means of invoking nostalgia, but rather filtering them through his own polytonal and dissonant aesthetic, forcing the listener to hear in a new way what at first seems familiar.

Both Ives and Foote regard the "melodies" remembered from childhood with an almost reverential respect. As a child Foote listened, and what he heard eventually assumed—in the realm of his memory and imagination—a musical structure and dimension. He remembered the storytellers he listened to as a child, each teller lending his or her own unique perspective so that the story became a theme, with each version a distinct but recognizable variation, just as in a musical composition (Foote 1989, 6). Foote used many of these stories in his plays "like recurring themes, sometimes only alluded to, sometimes the central action" (Foote, Spalding Lecture, 1987).

Not only do childhood memories function as artistic impetus, but Foote consciously and consistently draws on "found material," a trademark of Ives's compositional style. Foote recalls impressions from his childhood, modified and transformed as material for his plays. This "authentic" material lends a resonance and objectivity to Foote's work which, again, bears a great similarity to that of Charles Ives's compositions.

Throughout his life, Ives returned obsessively to the music and the experiences of his New England childhood, and a quintessential similarity between Foote and Ives is the deep impression childhood experiences left on the artistic psyches of both men. Foote has written:

> One of the mysteries of the creative process is what makes us choose what we write about and the style we choose to share it with others. I wonder if the themes and material we are drawn to as writers aren't given to us at a very early age, before we have done much reading of the works of others, or even begun to think of writing, and that the works of the writers we are later drawn to is because we are instinctively searching to reinforce the sense of style inherent in us. I wonder, too, if our writing style can be changed in any really profound way, any more than the color of our eyes or our skin. (Spalding Lecture, 1987)

Most importantly, Foote and Ives share underlying artistic and philosophical/spiritual principles from which their techniques derive. The best, and most vivid, explicator of the philosophical and aesthetic principles of Charles Ives is Ives himself. Ives's *Essays before a Sonata* (1962), drafted as an explanation of his *Concord Sonata*, demonstrates the composer's great admiration for Emerson and the transcendentalists and reveals the vital spiritual and philosophical underpinnings of his compositions.

In Ives's aesthetic, truth would be achieved through the rejection of conventional ideas of beauty and art and the strict adherence to the artist's perception of the world as he saw it. Foote's rejection of those tenets of dramatic writing that have guided the majority of contemporary playwrights—the reliance on Aristotelian structure, overtly heightened language, and dramatic conflict—parallel Ives's insistence on the value of substance over manner.

When, in the *Essays*, Ives (1962) wrote of ideals that coincide with spiritual consciousness, he was describing something very close to the "sense of truth" that Horton Foote's Russian mentors had advocated, and of the universality achieved through the true portrayal of the specific, which the American Actors' Company had taken as its primary goal. With characteristically colorful style, Ives described ideas of conventional beauty as those which "let the ears lie back in an easy chair." He felt that "ideals" of beauty were too often those sounds that did not offend because of their familiarity, and those compositions most easily accepted as sublime were those that "put the mind to sleep."

Both Ives and Foote demand that their audiences "be quiet and listen"

(Foote 1992). The art of both composer and playwright is the antithesis of escapist. It encourages the listener, the viewer, to look at the world around him or her in a new way—to hear the music that is present in everyday life. And in the work of both artists the aesthetic is powerfully molded by the spiritual. During his twenty years of "exile," Horton Foote was bringing to culmination the merging of substance and form that had engaged him from the beginning of his career and that would finally result in his "transcendent" style, a style which sought to achieve for dramatic writing the same divine purpose that Ives envisioned for music.

Transcendental style can be defined as a way in which various artists of diverse cultures have sought to express the holy. It is a style that seeks to "maximize the mystery of existence" (Schrader 1972, 11). With this goal in mind, transcendental style avoids the traditional ways in which artists have interpreted reality, refusing to adhere to the tenets of realism, naturalism, expressionism, or any of the other genres that have flourished since the birth of modern drama at the turn of the century. Ultimately, transcendental style denies the necessity of rational thought. Abbot Amdedee Ayfre described a basic tenet of the transcendentalist aesthetic when he wrote, "If everything is explained by understandable causal necessities, or by objective determinism, even if their precise nature remains unknown, then nothing is sacred" (Schrader 1972, 11). Paul Schrader wrote:

> Transcendental style stylizes reality by eliminating (or nearly eliminating) those elements which are primarily expressive of human experience, thereby robbing the conventional interpretations of reality of their relevance and power. Transcendental style, like the mass, transforms experience into a repetitive ritual which can be repeatedly transcended. (1972, 11)

If, as Gerardus van der Leeuw wrote, "religion and art are parallel lines which intersect only at infinity and meet in God" (Schrader 1972, 11), then Horton Foote's long apprenticeship culminated at that infinite point at which his vision and craft finaly converged, allowing him to express the ineffable.

In transcendental dramatic works, the whole world may exist in one family. The specific, the mundane—family, domestic concerns, the day-to-day realities of life—become the universal. The conventional emphasis on plot, action, and dramatic device is eliminated; instead, the transcendental writer seeks to communicate the essence of human existence without focusing on those dramatic moments most often chosen as the subject of plays and films.

In the philosophical and spiritual realm of the transcendental aesthetic, the opposing forces of human existence cannot be reconciled by anything as obviously manmade and controlled as plot (Schrader 1972, 19). The actions of a transcendental work might seem ordinary: the estrangement of parents and children, marriage, relocation, the birth and death of a baby, small-town life. But these seemingly mundane incidents take place in a much larger context. If the erratic behavior of a local businessman or the reconciliation of two families after a divisive elopement are the actions that drive the plot, these everyday events are set against a backdrop of such major American experiences as Reconstruction, the First World War, the flu epidemic of 1918, and the migration of people to the cities as the American economy moved from an agrarian model to one of industry and business.

There is a sameness to Foote's work, especially the plays written during the late 1960s and afterwards. Critics have objected to this homogeneous quality in which not only thematic preoccupations, but characters and even specific stories appear again and again. Also fodder for criticism has been Foote's penchant for setting all of his original work in the fictional town of Harrison, Texas. Yet the sameness, or "predictability," of Foote's works is not evidence of a lack of imagination or originality on the part of the author; Foote consciously chooses to repeat rather than to strive for a sense of variety usually demanded by American culture. In so doing, the playwright is consciously, and in the most subtle ways imaginable, instilling a sense of ritual in his work.

The underpinnings of transcendental style have much more in common with Asian than with Western aesthetic traditions. In traditional forms of Asian art, an artist might spend a lifetime painting and repainting certain scenes in order to perfect his brushstrokes. Horton Foote worked and reworked the same material, refining and moving toward a fully realized transcendental style. In a sense, the works Foote created, beginning in the 1970s, may be called his definitive "play" in the same way that a single painting might be the culminating product of a Zen painter's entire career (Schrader 1972, 33).

Most twentieth-century plays follow a model of psychological revelation. The influence of Freud was a determining force in the development of realism, and the model continues to dominate dramatic writing,
especially in America. Foote does not fit into this dominant trend, and,
again, his avoidance of conventional dramatic structure, which demands
the revelation of personal/psychological truth as a focal point, has
brought him criticism. But like traditional Asian artists, Foote wishes to
prepare a thesis, not emphasize his own personality in his storytelling.
The individual emotions of his characters are only of passing importance; it is the broader, philosophical/spiritual context that gives them
lasting value. The transcendental style frustrates audiences who attempt
to decipher the familiar expression of individual psychology. Instead,
their attention is subtly directed to recognizing something much different: an expression of the transcendent. Shared philosophical facets of
Buddhism and Christian Science (a belief system of which Foote has
been a student for many years)—despite their very real and important
differences—could explain why Foote is drawn to an aesthetic that
seems to owe much more to Eastern than to Western thought and tradition. The basic principles of Zen art emphasize negation, emptiness, and
stillness; most importantly, these are *positive* elements. Silence and stillness represent the *presence* rather than the *absence* of something. In a
haiku, the lines give meaning to the unwritten transitions. Silence and
emptiness are active ingredients in Foote's plays, as they are in the works
of the modernist poets whom Foote loves. The playwright uses silences
and voids as ways of communicating that for which there are no
words—a reflection, again, of the influence of Martha Graham and the
modern dancers who taught Foote to transcend the limitations of verbal
communication.

The structure of Foote's plays, always somewhat unconventional
and increasingly so as his style developed more fully, is much more comprehensible when viewed through the lens of Zen aesthetics. In Asian art
(and unlike Aristotle's model) ritual is not structured around a single,
cathartic event. If man and nature are truly one and eternal, then it is
necessary that any ritual evoking truth be cyclical in nature. In Zen, the
concept of *ekaksena* may be translated as the eternal present; such a concept is critical in understanding the philosophical/spiritual underpinnings of Foote's work. The structure of Foote's plays evoke the eternal

present by redirecting the emphasis from indiviual catharsis to the awareness of constant unity. Conflict between man and the material world is not resolved, but rather transcended. The material world is not "real" in the truest sense; consequently, there is no point in resolving that would preoccupy most playwrights. Indeed, focus on a more traditional type of resolution delays or prevents enlightenment. The seeming lack of resolution is actually a step in the process of transcending what only seems to be real in order to find ultimate—and eternal—truth.

The structures of Horton Foote's dramatic writings reveal the working of transcendental style. First, the writer establishes a determined focus on subject matter so close to reality as to seem almost nondramatic. This conscious and determined avoidance of the dramatic devices and heightened theatricality that characterize most plays can be difficult for audiences to accept. Audiences crave the vicarious excitement of conventional films, the theatricality and escapism of many plays. Foote eschews theatrical plots for a very specific reason: in the transcendental style, the events seem predestined, beyond the audience's control—and, more importantly, beyond the control of the writer/artist.

Foote consciously manipulates what is usually a theatrical/social medium in order to redirect its focus. If the internal drama is in the mind or soul, then emotional involvement with external plot distracts from it. This is not to say that the style favored by Foote evokes no emotional response from the audience, but the critical distinction from more traditional catharsis is that, in transcendental style, emotional involvement comes only after recognition of form.

Foote replaces what theatre audiences have come to expect as essential in engaging theatre—intricate plots, obviously heightened language and acting—with a form so subtle it takes audiences some time to become aware that they are watching anything other than simple naturalism. The audience member's desire to participate vicariously in the action is frustrated; emotional and intellectual engagement does not seem possible. Consequently, conventional catharsis is postponed. Yet, as the spectator's expectations go unrealized, it also becomes clear that the dramatic presentation is not a simple depiction of the everyday. The audience becomes cognizant of a controlling form that cannot yet be identified or interpreted; they are not being asked to view reality in a certain way, but are rather deprived of the comfort of the familiar. Just as Ives demanded audiences with new ears, Foote uses transcendental style to coax his audiences to apprehend with new senses.

After intimating the subtle form which underlies the seemingly every-day setting of his plays, Foote further disorients his audience by introducing a sense of the spiritual within an otherwise material environment. This spiritual dimension is revealed through the main character or characters and the way in which their actions seem motivated by a force that cannot be located in their material surroundings. The characters in Foote's plays suffer almost every affliction imaginable: children are drowned or deserted by their parents, men stab themselves and are shot down in the street, women lose their minds, sons succumb to alcoholism and compulsive gambling, the flu and war decimate a small town, young women die in childbirth or languish in loveless marriages. Yet sometimes, and for seemingly inexplicable reasons, some of the playwright's characters are able to transcend human tragedy. From the beginning of his career, Foote has been intrigued—even obsessed—with that which makes it possible for one person to survive what would have destroyed another. When asked how important the sense of mystery is in his writing, Foote replies:

> It's everything. It's the eternal fascination with life and looking around you at your fellow man and asking why did this happen to this man and not to that man. I think of this in terms of raising children. I happen to have very close associations with my children and I think they're remarkable human beings, but whenever I have any pride about that, I say to myself, "Now, wait a minute. I know men who are better than you whose children haven't turned out well at all." You look around and you can see wonderful people that have terrible things happen to them. It is a mystery, isn't it? (Wright 1997, 47)

The playwright remains true to the sense of mystery; in Foote's fictive world, conventional religious beliefs do not prevent tragedy, nor can they be relied on to supply the believer with the necessary courage and faith to go on. Yet some characters do survive, and it is in the mystery of their ability to vanquish death that Foote's employment of transcendent style is most clearly evident. The source of their seemingly miraculous salvation from destruction cannot be located in the material world around them, even in conventional religious beliefs. The source is transcendent—it is wholly other.

By presenting a seemingly naturalistic environment, then introducing in its midst a profound sense of the spiritual, Foote creates in his audience a strong sense of confusion, unresolvable through intellectual means. This delay in resolution creates an emotional intensity that cannot be released until the main character(s) confront and transcend what would seem to be unbearable in human terms. When a character such as the ruthlessly ambitious Leonard in *The Habitation of Dragons* or the alcoholic, country-western singer, Mack Sledge, in Foote's 1983 film *Tender Mercies*, is able to transform himself through seemingly suprahuman means, then that act must be acknowledged by the audience; in that moment emotion is released as the transcendent is recognized. It is the only way in which the audience member can make sense of what he or she has witnessed; in this way Foote guides his audiences to reach their own conclusion.

The moment of transformation is not one of resolution, but of acceptance, and this distinction is a critical element of transcendental style. That the spiritual exists in the material realm is an elemental paradox of human existence, and one which cannot be explained or resolved by the human mind. And that the audience member seems to have come to this conclusion through his or her own experience, without any discernible intervention on the part of the playwright, is a key element in the profound impact that a Foote play has on those who are open to the experience. In these final moments, audience members experience what in Zen aesthetics is called stasis: the eternal, symbolized by nature, is juxtaposed against ephemeral, material existence, and the viewer is left with a sense of the oneness of all things.

Paul Schrader has written that transcendental art distills the essence of man's relationship to the holy; transcendental style provides the vehicle which conveys the viewer "through the trials of experience to the expression of the Transcendent." But the journey does not end in that "calm region untouched by the vagaries of emotion or personality." Instead, the viewer returns to the realm of human experience; but, having been brought "nearer to that silence, that invisible image, in which the parallel lines of religion and art meet and interpenetrate," the traveler is forever transformed. And having completed its function, transcendental style "may now fade back into experience. The wind blows where it will; it doesn't matter once all is grace" (Schrader 1972, 168–169).

When one of Horton Foote's recent plays received its world premiere at the Signature Theatre Company in New York City in December 2000. Ben Brantley (2000), reviewing the production for the *New York Times*, wrote:

> We are all orphans, Mr. Foote keeps suggesting in his polite, laconic way. It is an existential given. The years have tempered neither the basic bleakness of this perspective nor the eloquence with which it is rendered by Mr. Foote, who is a singular artistic mix of ruthlessness and sentimentality. "The Last of the Thorntons" is, in its way, as unrelenting an assessment of the human condition as "Waiting for Godot."

The comparison is apt; but in the final moments of Foote's play, audience members are propelled to a destination never reached by Beckett's tramps. In *The Last of the Thorntons*, the denizens of a small-town nursing home endlessly repeat stories from the past as a way of dealing with a present that has passed them by. One and all, they long for homes that no longer exist. The central character is Alberta Thornton, an early victim of Alzheimer's. Throughout the play Alberta talks of her home in Houston, which she fears is about to be sold by an unscrupulous nephew. She yearns to return to the house she shared with her three sisters, now all dead. In the final moments of the play it becomes clear that the home was sold long ago; Alberta lives in a limbo in which time and place no longer have meaning. But it is not the often repetitive exchanges between the sad victims of age and time that so impact the audience of the play, nor is it Foote's ability to evoke that existential terrain so familiar from Beckett's plays. The play ends as it begins, with the nursing home residents seated in their customary places in the institutional waiting room. The audience waits for the inevitable light fade. But it does not come. Alberta stands, frozen in time and place, for a full two minutes before the lights finally come down. And in that unbearable moment of stasis, the audience is brought face to face with the eternal.

For Foote, this transcendental playwright—our "mystic of the American theatre"—ultimately there are no more words. The wind blows as it will. All is grace.

Works Cited

Balcom, Lois. 1944. Review of *Daisy Lee* by Horton Foote. *Dance Observer,* February, 15, 20.

Brantley, Ben. 2000. Wry Smiles Temper the Anguish of Old Age. *New York Times,* 4 December, nat. ed., sec. E, 1.

Burkholder, J. Peter. 1985. *Charles Ives: The Ideas Behind the Music.* New Haven, CT: Yale University Press.

Ellermann, Robert. 1996. Introduction. In *Horton Foote: Collected plays. Vol. II.* Lyme, NH: Smith and Kraus, pp. vi-viii.

Foote, Horton. 1944. Dance and the Playwright. *Dance Observer,* January, 7–8.

———. 1986. Symposium, American Film Institute, Los Angeles, 26 February.

———. 1986. McDermott Lecture. University of Dallas, 20 November. Horton Foote Papers, Southern Methodist University.

———. 1987. Fairleigh-Dickinson University Lecture, 30 March, Horton Foote Papers, Southern Methodist University.

———. 1987. Spalding University Lecture, 13 November. Horton Foote Papers, Southern Methodist University.

———. 1989. *Seeing and Imagining,* Louisiana State University, 19 April. Horton Foote Papers. Southern Methodist University.

———. 1989. *The New York Theater,* Louisiana State University, 19 April. Horton Foote Papers. Southern Methodist University.

———. 1990. Interview by the author, tape recording. 6 September.

———. 1992. Interview by the author. 28 September.

———. 1993. Interview by the author, tape recording. 15 March.

———. 1995. Interview by the author, tape recording. 8 April.

Ives, Charles. 1962. *Essays before a Sonata, the Majority and Other Writings,* ed. Howard Boatwright. New York: Norton.

Jilinsky, Andrius. 1990. *The Joy of Acting; A Primer for Actors,* ed. Helen C. Bragdon. New York: Peter Lang.

Kalstone, David and Patricia Wallace. 1989. Introduction to Randall Jarrell. *The Norton Anthology of American Literature, Volume II.* New York: Norton. 2462–63.

Price, Reynolds. 1987. Introduction. In *Three Plays,* by Horton Foote. New York: Grove, pp. ix–xiii.

Rossiter, Frank R. 1975. *Charles Ives and His America.* New York: Liveright.

Schrader, Paul. 1972. *Transcendental Style in Film: Ozu, Bresson, Dreyer.* Berkeley: University of California Press.

Swafford, Jan. 1996. *Charles Ives; A Life with Music.* New York: Norton.

Wolf, Mary Hunter. 1991. Interview. 16 September.

Wright, Tim. 1997. Horton Foote: An interview. *Image: A Journal of the Arts* (Spring): 47.

INTERVIEW WITH HORTON FOOTE

Interview conducted by Crystal Brian
in October 2000

Crystal Brian: What inspired you to write plays as opposed to any other form?

Horton Foote: I went into it because I was an actor. And I wanted to write parts for myself. [Laughs] And I got very interested in it, in the form. And I think, because my inclination is always to tell things through dialogue, that it's the most natural form for me. And, you know, I don't know that one chooses what one writes about or one's form as much as it chooses you. First of all, I was around plays all my life. And though I was a reader and read novels, I just have never been as interested in, let's say, describing the room or the scenery outside the room as I have been in what goes on between people. That's really what interests me as a writer. And I guess that's why I love Beckett so much. At least his plays. I'm not as familiar with his novels. But his plays. And, you know, it's a constant struggle for me to keep focused on the form, and to see its purest aspects, and which I feel essentially is language.

CB: And that's where the influence of poetry would come in.

HF: I'm sure so. I mean, all of those things influence you. I think the writers I like and admire and love are the novelists and the short story writers who all have fed my—whatever, you know—talent I have and whatever technique I have as a playwright.

CB: I found in your archives a poem you wrote when you were living in New York. I wondered if you ever seriously tried to write poetry?

HF: Not really. You know, once in a while I maybe did. I'm just too much in awe of poets. I would never attempt it. I mean, because I think their discipline is so different than a playwright's discipline.

CB: What are the greatest challenges or obstacles that you as a playwright have faced?

HF: Well, I think they vary, you know, from time to time. I think sometimes they're external forces. I think the internal forces are pretty constant in all art forms: to struggle to find what you want to say and how you want to say it. But playwrights increasingly are faced with diminishing audiences and places to have their plays done or to make a living at their craft. And it's not heartening. I mean, I think curiously that the quality of playwriting has increased and that the talent is there. If you're realistic about it, you know the better it is, maybe the more difficult it will become. Because you think of poets. I mean, how many poets even conceive of making a living off of writing poetry? And so maybe that's really not our business. I get concerned for the theatre itself. I've seen many phases and I've remained an optimist about the theatre because I think it will always survive, but—and I guess we're going through probably the most difficult, at least in America, transition that we've ever gone through. So that the big kind of Broadway houses are just becoming moribund. And so more and more you just have musicals filling them up. And it's all the places outside of New York that really are sustaining playwrights. Regional theatres and colleges, wherever.

CB: You have been writing for such a long time and have seen so many transitions and changes. What strikes you as being the most important ways in which things have changed since you began writing?

HF: I think that the encouraging thing is that the literacy and the quality of playwriting has not diminished. I mean, there are constantly young writers coming along that are interesting and vital. They always talk about the golden age of American theatre. Well, I wasn't a playwright necessarily then. But I was around as an actor. And it wasn't so golden. I mean, how many of the plays have survived? Whereas, you know, when you take men like Mamet and Shepherd and Arthur and Tennessee, their plays are surviving. But the Elmer Rices and the Maxwell Andersons and the S. N. Behrmans—and those are the better of the bunch. But if you look at the others, the only one, really, that I would even think twice about being interested in seeing his work is

George Kelley. Maybe that's too harsh. I don't know. I don't mean to detract from them. Because I think they were all serious workers. It's just that—what they were interested in . . . Maybe that's how it should be. Maybe they'll look back at us and say, well, we were a product of our times. But a lot of that theatre was, you know, based on the times. And the best of them were mostly plays socially impelled.

CB: What particular satisfactions or dissatisfactions come with playwriting?

HF: It's just enormously satisfying. The writing. Now the dissatisfaction often comes when you try to get a production together. And then you wonder, you know, because it's a question of money and the question of budgets. And you wonder if you just were a novelist or a short story writer, would it be easier to get the work done? And then you realize that playwriting is not a solitary thing. It basically has to be a cooperative venture. And you'd better get good actors and you'd better get a good director. And that's the part that then, well, it also can be very joyful because, you know, you sometimes get those and then it all works well.

CB: Since you direct your own work sometimes, does that contribute to the satisfaction?

HF: Well, it isn't that I want power. Because I do welcome directors. You know, I get along with them mostly wonderfully. It's just that it is interesting, because it keeps you alive and involved in the work a little bit longer. Because essentially when you're not directing, you have to almost mentally turn it over to somebody else. And welcome their input and welcome what they feel and welcome their ideas. And welcome the whole collaborative process. Because it's just hell if you don't.

CB: If you weren't a playwright, what do you think you would have done artistically?

HF: My first instinct is to say that I would have tried poetry. My fantasy is that. If I wasn't a playwright, I'd have been a poet.

CB: Do you regret not being an actor at all?

HF: No. [Laughs] I really don't. I'm so satisfied writing. As you know, I admire and respect and love actors. And depend on them greatly. But no, no. . . . I've just finished a new play. And I just sometimes don't think I'm alive unless I'm writing.

JONATHAN LARSON ROCKS BROADWAY

Amy Asch with Maggie Lally

At the 1996 Tony Award ceremony, where *Rent* was awarded Best Musical, Best Score, and Best Book of a Musical, Julie Larson said, "My brother Jonathan loved musical theatre. He dreamed of creating a youthful, passionate, pertinent piece that would bring a new generation to the theatre, so they would find as much joy in it as he did." Audience responses to *Rent*, and the Tonys, Obies, Drama Desks, and the Pulitzer Prize it won, confirm that Jonathan Larson met his goal. But *Rent*'s composer/lyricist/librettist was not able to enjoy his success. An aortic aneurysm killed Jonathan Larson (1960–1996) the night before *Rent* was to begin previews for a small off-Broadway production.[1] The thrilling show and the tragic circumstances generated tremendous press. To the general public, it seemed that Larson had sprung from nowhere. Actually, he had devoted seventeen years to honing his craft, exploring the issues raised in *Rent,* and trying to get his shows produced. The rock opera *Rent* is a vibrant synthesis of Larson's personal, social, and artistic influences and is informed by every one of his earlier projects.

Many of Larson's theatre pieces focus on characters outside the mainstream, how bottom-line thinking diminishes humanity, and the denial or apathy of those who don't resist. The seeds of all these themes can be traced to his childhood. The 1960s and 1970s were a time of progress for minorities, women, homosexuals, and ecological causes. They were also a time of political disillusionment, with the assassination of President Kennedy (which Larson cited as his earliest memory), the

Vietnam War, and Watergate. The Larson family passionately discussed all these issues. As an adult, Larson's interest in current events verged on obsessive.

From his earliest childhood, Larson believed he would have a life in the theatre. He was deeply engaged with music and listened to an eclectic mixture of show tunes, opera broadcasts, folk songs, and current pop music. Larson played piano by ear, accompanied various singing groups, and played tuba in his school marching band. But his primary interest was acting. Classmates and teachers remember his charisma and timing and, especially, his focus. Being in a show was not merely an after-school activity for him; it was preparation for a professional career. His classmates were also struck by Larson's approach to life. Small moments could give him great pleasure. He was emotionally open and eager for new experiences. These traits intensified during his college years.

Larson auditioned for Adelphi University's BFA acting program and was awarded a full-tuition scholarship. Adelphi's young actors studied acting, movement, speech, and text analysis, and the faculty pushed them to prove they had the creativity, dedication, and discipline a life in the theatre would require. It was an environment where students could take risks, learn by doing, and value process as much as results. In 1979, department chair Jacques Burdick was adapting a theatre piece from a thirteenth-century Spanish epic, *El Libro de Buen Amor*, and invited Larson, then a sophomore, to collaborate. Larson was an experienced accompanist and his elementary school piano teacher had encouraged him to experiment with rhythm, harmony, and setting text—but he had never tried to write songs, let alone a full score. However, he instinctively understood how theatre music must set the mood, convey character, and propel the story. He knew just which rhythmic patterns and instrumental colors would evoke the medieval Spanish setting. The songs included a hearty waltz tune for an active character and a quiet Satie-type melody for a meditative one. And, in a virtuoso display for a novice composer, these songs could be sung simultaneously as the characters expressed their conflicting points of view.

There were many opportunities to write at Adelphi. Students were taught to appreciate the nuances of fine work by imitating the masters. For example, they would analyze songs by Irving Berlin, Cole Porter, Rodgers and Hammerstein, and Sondheim for internal rhyme, character development, and structure, then write their own. The faculty cultivated a make-it-happen atmosphere. No one said "no" to an idea; they said "try it." The example of their commitment to process served Larson well as he did rewrite after rewrite of his major works.

Another hallmark of Adelphi's theatre program was the original cabarets presented twice a semester. Modeled on the political and cultural satires performed in France and Germany in the late nineteenth and early twentieth centuries, the shows consisted of short scenes and songs intended to produce shocked laughter and discussion of topical issues. In program notes, Burdick described their goal:

> The Adelphi Cabaret is a showcase where student writers, composers, designers, technicians, directors and performers can demonstrate their talents in a free satirical mode. We consider everyone and everything fair game . . . Far from wanting to offend, our objective is to evoke laughter, thought and dialogue. Our cry: Live and let live, and may God help the humorless.[2]

Larson was drawn to this form, which used the energy of live theatre to bring attention to social concerns. He wrote music and sometimes lyrics for four cabarets during his undergraduate years and for three more in the mid-1980s. *Herstory* (1980), book and lyrics by faculty member Nick Petron, had songs about race, empowerment, and menopause. Early on, Larson became known for his elaborate fugal numbers. In Petron's *Steak Tartare Caper* (1981), he set six suspects' weak alibis in a round. Classmate Maggie Lally's cabaret *Great American Letdown* (1982) began with eight characters introduced by appropriate songs, which were eventually all sung in counterpoint. *Sacrimmoralinority* (1981), book and lyrics by classmate David Armstrong, took on prayer in the schools, abortion, the shuttered life of a housewife, anti-gay activist Anita Bryant, and how to teach creation. The show began with an upbeat anthem, "We're the New Christian Right," and led into a gleeful list of the types of people and things they'd been saved from, including commies, druggies, Dallas, Satan, Arabs, and BeeGees. For the finale, the cast lined up in the shape of a cross to reprise the "New Christian Right." As this theme song morphed into "Deutschland Uber Alles," the cross became a swastika.

Larson's interest in theatre as a vehicle for social change was further stimulated in "Radical Theatre" class, where he studied the theories of Robert Brustein, Peter Brook, and Bertolt Brecht. Larson would retain these lessons for many years as he attempted to live up to Brecht's "Five Rules for Expressing the Truth."

> You must possess:
>
> 1. the courage to express the truth,
> 2. the intelligence to recognize the truth,
> 3. the art to fashion a manageable weapon of the truth,
> 4. the ability to choose those in whose hands truth will be effective,
> 5. the cunning to spread the truth among the greatest number.
> (quoted in Larson's personal papers[3])

Larson's work would also reflect Brook's view that "It's always Popular Theatre that saves the day. Through the ages it has taken many forms, and there is only one factor that they all have in common . . . that roughness" (Larson papers[4]).

When he graduated from Adelphi in the spring of 1982, Larson planned to pursue both writing and acting. What he had learned about pacing a scene, projecting character, and the function of rhyme and rhythm in dramatic verse and song lyrics would be useful in either field. That summer, he supported himself as a busboy and bar pianist while adapting George Orwell's *1984* for the musical stage, with what Larson described as "an epilogue that compares it to today's world."

> At the end of Act II, sc. 14, [the protagonist] Winston Smith has lost his battle for love, truth and the human spirit and confesses, "I love Big Brother." Immediately, the set explodes—smoke pours on stage, sirens wail, etc. Orwell's *1984* ends. The epilogue is basically the opening number over again, the difference is that the epilogue is done by the cast of actors in present-day dress, choreography, and most importantly, modern language. My overall premise is that Orwell's vision was beyond mere speculation and "science fiction"—because it has already become truth.
> (Proposition for *1984*, Larson papers, 1983)

The show opened with Winston filming typical aspects of his world on a video camera, introducing the audience to Big Brother, Newspeak, the Thought Police, and the Proles in a ten-minute montage of scenes and songs. In Larson's epilogue, the opening sequence is repeated with pointed changes: "CIA" is substituted for "Big Brother" and our own mumbo jumbo—"CBS, HBO, IRA, ABC, AFL, CIO, CIA, FBI, ERA"—stands in for Newspeak. Larson's observations were astute, but in *1984* and most of his later works, his romantic side overruled his intellect. Larson was familiar with the ways Brecht would have kept the audience squirming, denying them a comforting catharsis, but he chose to end *1984* on a positive note. In the opening, lyrics threatened death to those who question the system. As the epilogue finishes, the melody recurs with the message that we *must* question the system, while other cast members sing "Love is the key, love is the answer."

Larson hoped to be on Broadway by January 1, 1984 with Jerome Robbins or Harold Prince directing, and Alan Alda playing the main character. When he had finished two drafts of the script and recorded a demo of the songs, he engaged a theatrical lawyer. But the stage rights had been optioned by the producers of a film version, and Larson got no further. The effort, however, was not entirely wasted. Those familiar with Stephen Sondheim's career[5] know that Sondheim learned his craft by following a curriculum set for him by Oscar Hammerstein II: make a musical from a successful play, make a musical from a flawed play, make a musical from a nondramatic source, write an original musical. With *1984*, Larson continued to develop his voice and experiment with forms and themes that would recur throughout his work. Adapting the novel gave him practice dramatizing dense exposition and writing the scenes-in-music that distinguish a theatre craftsman from a pop songwriter.

Before he left Adelphi, Larson had written a fan letter to Sondheim, who responded with an invitation to meet. Larson's family and friends cite that conversation as a turning point in the younger composer's life. He often recounted Sondheim saying, "Don't be an actor. There's more dignity playing piano in a bar." During the development of *1984*, Larson still went to a few auditions. But he was a character actor, not a chorus boy, and would usually be typed out before he had a chance to speak. Although *1984* had not panned out, Larson felt that as a composer he was "taken seriously." There were encouraging developments. Larson and a college collaborator had mounted their cabaret about the New Christian Right as an Equity showcase and ASCAP gave them a cash award. The head of the public relations firm where Larson worked as a messenger heard the young songwriter's demo, liked it, and was introducing him to agents.

Larson's ambition was enormous. In a 1986 grant application, he wrote, "I want to add my generation's voice to and build a new audience for the American musical theatre—continuing in the traditions set by such people as George Gershwin, Rodgers & Hammerstein, Jerome Robbins, Harold Prince and Stephen Sondheim" (Larson papers). Moreover, he had tremendous faith in the power of art. When his high school music teacher's job was eliminated during budget cuts, Larson prepared a letter to the editor: "What happened to a healthy mind, body and spirit being the keys to a happy existence? It seems that the human spirit, which feeds on the Arts, isn't important to students, parents, and administrators." So many of America's social priorities seemed dangerously warped to him. Why did people play it safe, think small? Why did people only value what can be measured in money? Didn't they see they were being "infotained" into complacency? Since Larson couldn't use Orwell's dystopia to show where such thinking leads, he invented his own totalitarian society.

In his new project, *Superbia,* the whole country is told what to do by a central television broadcast. Everyone but the hero and heroine has been surgically stripped of the capacity to feel. This pair, Josh Out and Elizabeth In, are "idealistic misfits" in a nation devoted to celebrity worship, buying worthless objects, and getting high. They meet, fall in love, and try to make their "unfeeling plastic world" more like the situations they've been reading about in a contraband volume of Broadway lyrics. In a letter to Harold Prince, Larson explained:

> *Superbia* is an attempt to bring a new audience to the American Musical
> Theatre. People aged 22 to 35, so called "yuppies," who can afford to go
> to a show, but don't because
>
> a) it doesn't deal with topics that concern them
>
> b) the music isn't hip
>
> c) it isn't fashionable. (Larson papers)

Larson applied and was accepted into ASCAP's musical theatre workshop, where young writers meet weekly to hear selections from works-in-progress and the reactions of musical theatre professionals. During the 1985–86 workshop, he presented four songs from *Superbia.*

"After the Revolution," a hold-over from the *1984* score, was the lovers' vision of their future, set to a music box melody. Stephen Sondheim, a panelist the first afternoon, told him that his mis-setting of word accents was amateurish (Larson had fudged the stresses of certain syllables to make the lyric fit the music), and pointed out that the song's old-fashioned melody contradicted the repeated title phrase. But Sondheim was quite impressed by "Face Value," a song for the bouncer outside Incity who fawns on the famous and sneers at the unknown to frenetic 1980s pop music. In "Eye on Her/Mr. Hammerstein II," Elizabeth's parents flirt to an S&M madrigal melody and discuss ways to monitor their daughter's unseemly behavior, while she sings of musical-theatre happily-ever-afters. "Sextet" was the Act II opening, a bravura set of sung conversations and monologues (not unlike the "Tonight" quintet in *West Side Story*). At the end of the workshop season, ASCAP recommended Larson for a more advanced program sponsored by the Dramatists Guild, where he presented a full act.

The feedback from the professionals at these workshops sent Larson and *Superbia* in various directions. Some panelists thought the case against Superbian society was too one-sided to be worth telling the story. Others were distracted by logic gaps in Larson's imaginary universe and asked him to make the Superbian world more concrete. The panelists rarely agreed on what, exactly, would make Larson's script work. In response, Larson tinkered with many structural and character elements: Should Elizabeth In be immediately sympathetic to Josh, or disdainful, or a numb Out girl who is somehow brought "to her senses," as one song puts it? Should Josh's mission to Incity be self-motivated or triggered by disastrous news? Does Josh get his message out? Initially Josh and Elizabeth's naivete was meant to be a wink at old-fashioned musicals. But the humorous theatre references were all dropped. As the characters changed, the music became more edgy. Instead of a "Broadway sound played with synthesizers," Larson used the contemporary styles of Prince and The Police to convey modern anxieties. With each rewrite, the show's tone got darker, possibly reflecting the author's frustration that no one seemed to understand his show. Whatever the motivation, the optimist who had found a positive way to conclude *1984* made Elizabeth's accidental electrocution/suicide the climax of *Superbia*.

In 1988, Larson won a Richard Rodgers Award that funded a staged reading at Playwrights Horizons. He plunged into more rewrites, based on feedback from R. J. Cutler, the reading's director, and Ira Weitzman, director of new-musical development. But the experience soured as pre-production began. The script had specified: "Sound design is as important a factor as costumes or sets. The music mix must be clean, current and digitally enhanced—closer to today's standards for pop music than 'Broadway' sound." But he wasn't permitted to use electronic instruments, and the cast didn't have the pop/rock voices he wanted. The next year, he and his friends staged a one-night concert version of the show with a full band, but the record producers and theatre people they invited just weren't interested. Sondheim encouraged Larson to move on. The young songwriter had spent five years on the show and thought he could make *Superbia* work as a screenplay. But he also began a new stage project.

Larson had sent *Superbia* to many regional theatres. Often the rejection letters said the show was too complicated. So, Larson decided to take a lesson from Eric Bogosian and Spalding Gray, whose work he admired. His new project, *Boho Days*, needed "no sets, no costumes, no cast. Just me, a piano and a band." He called it a "rock monologue" and hoped it would show a hip young audience that musical theatre could speak to them. In the course of twelve songs and twelve monologues "Jonathan," an aspiring writer of rock musicals on the eve of his 30th birthday, takes stock of his career, his relationships, and the way he lives. For ninety minutes, Larson detailed "Jonathan's" dilapidated apartment, his job as a waiter, the reactions to *Superbia*, his "audition" for a market research firm. He wondered aloud if his generation, which had excelled in money making, addictions, and apathy, would ever grow up, and if he would ever get a show produced. His frustration with the commercial theatre—vapid spectacles, marquee names, revivals—was the basis for a rap song, dropped after script revisions, called "The Theatre Is Dead":

Even off Broadway
There's no guarantee
That some M.B.A.
Won't decide what you see.

Just like America
Lacking innovation
Just getting by
On glitz and reputation

. . .

Write for the movies
Write for TV
So what if it's crap
At least you won't write for free.

Make thousands of dollars
For a first draft
And your life won't depend
On whether Frank Rich laughed. (Larson papers)

Then "Jonathan" finds out his best friend from childhood is HIV-positive and is shocked out of his self-pity. The show ends with "Jonathan" writing down an idea for a new show.

Larson performed *Boho Days* in his agent's office for the artistic directors of the Second Stage theatre. They offered their auditorium for five performances if Larson could raise several thousand dollars to cover the expenses of a band, sound, and lighting. He hoped that Second Stage would pick up the show; at the very least, he would have audience feedback to guide his rewrites. A *New York Times* critic attended in an unofficial capacity but wasn't enthusiastic. On the positive side, Jeffrey Seller, an aspiring producer, praised Larson's contemporary style and said he hoped they would work together someday.

Larson made some adjustments to the script and renamed the piece *Tick, tick . . . BOOM!* to emphasize the pressure he felt to achieve something noteworthy and the time running out on his boy-wonder years. In 1991, he performed the show twice at the Village Gate. Larson loved to be on stage, and his sincerity compensated for any weaknesses as a vocalist. But the audience he was wooing was much more interested in *The Real Live Brady Bunch*, which was playing down the street. In January 1992, Larson recorded a professional demo for Geffen Records, hoping that the songs might get airplay if they were marketed as an album by a new singer/songwriter. But his work didn't fit neatly into any music industry category, and Geffen passed. He continued to perform *Tick* a few times a year through 1993.[6]

In 1989, Larson had begun working with playwright Billy Aronson, who wanted to update Giacomo Puccini's *La Bohème* to present-day New York City. The opera is based on a series of stories about a painter, a writer, a musician, and a philosopher who share a garret in Paris. Marcello, the painter, has an on-again/off-again relationship with a social-climbing flirt. Rodolfo, the writer, falls in love with Mimi, a seamstress who dies of tuberculosis in the last act. Larson suggested the title *Rent*, alluding to the debt the characters owe their landlord and to the torn fabric of the characters' lives. He and Aronson wrote three songs together, but had different ideas about the direction the show should take, and amicably separated. In the fall of 1991, when three more of Larson's friends were diagnosed HIV-positive, he "felt the need to act." He volunteered at a support center, but knew that his main form of communication was songwriting. With Aronson's blessing, Larson went back to work alone. *Rent* moves *Bohème*'s young artists to Alphabet City in the age of AIDS. Roger (a songwriter), Mark (a filmmaker), and their friends—a transvestite street musician, a self-described "computer anarchist," a lesbian performance-art diva—have their own struggles with creativity, relationships, poverty, and illness. Several characters, including Roger and Mimi, are HIV-positive.

Larson brought an outline and a demo tape to New York Theatre Workshop (NYTW) and was invited to join the company's artistic community. There were readings and workshops of increasing sophistication in 1992, 1993, and 1994. Audiences and theatre professionals loved the score but found the story hard to follow. Director Michael Greif, NYTW artistic director Jim Nicola, Sondheim, and many others gave Larson extensive notes. He experimented with structure, plot, and form: Larson tried telling the story as a flashback, he reconsidered issues of the characters' sexuality, and he dropped an elaborate subplot about an unfeeling politician who winds up homeless. But he never changed his ending: Mimi revives.

Although neither *Superbia* nor *Tick* had broken through, and *Rent* was only in an early stage of development, Larson's reputation and skill as a composer/lyricist and as a social commentator were growing. In 1989, American Music Theatre Festival, a new works producer in Philadelphia, gave him its Stephen Sondheim award. Producers began to seek him out for projects, giving him credibility and a chance to do the work he loved. Nelle Nugent invited him to submit material for a National Lampoon revue about life under the Republicans in the year 2076. In three musical scenes, Larson ridiculed presidential campaign practices: Every sound-bite is tested on a snack-munching family whose couch is enclosed in a giant cage; the candidate gets special training in a mud-slinging room; and a practice debate turns into a square dance with the chief handler calling the moves: "Shuffle and waffle/Jiggle and fudge/Never give answers/Don't ya dare budge." (When a Democrat won the 1992 election, the show lost its hook and was canceled.) With veteran lyricist Hal Hackady, Larson was commissioned to write a revue to be performed in New York City middle schools. They called the show *Blocks* and wrote songs about child abuse, prejudice, making excuses, and expressing your feelings. Larson used the same contemporary musical styles he was bringing to *Rent*. *Blocks* was performed in 1993 and revived in 1995.

Larson also worked on television and video projects. None of them was as important to him as *Rent*, but he kept trying to find a way to reach a larger audience or generate an ongoing source of income. Writer/performer Paul Scott Goodman invited Larson, Bob Golden, Rusty Magee, and Jeremy Roberts to work with him on a series of twisted biblical and mythological tales they could sell to MTV or Saturday Night Live. Like Larson, Goodman believed the music in musical theatre was decades behind the times. "We need to hear more from writers who were brought up with rock-and-roll, funk, jazz, reggae, and rap" he told *Backstage* (Hersh 1994). In their pilot episode, set in the Garden of Eden, Yves is a naive naked country boy with a guitar slung over his private parts. Adame is an urban rapper. She's totally bored and looking for action. God is a Kurt Cobain–type, attended by grunge angels. The tempter is a team of marketing specialists who break down Yves's resolve with a series of jingles. The five songwriters recorded an elaborate demo but did not take their own marketing efforts very far.

Larson also tried making a children's video. A regular at the diner where Larson worked pointed out how lucrative it might be and offered to fund three days of shooting. Larson invited Bob Golden, who had written for children's television, to work with him on the writing, producing, filming, and editing. The result was *Away We Go!*, in which two children and a puppet travel around New York City in an elevator, a taxi, a ferry, a bus, and finally an airplane, to the strains of four songs by Golden and four more by Larson. Distribution was very limited, but the tapes became something of a collector's item after *Rent*'s success. Larson makes a cameo appearance in the elevator scene.

Another video project came to Larson through Victoria Leacock, a friend who tirelessly promoted Larson's work and helped produce his readings and concerts. She had been hired to cull entertaining shorts from home movies taken by *Rolling Stone* publisher Jann Wenner and immediately brought Larson in to provide musical backgrounds. He wrote original songs about the Wenner children, set nursery rhymes to rock beats, and composed pirate music for footage of a Caribbean sail. Larson's pride and joy was a sound collage of the words "daddy," "papa," and "father" sampled from eighteen pop and rock songs. He received a small fee and his studio expenses—and the unusual job got him a small profile in *New York* Magazine.

Larson unexpectedly got involved in another theatre project in 1995, when En Garde Arts, known for site-specific pieces, asked Larson to join playwright Jeffrey M. Jones on *J.P. Morgan Saves the Nation,* a work-in-progress about the nineteenth-century capitalist. Anne Hamburger, En Garde's artistic director, had seen a reading of *Rent* and thought of Larson when *J.P. Morgan*'s original composer was unable to finish the project. Larson signed on early in the year, and the show was performed at the intersection of Wall Street and Broad that summer. Referencing Nine Inch Nails, Madonna, marching bands, and old-time melodramas, Larson's music added emotion and humor to a confrontational allegory laden with economics and history. The reviews for *J.P. Morgan Saves the Nation* were lukewarm to downright hostile, but the composer got a nod in the *Times*: "Mr. Larson works adroitly in an assortment of musical pastiches, from ragtime to rap: his music-hall hymn to capitalist hunger, 'Appetite Annie,' is charming" (Brantley 1995). And the *Village Voice* ran a profile of Larson, titled "Rescuing the Musical."

> *J.P. Morgan* is only the latest endeavor in [Larson's] personal crusade to reclaim for theater whatever popularity it once had on the radio. The last time theatre and pop music were in sync, according to Larson, was in the late 1960s, with the advent of rock musicals like *Hair* and *Jesus Christ Superstar*. "I'm on a quest," he insists. For instance, in *Rent* . . . he plun-

dered a full range of 1980s and '90s pop styles. "I find different types of contemporary music for each character—the hero sings in a Kurt Cobain-esque style, the street transvestite sings like De La Soul, and there's a Tom Waits character." (Istel 1995, 73)

Rent was progressing steadily. In 1994, Larson had won a second, larger, Richard Rodgers Award. The grant partially funded a two-week workshop production of *Rent* at NYTW. The show still needed work, but NYTW scheduled it for their 1995–1996 season. With a cast of twelve, a small band, a choreographer, headset microphones, and other costs, *Rent* was, by far, the most expensive show they'd ever undertaken. Jeffrey Seller, Kevin McCollum, and Allan S. Gordon put up the extra cash NYTW needed and negotiated an option for future commercial rights. The director and producers continued to press Larson to simplify or clarify his story, and the show was postponed from fall 1995 to January 1996, with a February opening. At the end of October, Larson finally quit waiting tables. He told his family the cast was "the sexiest, most talented, most exciting group of people he had ever seen assembled." He told the cast, "This is the best thing that ever happened to me."

In the eyes and ears of many critics, *Rent* was the best thing to happen in years. The drama jury for the Pulitzer Prize wrote:

> The strength of Mr. Larson's lyricism is great, and the power of his music is immense. Writing book, music and lyrics, he has sounded a fresh, ringing voice in our musical theatre. The characters, the setting, the music of this musical are particularly and triumphantly American in the vividness and force of their presentation. The young people so dynamically presented in his story are alienated bohemians . . . but they are also people of immense vitality and humor, facing their uncertain future with hope and expressing their concerns with rugged elegance. (Pulitzer Prize Administrator's Office 1996)

In notes for *1984*, the first project for which Larson wrote book, music, and lyrics, he had copied out Peter Brook's words: "Obscenity is joyous: Popular Theatre is anti-authoritarian, anti-traditional, anti-pomp, anti-pretense. . . . It is always popular theatre that saves the day." In the act one finale of *Rent*, "La Vie Boheme," Brook's ideas come alive in words, music, and gyrating bodies. In that same scene, Mark, the narrator, announces, "The opposite of war isn't peace. It's creation." *Rent* was Larson's creative response to the illness and addictions that were killing his friends; to the way advertising distorted politics and news became infotainment; to attacks on the NEA and to budget cuts in arts programs; to the way technology was encroaching on human contact.

Even listening to music had changed. When Larson was in high school, playing albums was a social activity. Now, people carried personal cassette players everywhere and listened alone, isolated by their headphones. The headphones also provided an excuse for ignoring panhandlers and, by extension, the situations that left more and more people living on the street. *Rent's* choral moments, particularly "Will I . . . ?" and "Seasons of Love," are a reminder of how a community can come together. The way the characters accept each other sets an example for the audience. "In our desensitized society," Larson wrote in 1993, "the artists, the bohemians, poor, diseased, 'others,' recovering addicts—all are more in touch with their human-ness than the so-called mainstream. Despite everything, human-ness, love, life, art survives" (Larson papers).

Notes

1. The condition, possibly caused by Marfan Syndrome, had gone undiagnosed during two emergency-room visits that week.
2. Quotations from Jonathan Larson's working notes, scripts, lyrics, and letters appear with kind permission of Unky's Music and the Larson family.
3. This is Jonathan Larson's adaptation of Brecht's "Writing the Truth: Five Difficulties," contained in *Galileo*, New York: Grove Press, 1966.
4. Jonathan Larson's adaptation of Brook from *Empty Space,* 1968.
5. Larson had read Craig Zadan's book *Sondheim & Co.* (Harper & Row, 1986) so many times, the spine had to be bound with duct tape to hold the chapters together.
6. Editor's Note: In 2001 a revised version of *Tick, tick . . . BOOM!* was presented at the Jane Street Theatre in New York City (opening June 13; last performance January 6, 2002). The show was modified from a solo performance to a three-hander. One actor plays "Jonathan." Two others play his girlfriend, his best friend and assorted other characters. David Auburn (Pulitzer Prize, 2001, for *Proof*) worked with Larson's three earlier drafts to prepare the adaptation. Scott Schwartz directed. The cast album, with Raúl Esparza, Amy Spanger, and Jerry Dixon, is on RCA Victor.

Works Cited

Brantley, Ben. 1995. "J.P. Morgan" and Some Heavy Site Specificity. *New York Times,* 16 June, C2.

Hersh, Amy. 1994. Innovative Forms of Musicals are Explored in BMI workshop. *Backstage,* 22–28 April.

Istel, John. 1995. "Rescuing the Musical. *The Village Voice,* 4 July, 73–74.

Pulitzer Prize offices. 1996. Extract from the 1996 Drama jury report.

CONVERSATIONS WITH JONATHAN LARSON

Compiled by Amy Asch

The material that follows is excerpted from previous interviews with Jonathan Larson and statements that Larson made about his work and his goals in grant applications, pitch letters, and other materials. Scott Gordon, an eighth-grade student, interviewed Larson in November 1995 for a school project. John Istel, an editor at Stagebill, *wrote about Larson for the* Village Voice *in the summer of 1995, and a transcription of his conversation with the composer was published in* American Theatre *after Larson's death (1996). Music journalist Barry Singer interviewed Larson for* New York *Magazine in 1993. Larson even asked himself some questions. In 1990, during the writing of his autobiographical show,* Tick, tick . . . BOOM!, *he designed a questionnaire about the experiences, ambitions, and concerns of his contemporaries. His own answers were found among his notes for that show.*

Gordon (1995): What made you decide to go into theater?

Jonathan Larson: I always, always, from the day I could talk, loved putting on plays. My older sister and my cousins and I used to put on plays at the beach every summer for our parents. . . . I was in third or fourth grade when I was on stage for the first time. And I just was a natural and loved being on stage, loved acting and everything about the theater and found that I was pretty good at it. So I just kept it up. I went to college and studied theatre and wrote a lot of shows. I've never personally had any question that this was what I wanted to do.

Gordon: What do you enjoy most about being a playwright?

JL: I most enjoy having audiences listen to my music and care about the story that I'm telling.

Questionnaire (1990): If you had the opportunity to meet anyone— living or dead—who would it be and what would you talk about?

JL: Shakespeare. How to "see" humanity more clearly—simply.

Questionnaire: If you were stranded on a desert island and could have only one book and one record, what would you bring and why? What one possession would you miss the most?

JL: Complete Works of Shakespeare—you could spend a lifetime and not know it all. *West Side Story* soundtrack—beautiful, entertaining, uplifting. Piano—it's my greatest outlet.

In many of his writings, Larson mentioned his musical influences:

JL: I grew up listening to the Beatles and Billy Joel as well as Andrew Lloyd Webber's *Jesus Christ Superstar* and *Evita*, Steve Schwartz, and Stephen Sondheim. (Letter to Harold Prince, 1984)

JL: I was a piano player. I loved old Elton John, Billy Joel. That's what I grew up with. They both knew how to write a pop tune that you couldn't get out of your head. (Barry Singer interview, 1993)

JL: I loved Pete Townshend growing up, and I loved the old Police and Prince—or whatever his name is—he's brilliant. I love Kurt Cobain and Liz Phair, the Beatles. And in the theatre—Leonard Bernstein, Sondheim. I absolutely love them. (Istel 1995 interview, *American Theatre* 1996).

JL: Never had a band. Although now, I have a band who I work with whenever I do my one-man show. (Singer, 1993)

Istel (1996): Do you see your music as part of the American musical theatre tradition?

JL: My whole thing is that American popular music used to come from theatre and Tin Pan Alley, and there's no reason why contemporary theatre can't reflect real contemporary music, and why music that's recorded or that's made into a video cannot be from a show. Popular music being part of theatre ended with *Jesus Christ Superstar* and *Hair* and rock musicals in the late 1960s. A number of things happened. One was that there had been singers in the '40s, '50s, even early '60s, who would sing anybody's material—Frank Sinatra, what have you. Then, beginning with the Beatles, you had songwriters and bands who were singing only their own material. So you didn't have that venue for theatre music to be popular.

In grant applications and in conversation with Scott Gordon, Larson described some of the obstacles he faced:

JL: I'm 29 and support myself primarily by waiting tables. Although it's a grind, I usually have found time for my real work. But lately, the more ruthless I am with myself as a writer, the longer it takes to complete a song—yet the results are better and better. Last year I received the Richard Rodgers Development Grant, which funded a staged reading at Playwrights Horizons of my musical *Superbia*. The stipend allowed me to excuse myself from the restaurant during the two weeks of rehearsal. Besides the euphoric feeling of being in my element (in rehearsal), I accomplished more on rewrites than I normally would have in three months. Needless to say, going back to the diner was a drag. That's why I'm applying for the Kleban Award. . . . The grant would afford me the time and financial flexibility to concentrate on [*Rent*, National Lampoon Tricentennial Revue, and *Superbia*] and other projects and to expand my voice as a writer. (Grant application, September 1989)

JL: A problem with a rock score is that in order to see if it works, you must fully produce your music. A simple piano-vocal cannot convey the feel of rock, "sampled" hip hop or rap music . . . [which] technically limits your creativity. So to develop my sound, I must either rent studio time or purchase state-of-the-art equipment. (NEA grant application, 1992)

JL: It's unfortunate but true that the critic's review, especially in the *New York Times*, is the determining factor [of whether an off-Broadway show transfers to Broadway] in almost all cases. There are a few exceptions, but almost always a review that's really positive and good is what's going to make a producer decide to take the financial gamble and move a show. It's too bad that one man who's the reviewer for the *New York Times* has all this power. (Gordon interview, 1995)

Writing about his life and work, Larson described his very specific goals:

JL: I am a sentimental romantic who loves old-fashioned musicals, in a generation of very unsentimental unromantic people, who could basically care less about that stuff. . . . If I want to establish myself with the "powers that be" in the theatre, I must compose music that appeals to the older ears in the audience and producing houses. But if I want to try to cultivate a new audience for musical theatre, I must write musicals with music that MTV ears will accept. (Larson papers, 1984)

JL: My goal as a lyricist-composer is to take the best aspects of traditional American musicals—well-made plot, three-dimensional characters, sense of humor, and integrated choreography—and combine them with current themes, aesthetics and music. I believe theatre should (and could) again be a source of pop music, which would attract a new audience. Generally, my music is contemporary, yet I take a more theatrically conservative approach with my lyrics. I've found it tricky, but not impossible, to advance the plot and theme lyrically on top of a happening beat. (Grant application, September 1989)

JL: I write for the twenty- to forty-year-old audience. People who don't usually attend musicals yet spend money on Eric Bogosian or the Rolling Stones. I've studied the traditional form—(I've won the Richard Rodgers and Stephen Sondheim Awards)—but grew up listening to Springsteen, Paul Simon and The Who, and my music reflects that. (Pitch letter, February 1992)

JL: I've created a lot of work in a relatively brief amount of time, while waiting tables. My immediate short-term goal is to keep doing what I've been doing for the past eight years, only without having to worry about money. I think ultimately my work can make a lot of money and I'm not afraid of that. I want that. But I'm not interested in using my talents strictly to make a buck. My primary goal is, with integrity and class, to fulfill my artistic talents. (Larson papers, My Goals, April 1994)

Many of Scott Gordon's questions had to do with the differences between a Broadway production and an off-Broadway one. Concluding that discussion, Larson expressed his concern about the state of American theatre, explaining that money is one of the major factors in what gets produced and, hence, what gets written.

JL: It's mostly financial. . . . If you have a play like *Glass Menagerie,* you have five characters and one set. And that's a pretty basic little cost.

But if you have a musical off-Broadway, you have ten or fifteen cast members, maybe a choreographer, you have a band of some kind that you have to pay. The expenses just quadruple doing a musical. . . . It's gotten to a point where the American Musical is sort of an endangered species, because it's such a gamble to produce. If you're young and just starting out writing a musical—it's almost impossible to break in.

In the old days, twenty-five Broadway musicals were produced a season. Some of them were bombs and some of them were hits, but it wasn't as big a gamble, it wasn't as costly. Now you maybe have six musicals a year produced. And they're huge productions like *Sunset Boulevard*—where having a movie star like Glenn Close in the cast is the only way that producers can guarantee that they'll get enough people to spend $75 on a ticket. Or they do a show like *Beauty and the Beast,* which already was a movie that sold millions and millions of dollars in videos, so it's a sure thing. Or you have revivals. . . . But if I have my say, as a young writer who writes in rock-and-roll mode, I say that the walls are going to have to come tumbling down and they're going to let new talent in, because people are getting tired of the same old thing. (Gordon 1995)

Note
Quotations from Jonathan Larson's working notes, scripts, lyrics, and letters appear with kind permission of Unky's Music and the Larson family. Interview with Scott Gordon reprinted with the permission of Scott Gordon.

Works Cited
Gordon, Scott. 1995. Interview by author, November.
Istel, John. 1995. Rescuing the Musical. *The Village Voice,* 4 July, 73–74.
Istel, John. 1996. Interview with Jonathan Larson. *American Theatre*, July/August, 13–17.
Singer, Barry. 1993. Interview by author, March.

SEDUCING THE AUDIENCE: POLITICS IN THE PLAYS OF PAULA VOGEL

Ann Linden

I remain scared of the dark—scared of our darkness—and I seek a communal light in the darkness of our theatres.

—Paula Vogel, preface to *Hot 'N' Throbbing*

Paula Vogel was introduced to the theatre at an early age, attending her first theatrical production through an elementary school field trip to the National Theatre in Washington, D.C. What she remembers most vividly about the experience was watching her male classmates ogle the lead actor's cleavage from the upper balcony. "I think I knew even then," she recalls, "that theatre had to be seductive in order to work" (Vogel 1999, 267). Vogel capitalizes on this early recognition of the seductive potential of performance in her own work: "I want to *seduce* the audience. If they can go along for a ride they wouldn't ordinarily take, or don't even know they are taking, then they might see highly charged political issues in a new and unexpected way" (quoted in Drukman 1997, 6). Vogel seduces her spectators to go along for a ride that often takes them over previously uncharted terrain through her unconventional dramaturgy and provocative subject matter. Vogel herself seemed to find the world of theatre seductive, particularly as she became aware of her double marginalization as both a woman and a lesbian in the 1960s. Born in 1951, Vogel grew up in the Washington, D.C. area. At the age of five, she "fell in love with" Mary Martin's performance of Peter Pan (Vogel 1999, 268). Finding characters for women "extremely flat" in the plays she saw in the 1950s and 1960s, Vogel continued to gravitate towards musical theatre because she found it to be "a very female centered form" (268). In her sophomore year of high school, Vogel "stumbled into a drama class" and began to get involved with her school's productions (267). She also recognized that she was attracted to women in high school and recalls the struggle of figuring out where she fit in. After having her first affair with a woman during her senior year, Vogel knew that she would never choose to relinquish the gay lifestyle, even though she knew she would have to alter other aspects of her life. As she explains in an interview with David Savran:

> At that point I was a good public speaker. I was class president but I suddenly became aware that if I went in the track of law school and politics, my sexuality could not be hidden, which was unthinkable during the sixties. I realized immediately in my first moment in bed with another young girl, "I can never stop doing this. I can never not have this be a part of my life." And I immediately said, "Good-bye politics, good-bye being a public servant." (Vogel 1999, 268)

Vogel decided to put her energies into theatre because it seemed to offer her "a spectrum of possibilities in terms of gender" and "was a home that could include [her] sexuality" (Vogel 1999, 268–69). She tried acting in high school, but stopped in part because she was "petrified of exposing [her] own body" (267). She considered directing, but her awareness of the gender politics and discrimination of the time discouraged this path. "Directing," she explains, "seemed to be the province of straight men— prescribing the roles that everybody else played" (269). Finally, she tried her hand at stage management, discovering that "for gay women, tech theatre was perfect—you were out of sight, you could watch everything" (269). The comprehensive knowledge of all aspects of theatrical production Vogel gained through these high school experiences is evident in her plays, which she began writing in college.

Encouraged by her brother Carl to apply for college despite their family's lack of economic means, Vogel received a scholarship to Bryn Mawr, where she wrote her first play, a musical version of *The Hunchback of Notre Dame* (Rosenfeld 1999, G1). After two years at Bryn Mawr, Vogel transferred to Catholic University, where she continued to write, though she again recognized a lack of gender equality in the discipline: "More and more I thought maybe I could write, but I didn't know any women writers" (Vogel 1999, 269). Despite the lack of role models in the curriculum of the late 1960s and early 1970s, Vogel hoped to persevere with her writing. She applied to the Yale School of Drama, the only graduate playwriting program she knew of, but was turned down. She frequently mentions this rejection, noting with irony that she was turned down in the same year that Christopher Durang and Wendy Wasserstein were accepted. Vogel cites this as yet another instance of feeling like an outsider: "I've charted the impact that being admitted to Yale has had in people's lives, and it seemed in one more way I was outside the club when Yale turned me down" (269).

Despite the Yale rejection, Vogel did not give up her writing. She applied to and was accepted by the Ph.D. program at Cornell University. She admits, "I pretty much used Cornell as a backdrop to continue playwriting and try to figure out how to do it my own way and teach myself a method" (Vogel 1999, 269). In retrospect, Vogel sees her early struggles to be instrumental in developing the writing process she still uses today:

> I've been very lucky. I didn't come from a family with trust funds. I was lucky in that. I was also lucky that I wasn't accepted into Yale School of Drama. All along, I knew there was not family money and that I knew no one in the arts. If I was to make it in this world, I would have to do the writing on top of at least forty hours a week or more of work. In my 20s and early 30s, when I was struggling in New York, I was working sixty hours a week and writing plays. No one in my circle of friends was being produced, so we all got together as a group. . . . We dared each other to write a play in 48 hours, then in a week or two, because theater is a time-oriented form. ("Coast to Coast" 1999)

Vogel continues to write the first draft of her plays in a matter of a few weeks. The first draft of *How I Learned to Drive*, for instance, was written in two weeks. While her plays then typically go through numerous rewrites (*The Mineola Twins* went through nearly twenty drafts), Vogel finds that the "rush to get to the end gives the play energy" ("Coast to Coast" 1999).

Vogel acknowledges that her personal experiences play a role in the content of her work as well as in her writing process: "I'm using sides of my history, of my own life, in order to enter a subject" (Vogel 1999, 278).

However, there is rarely the direct correlation between her life and her plays that is characteristic of traditionally autobiographical works. Instead, as Vogel explains, "I use the actual relationships between my self and the material. But it's translated, it's not direct" (279). Vogel often translates these autobiographical impulses into political explorations intended to provoke a dialogue between her plays and her audiences:

> In this time of political correctness . . . you have to go against the grain. If the audience [doesn't] embrace both sides of an issue, there can be no real political dialogue. . . . In my sense of political, you can never be politically correct. To be political means to open up a dialogue, not to be "correct." (quoted in Drukman 1997, 6)

She promotes such political dialogues around some of society's most highly charged issues, from pedophilia and domestic violence to sexism and homophobia.

Vogel explores these controversial issues in unconventional ways. She uses a number of theatrical techniques and dramaturgical approaches, many of which are inspired by defamiliarization strategies formulated and practiced by her acknowledged model, Russian formalist Viktor Shklovsky. She often rejects causal, linear structures in favor of episodic, circular forms, juxtaposes visual elements with dialogue rather than aligning them seamlessly, and displaces unified subjects through fragmentary characterizations. By combining the familiar with the unfamiliar and identification with alienation, Vogel encourages her spectators to consider the issues she explores in a new, more critical light. As a discussion of some of her most well known plays will indicate, in Vogel's work no topic is taboo, no formal experiment discounted, and no clear-cut answers are handed out on silver platters.

One of Vogel's earliest published plays, *The Oldest Profession* (1980), reflects three of the common impulses behind Vogel's writing— a response to a personal experience, a desire to experiment with formal elements, and a reconsideration of another (usually male) author's work. Vogel's aunts and her grandmother, who had suffered a heart attack shortly before she started writing the play, inspired the characters in *The Oldest Profession*. First produced as a reading in 1981 by the Hudson Guild in New York and then produced in 1988 by the Theatre Network in Edmonton, Canada, the play features five women between the ages of seventy-two and eighty-three—all of whom have been "working girls" together for decades in the oldest profession.

Vogel states that she wanted to write a play that employed "repetitive form" (quoted in Bigsby 1999, 301). Consequently, each scene takes place on the same sunny park bench, where the old friends and colleagues discuss their lives, loves, and fears. In each scene the content of the conversation invariably features food, money, clients, and security (both economic and emotional). Each of the six scenes ends in a blackout. In all but one instance, when the lights come back up, there is one member missing from the group. One by one, the women pass away until, in the final scene, only one character remains on the bench. The final image of the play describes Vera, the one remaining woman, as sitting "plaintively quiet, at times watching the traffic. But she sits still, looking very frail, and a bit frightened" (Vogel 1996, 172).[1] Although the play ends here, the audience cannot help but assume that the cycle will repeat one last time.

Vogel states that she had David Mamet's *Duck Variations* on her mind when considering both the repetitive structure and the elderly protagonists of *The Oldest Profession*. However, while the political, cultural, and historical significance of Mamet's play is often veiled in his characters' metaphorical contemplations of ducks and their habitats and behaviors, Vogel's characters explicitly engage with the political and social issues of their time. Vogel's opening description of the play's setting reads, "Time and Place: A sunny day shortly after the election of Ronald Reagan in 1980" (130). Throughout the play the characters express a keen awareness of the political climate in which they live. In the first scene, for example, the characters launch into a discussion of Medicare, social security, and free market economy. After a debate on the moral ramifications of accepting governmental "hand outs," one of the characters proclaims, "I wouldn't mind being eligible for a government subsidy each month in recognition of all my years in public service" (135). Through this exchange, as through many others in *The Oldest Profession*, Vogel foregrounds the ways in which her characters' ages, gender, and professional/social status position them as outsiders √ within the socially and fiscally conservative new administration.

Personal experience, politics, and the influence of another playwright also feature in Vogel's next play, *And Baby Makes Seven* (1984), first produced in 1984 by Theatre with Teeth at the 18th Street Playhouse in New

York (directed by Vogel) and later staged by Circle Repertory Company in 1993. In an interview in the gay/lesbian publication, *Advocate*, Vogel explains that *And Baby Makes Seven* was inspired in part by her own childlessness: "I wanted to have children badly. That's why *And Baby Makes Seven* was written. I went through planning having a baby with my best friend and my lover at the time, and when it fell through I wrote this play" ("Role Models" 1999, 43). The play chronicles the increasingly anxious lives of two lesbian partners, Ruth and Anna, and Peter, the gay male father of their child, through the final months of Anna's pregnancy and the first months of their parenthood. We see them going through what Vogel describes as "that kind of insane crisis period just before you have a child, when you know that your entire life will change but you're not sure how" (quoted in Bigsby 1999, 304). Also active in the family dynamics are Ruth and Anna's three imaginary sons: Cecil, a precocious nine-year-old prodigy (played by Anna); Henri, a sensitive French boy of eight inspired by the protagonist of *The Red Balloon* (played by Ruth); and Orphan, a stuttering wild child raised by dogs and rescued from behind the Greyhound bus station (also played by Ruth).

The imaginary children were, as Vogel admits, inspired in part by George and Martha's imaginary son in Edward Albee's *Who's Afraid of Virginia Woolf?* In *And Baby Makes Seven*, however, the children, whom Ruth and Anna actually enact, are an integral part of the on-stage action. The partners slip in and out of character effortlessly, and the boys' presence adds a level of fantasy and play to the family's life. Furthermore, in contrast to the dark, biting humor of Albee's play, the humor in *And Baby Makes Seven* is light and at times even slapstick. In one scene, for example, Henri and Orphan, both played by Ruth, get into a fight over a peanut butter sandwich that culminates in Ruth's hand conducting "*a Dr. Strangelovian battle with her other hand, fighting for possession of the peanut butter and jelly*" (81).

As in *Virginia Woolf*, the deaths of the imaginary sons feature prominently in *And Baby Makes Seven*. But unlike in Albee's play, their eventual "murder" is not a retaliatory act perpetrated by one partner upon the other in a moment of passionate frustration. Instead, instigated by Peter's unease over his sense that the line between fantasy and reality is "getting dangerously thin" (70), the deaths in *And Baby Makes Seven* are the result of a mutually agreed upon decision between the three characters. Furthermore, the deaths of the children in *And Baby Makes Seven*, unlike the shocking trauma of the son's death in *Virginia Woolf*, are almost whimsical in their fittingness. Orphan, the first to go, succumbs to rabies. Henri, like his film counterpart, is carried away by a flock of red balloons. Cecil, in a fittingly noble act, "runs his sword" while reciting lines from *Julius Caesar*. Ruth, the most reluctant of the partners to give up the children, devises the detailed scenarios for their deaths because she wants to get her "last inch of fantasy out of them," underscoring the centrality of fantasy in the family's dynamics (84).

Whereas Albee's play ends after the characters have stripped away the layers of fantasy and illusion with which they have surrounded themselves, Vogel's characters ultimately acknowledge and accept the pleasure that fantasy and play can provide. The play's penultimate scene is set shortly after the birth of their real son, Nathan, and takes place in the kitchen as Ruth, Anna, and Peter prepare for dinner. Now that they no longer have the imaginary children in their home, the discussion of the three adults reverts to the various events of their day, from car mechanics and incompetent bosses to dirty diapers and Xerox machines. Peter becomes increasingly agitated during the recital of mundane minutiae until, finally, he "falls from the chair and rolls on the floor" screaming, "Orphan! Revenge! Oorrrppphannnn!" (121). Peter has come to realize the allure of fantasy and revives the three children, highlighting the idea that fantasy and reality can coexist productively. In fact, this coexistence is what also grounds the structure of the play. The free play of fantasy in which the characters engage creates a fluid sense of characterization and a constant fluctuation between fantasy and reality.

The final scene of *And Baby Makes Seven* crystallizes the larger social issues raised by Vogel's representation of a nontraditional family structure. As Peter plays with Nathan, Anna and Ruth join them, and the lights begin to change. As they do, "The walls become more transparent, and we become aware of the sounds in the street below: New York City at night" (125). The final stage direction reads: "We see Peter, Anna and Ruth cradling Nathan in their apartment—one apartment among hundreds of their neighbors. The lights stream from adjacent windows where other families in privacy keep their own nightly vigils" (125).

As the boundaries of the play's environment expand, so, too, Vogel hopes, will spectators "expand the boundaries of what [they] think parenting is" (quoted in Bigsby 1999, 305). "We're not," Vogel noted at the time of the play's original production, "happy little nuclear families with two children and Mummy and Daddy. We're not pretending that we're perfect American sitcoms. But we're all anomalies at this point; we're all exceptions to the rule" (297). Vogel hopes that by staging experiences that many people share, but by representing those experiences through characters that many people believe to be very different from themselves, spectators may "feel a sense of inclusion when they leave the theatre" (305).

Desdemona: A Play about a Handkerchief (1986) was given its first staged reading under Vogel's direction at Cornell in 1977. It was first professionally coproduced by Circle Repertory Theatre and Bay Street Theatre Festival in Sag Harbor, New York in 1993. In this early piece, Vogel's experiments with form and content are again inspired by her reactions to other writers' works as well as contemporary cultural attitudes. Vogel's notes to the published play acknowledge that "*Desdemona* was written as a tribute (i.e., 'ripoff') to the infamous play, *Shakespeare the Sadist* by Wolfgang Bauer" (176). Bauer's play is divided into "takes" separated by blackouts and featuring cinematic devices such as film music, slides of studio trademark symbols, and slow and accelerated motion (Bigsby 1999, 298). While Vogel stipulates that blackouts should not be used between scenes, she does describe *Desdemona* as being "written in thirty cinematic takes" and her production notes encourage directors to "create different pictures to simulate the process of filming: Change invisible camera angles, do jump cuts and repetitions, etc." (176). Accordingly, a number of the play's thirty scenes contain no dialogue. Instead, they resemble screenplay-style stage directions, using the minor changes in a series of scenes to denote the passage of time. But while Vogel's play relies on a cinematic structure and style, it does not, as Christopher Bigsby (1999) noted, feature characters whose "imagination has been commandeered by screen images and whose language has been infiltrated by the language of cinema" as does Bauer's play (299). Instead, Vogel contrasts her characters' language and attitudes with her play's structure as a defamiliarization strategy, which she uses to foreground constructions of gender and processes of identification.

The content of *Desdemona* seems to owe more to Shakespeare than to Bauer. Bauer's play features a Swedish pornography star, who identifies himself as Shakespeare, as its protagonist. Pornographic film images (depicting incidents such as rape, torture, and decapitation) are reenacted and referred to throughout the play (Bigsby 1999, 298). While Vogel's play certainly contains sexual undertones, it lacks "the aggressive and literal nature of the violence and sexuality of Bauer's play" (299).

Nonetheless, Vogel includes a take she entitles "the beating scene," in which Bianca, a prostitute, instructs Desdemona on the fine art of "fakement" (211). Highlighting the constructed nature of the sexual fantasies in which the women engage, Bianca first shows Desdemona how to raise and lower her "tail" so that the impact of the blows appears harder than it actually is, much like in stunt fighting. Next, Bianca directs Desdemona to add sound effects. They then put all the elements together, building to a climax in which Desdemona breaks into "peals of laughter" (211–12). Unlike the more realistic sadism in Bauer's play, Vogel portrays the women in control of their sexual fantasies by placing them in the subject rather than object position.

It is this notion of women as subjects of identification that most directly connects Vogel's inspiration for this play to Shakespeare. She has declared that the identificatory processes aroused by her own early readings of *Othello* disturbed her:

> In the 1970s, when I had read *Othello*, I was struck by the fact that my main point of identification, of subjectivity, was a man who is supposedly cuckolded, that I was weeping for a man who is cuckolded rather than for Desdemona. And, of course, at that point in the seventies, in terms of women's studies, there was all the virgin/whore analysis coming out, and it wounded me a great deal that Desdemona is nothing but an abstraction and that I didn't find any way of identifying with her. (quoted in Bigsby 1999, 299–300)

Vogel draws on the storyline and characters of *Othello*, but rather than focus on the dilemmas of a Venetian General and his evil antagonist, Vogel places their wives, Desdemona and Emelia, center stage. The third character rounding out the all-female cast list is Bianca, playing a brothel owner for whom Desdemona occasionally fills in to give Bianca a night out with Cassio. Vogel troubles the traditional virgin/whore binary by blurring the distinction between the virtuous Desdemona and promiscuous Bianca of Shakespeare's play. Furthermore, rather than portraying these characters as abstractions or extensions of their husbands or lovers, Vogel highlights issues of importance to the women of the play, including sexual subjectivity, domestic violence, and economic dependence.

While *Desdemona* reveals Vogel's reactions to other playwrights' works, her first play to earn widespread acclaim, *The Baltimore Waltz* (1992), reflects her response to a personal loss, the death of her brother Carl. She began writing the play in her head in the hospital waiting room when she was visiting Carl during what would be his final hospital stay before he died from AIDS complications. "It was a survival technique," she explains. "One time he smiled at me and said, 'You're writing about this, aren't you?' I denied it, but I could never hide anything from him" (quoted in Hughes 1998, 99). Completed a year and a half after his death, she dedicated the play "to the memory of Carl—because," as she added, "I cannot sew" (3).

In the published version of *Baltimore Waltz*, Vogel includes the text of a letter Carl sent her before his death in January 1988. She encourages productions to reprint the letter in their program notes: "I would appreciate letting him speak in his own words" (4). Written with humor and poignancy that seem to be shared sibling traits, Carl explains the purpose of the letter in its opening:

> I thought I would jot down some of my thoughts about the (shall we say) production values of my ceremony. Oh God—I can hear you groaning—everybody wants to direct. Well, I want a good show, even though my role has been reduced involuntarily from player to prop. (4)

He goes on to outline his memorial requests, spanning the spectrum from "prayers that give thanks to the Creator for the gift of life and the hope of reunion" to the possibility of an "open casket, bum up," with the parenthetical note, "You'll know where to place the calla lilies, won't you?" (5). His music choices, too, run the gamut from Gluck's "Dance of the Blessed Spirits" to "I Dream of Jeannie" or Jeneatte MacDonald's rendition of "Nearer My God to Thee" (5). The eclectic combination of requests in Carl's letter is echoed in the juxtaposition of elements and images in Vogel's play.

Vogel describes *Baltimore Waltz* as "a journey with Carl to a Europe that exists only in the imagination" (4). From the moment the play opens, the suggestion of an alternative reality is apparent. Vogel's stage directions recommend the lighting be "highly stylized, lush, dark and imaginative" and that Anna, Carl's sister, be costumed in a negligee and trench coat and Carl in flannel pajamas and a blazer (6). The play's one other character, the Third Man/Doctor, plays over twelve minor roles. The Europe through which Carl and Anna travel is also filled with imaginative images: the Little Dutch Boy at age fifty (still sporting a Buster Brown haircut and oversized wooden shoes), who now makes money off the lustful fantasies of female tourists; clandestine meetings held on ferris wheels to negotiate over stuffed rabbits; and mad scientists wearing fright wigs and compulsively drinking urine. The imaginary journey of the play is connected to an actual travel invitation Vogel's brother extended to her in 1986. She explains in her notes to the published play that "due to pressures of time and money," she declined Carl's invitation to go to Europe with him, "never dreaming that he was HIV positive" (4).

Essentially the story of *Baltimore Waltz* revolves around siblings, Carl and Anna, who travel to Europe in search of a black market treatment for Anna's AIDS-like illness, Acquired Toilet Disease (ATD), contracted by sitting on public toilets. But in the final scene of the play, harsh white lights come up on Anna in a hospital waiting room receiving the news that Carl has just died of pneumonia. When the doctor brings Anna her brother's belongings, consisting of his childhood stuffed rabbit and some European travel brochures, it becomes clear that the journey of the play to this moment has taken place in Anna's imagination, and it is actually Carl, not Anna, who has been ill.

Although Vogel defines *Baltimore Waltz* less as a play about AIDS than as "a way of talking to [her] dead brother, being able to spend time with him" (Vogel 1997, 24), ATD is clearly paralleled to AIDS, as are the discriminatory attitudes circulating in the discourse regarding the disease. The high-risk group for ATD includes "single elementary school teachers, classroom aides, custodians and playground drug pushers" (18). Vogel may have chosen this selection of categories as an ironic gesture toward the rage she has said she feels whenever she hears the phrase "innocent victim" in association with HIV/AIDS, which for her implies that some people acquire the illness innocently while others deserve their fate (Bigsby 1999, 311). Early associations between AIDS and marginalized, often disenfranchised groups such as gay men, intravenous drug users, and prostitutes were considered by many to be major factors in the societal apathy towards AIDS-related issues. In the third scene of the play, Carl gives voice to the frustration and anger generated by such apathy:

> If Sandra Day O'Connor sat on just one infected potty, the media would be clamoring to do articles on ATD. If just one grandchild of George Bush caught this thing during toilet training, that would be the last we'd hear about the space program. Why isn't someone doing something?! (12)

Moments such as these, however, erupt only intermittently throughout *Baltimore Waltz*. This may be due to Vogel's consideration of playwriting as "structuring memory for an audience" (Vogel 1999, 271). She believes that overexposure to an issue often causes people to forget, stop looking at, or take for granted those things that are constantly in plain view. "As cultural animals, we do not forget because something is hidden, we forget because something is in our face and we don't see it anymore" (271). Therefore, direct references to the discriminatory or apathetic attitudes toward HIV/ATD-positive people in *Baltimore Waltz* are infrequent, which causes them to stand out distinctly when they occur.

Vogel also believes that the playwright can encourage spectators to "re-remember" those issues that have lapsed from conscious consideration by foregrounding the process through which overexposure leads to forgetting (or indifference). One distinct strategy by which Vogel attempts to enact this theory in *Baltimore Waltz* is through the use of the latex gloves worn by the Third Man. He is described as wearing them throughout the entire play until, as the Doctor, he peels them off in the final hospital scene. She recalls explaining this choice to Anne Bogart, who directed the premiere New York production of *Baltimore Waltz* at the Circle Repertory Company in 1992.

> I told [her] I wanted the Third Man constantly in latex gloves. And she said, "Isn't that awkward?" And I said, "If he's constantly in latex gloves we will forget that he's wearing them, and people will gasp at the end of the play when he pulls them off. (Vogel 1999, 271)

Through this moment, Vogel not only highlights the dehumanization of medical discourse but also calls attention to the process of forgetting, ideally creating a greater awareness of the process of remembering in her spectators.

The moment of conception for Vogel's next play, *Hot 'N' Throbbing*

(1993), which focuses on domestic violence, occurred in 1985. As she was driving late at night through the streets of Providence, she was struck with a sudden vision of the play's ending. She relates the power of this vision in her author's note: "I knew that I would have to face this play in my future, and that certainly fueled a fear that kept me driving the deserted downtown streets in circles" (229). Although she did not begin researching the play until five years after this sudden vision, the fear that drove her in circles that night in Providence is reflected in both the form and content of the play. She began assembling a file of clippings on incidents of domestic violence reported in the *Providence Journal*, and within less than a year, the file was two inches thick (230). Mirroring the repeated cycle of violence evidenced by these reports, *Hot 'N' Throbbing* uses a circular dramaturgical structure to tell the story of one family's encounter with domestic violence.

Hot 'N' Throbbing features six characters. The Woman, Charlene, left her abusive husband, took custody of their two children, and moved into an "empty nester townhouse." Once a nurse, she now makes her living by writing "women's erotica" and serving as story editor for a "feminist film company." The Man, Clyde, is her abusive ex-husband who, after downing a six-pack and discovering that he does not have enough money to hire a prostitute, ignores a restraining order and breaks into his ex-wife's home on the night the play takes place. Their fifteen-year-old daughter, the Girl (Leslie Ann), and their fourteen-year-old son, the Boy (Calvin), are both shown struggling with their burgeoning sexuality and the influence that living within an abusive atmosphere has had upon them.

The last two characters in the cast are Voice-Over, cast as female, and The Voice, cast as male. Voice-Over is a "sex worker" who narrates the script that the Woman is writing and serves as her "inner voice" (232). The Voice, described as "a presence more than a person" (232), often recites passages from famous literary works and represents a male voice of authority. While these two characters frequently intersect with the action in Charlene's living room, they exist physically in the second of what Vogel delineates as the two worlds of the play: "reality constructed as we know it; and the erotic dance hall, as we fantasize about it" (233).

In the dance hall, however, there are bouncers who maintain the line between fantasy and reality, voyeurism and violence. In the living room, there is no bouncer to protect such distinctions. Charlene, who has shot her husband in the backside after he broke down her door, ends up comforting and nursing him. Ultimately, she is swayed by Clyde's emotional tale of despair at having lost his job and potentially his virility. She tries to boost his sagging ego by enacting a fantasy with him, "just this once" (285). While Charlene is in the bathroom changing clothes, however, Clyde's mood shifts. The Voice-Over implies that he is disturbed by the notion of losing control, letting his wife write the narrative of their romantic encounter. Clyde's final act of regaining control over Charlene results in a highly stylized scene that culminates in Clyde beating and finally strangling Charlene to death while the children watch from the patio doorway.

The final moments of the play expose the cyclical nature of domestic violence. Not only has Clyde exhibited a repetitive pattern of violence and Charlene a repeated willingness to engage with him, but it also seems as if the effects of such dynamics will continue on in the next generation. When the lights come back up after a blackout immediately following Charlene's death, we see the Girl discover her mother's body and then step into a spotlight. "If this were a film script," Vogel's stage directions read, "we would see The Girl age before our eyes, transformed over the years by what she has just seen" (294). Instead, the Girl puts on clothes resembling her mother's, puts on Charlene's glasses, sits down at her mother's computer, and types the lines Charlene was writing at the play's opening. *Hot 'N' Throbbing* ends with a continuation of patterns and with unresolved questions regarding the relationships between sex, violence, love, hate, fantasy, and reality.

While Vogel's sudden vision that night in Providence may have led her to begin writing *Hot 'N' Throbbing*, she credits "Senator Jesse Helms and Congress" as having provided her with the "incentive to finish the play" (230). Vogel is referring, of course, to the so-called Helms amendment, which sought to deny NEA funding to art that, as Helms defined it, "is clearly designed to poison our culture" (quoted in Bolton 1992, 4). For over a year, artists seeking NEA grants were required to sign statements pledging not to produce "obscene" art with public funds (5). "Eager to test the censorship of the NEA pledge," Vogel writes in her author's note, "I applied for an NEA grant, received one and wrote *Hot 'N' Throbbing* to see just what would be perceived as pornographic"

(230). Although Vogel did not encounter censorship problems with the NEA, she met with resistance from many artistic directors, leading her to conclude, "Jesse Helms and the fundamentalist Right are not the greatest threats to the arts community. Rather, it is our own cooperation with the Right within the arts community" (quoted in *Baltimore Waltz* 1996, 230). When Peter Franklin, Vogel's agent, first read *Hot 'N' Throbbing* he predicted that she "may get two productions of this play—one here and one abroad" (230). The play was originally produced by the American Repertory Theatre and directed by Anne Bogart in 1994; more than a year later, this remained one of only two professional productions of the play—the other being that of the Harrogate Theatre in England (230). Vogel considers the stunning accuracy of Franklin's prediction and its reflection of the conservative nature of contemporary mainstream theatre in the final statement of her author's note: "Censorship is alive and well in 1995: a benign censorship, a censorship within. If we cannot confront domestic violence on our stages, we will not be able to eliminate it from our living rooms" (231).

In an interview with Kathy Sova for *American Theatre*, Vogel links *Hot 'N' Throbbing* with the motivation behind writing her next play, *The Mineola Twins* (1995), which premiered at Alaska's Perseverance Theatre under the direction of Vogel's long-time friend and collaborator Molly Smith in 1996. "*The Mineola Twins* was created by me thinking, 'Okay, I wrote *Hot 'N' Throbbing*, it's time for me to laugh" (Vogel 1997, 24). As with *Hot 'N' Throbbing*, however, there was also a political agenda at work in the inspiration behind her construction of the play:

> I have been extremely upset at the Republican right taking over our
> Government. So, I thought, okay, let's go back to the 50s, with its quintes-
> sential combination of comedy and terror. As a culture then, we went into
> science fiction, invaders from Mars, instead of looking at those who were
> invading us from within. There were Communists and queers and also Roy
> Cohn and Joe McCarthy. We used our fear of aliens to mask our terror at
> what was at the heart of America. In terms of theatricality, I chose the
> image of twins that war: Jacob and Esau, a blood hatred between them. It's
> where we are emotionally as a country. (quoted in Witchel 1999, 5)

The Mineola Twins, then, chronicles the personal and political comedies and tragedies of over thirty years in the lives of twin sisters,

Myra and Myrna. Physically, the twins are identical but for one notable exception—Myrna is "stacked"; Myra is lacking "in the chestal area" (Vogel 1998a, 96).[2] In all other aspects, it appears that the two sisters could not be more different.

The subtitle of *The Mineola Twins, A Comedy in Six Scenes, Four Dreams and Six Wigs*, suggests the formal symmetry of the play, which is essentially divided into three acts, each taking place in a different decade. Each act features two scenes and a dream sequence (with the fourth dream sequence concluding the play). The six wigs in the subtitle refer to the symmetrical casting requirements of the play. Myra and Myrna are to be played by the same actor, using, one would assume, padded bras and time-appropriate wigs to delineate the individual sisters. Vogel suggests further double casting, calling for the same actor to play each sister's son and the same actress to play Myrna's fiancé (Jim) and Myra's partner (Sarah).

The play begins in the 1950s, the Eisenhower administration, when the girls are seniors in high school. Myrna, the "good" twin, strives to win the Homemakers of America Senior Award and dreams of her future with her fiancé, Jim. In contrast, the "bad twin," Myra, drives her parents to distraction by sneaking off to Greenwich Village late at night and tries to satisfy herself by sleeping with the first string of varsity athletes. She also ends up sleeping with Myrna's fiancé. The second part of the play takes place during the early days of the Nixon administration in 1969. Still, the twins seem to lead diametrically opposed lives. Myrna has a successful husband and a teenage son. Having spent time in a mental institution, she now fills her days by volunteering for the Nixon for President Campaign and leafleting for "harsh control of subversives" (131). Myra, unlike her sister, remains unmarried with no children. She has gotten involved with a radical peace movement leader and is eventually arrested for having driven the get-away vehicle in a bank robbery her boyfriend supposedly committed as a Vietnam War protest. The last section of the play takes place during the first Bush administration in 1989. Again, we immediately see the disparity between the two sisters' lives. Myrna, now divorced, is involved in right-wing conservative politics including "Right to Life" groups. After being released from prison, Myra has settled into a long-term lesbian relationship with Sarah, has a child, and now runs a Planned Parenthood Clinic.

The sisters' political proclivities ultimately bring them into contact for the first time in twenty years when Myrna, as part of her right-wing organization's "Operation Jane Roe," is sent to bomb Myra's clinic. Myrna believes Myra to be out of town, but after she has planted the bomb, she discovers that Myra has returned early and is actually in her office while the bomb is ticking away. With only seconds left before detonation, Myrna is struck with the desire to protect her sister and runs into the building to save Myra. She succeeds in saving her sister, but loses her own life in the process.

Despite her depiction of their vastly different lifestyles, Vogel also weaves many similarities into the sisters' attitudes and experiences. In the first two scenes of the play, for instance, both sisters turn to Jim for fulfillment and both are met with condemnation from him. When Myrna stops their foreplay because she wants to be a virgin when they marry, he critiques her as a tease; after Myra accepts his advances, he proclaims her a whore. Although they go about it in opposite ways, both women have tried to do what is expected of them in order to gain a man's appreciation and respect, and both have come away disappointed and disillusioned by the essentialist assumptions behind patriarchal prescriptions for "proper" feminine behavior.

The later scenes further reinforce that while the sisters have chosen very different paths through life, they still operate under similar paradigms and experience similar challenges. For instance, the reality of both Myrna's domestic dream and Myra's revolutionary fantasy leaves each woman frustrated and unfulfilled. Furthermore, while both sisters feel trapped in the lifestyles they have individually pursued, they also wind up being complicit in physically constricting each other. Myrna turned Myra into the authorities, an act that resulted in Myra's imprisonment. Myra co-signed the papers that allowed for Myrna's commitment in a mental hospital. Each sister has conspired with institutional powers to entrap the other.

The personal and political differences between Myrna and Myra point to the societal divisions that inspired Vogel to write *The Mineola Twins*. Their similarities (and the formal symmetry of the play), however, represent Vogel's hope that such divisions might be bridged:

> I see *The Mineola Twins* as a way of figuring out how as siblings we don't
> talk to each other. There's a political schizophrenia that's dividing us,

> dividing us in communities, into warring factions, into enraged siblings. To me *The Mineola Twins* is working toward that moment—even if it's only in our dreams—that we'll talk to each other, that we won't be divided anymore. (Vogel 1997, 24)

Vogel highlights the connections between the two sisters, who at first appear to have little in common. By doing so she exposes the sexist, exclusionary ideology underpinning both conservative and liberal politics and encourages spectators to reexamine the divisions between both ends of the political spectrum.

Critics frequently summarize Vogel's next play, the Pulitzer Prize–winning *How I Learned to Drive* (1997), as a drama about pedophilia. Vogel rebukes this notion, stating, "This play is not a celebration of pedophilia. As a matter of fact, pedophilia is not even a way I would be thinking of this. This is a gentle plot compared to the extremities of reality around us" (Vogel 1998b, 13). First produced in 1997 by Vineyard Theatre in New York, *How I Learned to Drive* focuses on the complex relationship between Li'l Bit and her Uncle Peck. Arranged in nonchronological order, the play concentrates on pivotal moments in their relationship from the time he makes his first sexual advance towards her when she is eleven years old through her reflections of their relationship over twenty years later. The play also features three Greek Chorus members (Male, Female, and Teenage Greek Chorus) who portray various family members, friends, waiters, and others.

The relationship between Peck and Li'l Bit goes beyond that of abuser/victim. Li'l Bit is drawn to Peck, for instance, because he treats her differently than her family and peers. He acknowledges her intelligence and abilities and often intercedes on Li'l Bit's behalf in family squabbles. Although he clearly crosses over critical boundaries with her, Peck's affection and respect for his niece are portrayed as genuine. Nonetheless, while Peck recognizes and nurtures Li'l Bit's potential, he also triggers many of her struggles as she grows older, including a heightened degree of self-consciousness and a problem with alcohol. Li'l Bit has her final meeting with Peck on her eighteenth birthday, when she rejects his marriage proposal and informs the audience that afterwards Peck slowly drank himself to death.

Although she marks the day on which she was first molested by

Peck as the "last day [she] lived in [her] body," the final moments of the play (set in the present) confirm that Li'l Bit has moved on: ✓

> And now that seems like a long, long time ago. When we were both very young. And before you know it, I'll be thirty-five. That's getting up there for a woman. And I find myself believing in things that a younger self vowed never to believe in. Things like family and forgiveness. I know I'm lucky. (91)

The final image of the play confirms that Li'l Bit has managed to find forgiveness for Peck. As she prepares to go for a drive, she adjusts her rearview mirror, sees "the spirit of Uncle Peck" in the back seat, and smiles at him as she slips the car into first gear and drives off (92).

Vogel does not dismiss the very real trauma of pedophilia, but she sees the central journey of *How I Learned to Drive* as focused on Li'l Bit's ability and responsibility "to look the experience squarely in the eye and then to move on" (quoted in Bigsby 1999, 328). The ending of the play confirms that while Li'l Bit was certainly a victim, she is also a survivor. In part, this ending was motivated by the responses of some of Vogel's playwriting students at Brown to the ending of *Hot 'N' Throbbing*: "[They] found the play very painful because it said there was no way out" (quoted in Bigsby 1999, 316). The agency that allows Li'l Bit to move on at the end of *How I Learned to Drive* signifies Vogel's desire to create a more hopeful alternative for her protagonist and her audiences:

> I am paying more attention these days to endings. The fact that Peck doesn't get out of it doesn't mean that she doesn't. I think that the ending of *How I Learned to Drive* came very much as a response to some of my students being crushed by the ending of *Hot 'N' Throbbing*. *How I Learned to Drive* was a response to this young woman who just sat and cried in my office. (quoted in Bigsby 1999, 327)

While there is a "way out" in *How I Learned to Drive*, it is not the sort of "happy ending" one might expect of a more traditional treatment of such a sensitive issue. Vogel has said that she had "no interest in a movie-of-the-week drama about child molesting" (quoted in Drukman 1997, 6). One of the ways she avoids sensationalizing the issue is through her nonrealistic staging of the molestation scenes. In the first such scene, for instance, the stage directions indicate that the actors playing Peck and Li'l Bit "sit facing directly front. They do not touch. Their bodies remain passive. Only their facial expressions emote" (8). From this scene, the action moves back and forth in time, revealing bit by bit the complexities of the relationship between Peck and Li'l Bit. Although Peck frequently manipulates Li'l Bit, no other scene portrays explicit physical "contact" between them until the next to last scene. It is here, in one of the most painful and condemning moments of the play, that the audience learns that Peck first molested Li'l Bit when she was only eleven. In this scene the two actors do touch, but Li'l Bit's words are spoken by the Teenage Greek Chorus member who "stands apart on the stage" (88). Vogel, significantly, places this scene after the audience has witnessed the nuances of the characters' relationship, both the trauma and the tenderness, and after they are assured that Li'l Bit finally broke away from Peck and moved on. This structure deflates the sensationalism that would likely have ensued had this scene been enacted in the early moments of the play. Feminist critic Jill Dolan (1998) astutely contends that "Vogel's choice to remember Li'l Bit and Peck's relationship non-chronologically illustrates its complexity, and allows the playwright to build sympathy for a man who might otherwise be despised and dismissed as a child molester" (127).

That Peck is neither despised nor dismissed is crucial in achieving the sort of empathetic response Vogel strives for in *How I Learned to Drive*. Fascinated by Humbert Humbert in Vladimir Nabokov's *Lolita* and the fact that "the eroticizing of children is so prevalent in the culture yet so seldom acknowledged," Vogel carefully structures her play "to see if audiences will allow themselves to find this erotic; otherwise, they only see victimization without empowerment" (quoted in Drukman 1997, 6). If Vogel can seduce spectators into empathizing with both Peck and Li'l Bit, they can no longer easily deny the contradictions between representations that promote Peck's desire and public discourse that condemns his actions.

This empathy is crucial, Vogel contends, because "we're trained to be pedophiles in this culture; look at the messages we're receiving. It's all around us" (Vogel 1998b, 13). Vogel explicitly foregrounds the pervasiveness of such messages through the music and images inserted into the play. Her production notes recommend the use of sixties music "rife with pedophilish (?) reference: the 'You're Sixteen' genre hits" (5). Vogel also recommends the use of slides depicting advertising and media images of girls and young women: "models à la *Playboy*, Calvin Klein, and Victoriana/Lewis Carroll's Alice Liddell" (62). By combining these familiar songs and images with an unconventional dramaturgical style, Vogel provides something other than a sentimental, psychological portrayal of a troubled relationship. Instead, her character delineations, nonrealistic dramaturgy, and use of pop cultural references both encourage identification in her spectators and provide a critique of a society that perpetuates the objectification and sexualization of girls and women.

How I Learned to Drive was well received by the American theatre. Although Vogel admits that she "never thought the play would be produced" (quoted in Hughes 1998, 99) it was the most-produced new play in 1998, with twenty-six regional productions. It went on to receive the New York Critic's Circle Best Play Award and the Obie Award for Playwriting as well as the Pulitzer Prize.

Not all of Vogel's work has been met with such appreciation, however. Her untraditional subject matter, nonrealistic structure, and provocative political implications have repeatedly led artistic directors to reject Vogel's plays. Nonetheless, Vogel remains an outspoken advocate of the theatre as a cultural and political institution. While she is "not worried about the theatre dying" (Vogel 1999, 285), she is concerned about the state of commercial theatre and its ability and willingness to grapple with difficult issues in provocative ways, as she describes in her preface to *Hot 'N' Throbbing*:

> For some time now many theatres have been choosing their seasons from fear rather than conviction. We have quietly, silently, drifted to the Right in our seasonal offerings of benign and often vacuous theatre. . . . I worry that there is no longer a place for audiences to come to a civic space—the theatre—to confront the disturbing questions of our time. I remain scared of the dark—scared of our darkness—and I seek a communal light in the darkness of our theatres. (230–31)

In spite of the dwindling arts funding that compels many theatres to abandon risky political agendas in favor of high-grossing entertainment values when determining their seasons, Vogel remains committed to creating theatre that "confronts the disturbing questions of our time" and provokes political dialogue. Through her endeavors, she kindles the flame of theatre's potential to serve as a political forum and to function as a civic space.

Notes

1. All subsequent references to *The Oldest Profession, And Baby Makes Seven, Desdemona, The Baltimore Waltz,* and *Hot 'N' Throbbing* are from this volume.
2. All subsequent references to *The Mineola Twins* and *How I Learned to Drive* are from this volume.

Works Cited

Bigsby, Christopher. 1999. *Contemporary American Playwrights.* Cambridge, UK: Cambridge University Press.

Bolton, Richard, ed. 1992. *Culture Wars: Documents from Recent Controversies in the Arts.* New York: New Press.

Coast to Coast with Paula Vogel. 1999. *The Dramatist,* 1.6 (July/August). Retrieved 10 January 2000 from http://www.dramaguild.com/docs/vogart.htm.

Dolan, Jill. 1998. Review of *How I Learned to Drive,* by Paula Vogel. Vineyard Theatre, New York. *Theatre Journal,* 50.1, 127–8.

Drukman, Steven. 1997. A Playwright on the Edge Turns Toward the Middle. *New York Times* 16 March, late ed., sec. 2, 6.

Hughes, Holly. 1998. In the Driver's Seat. *Advocate,* 20 January, 99.

Role Models. 1999. *Advocate,* 2 February, 42–46.

Rosenfeld, Megan. 1999. One "Hot" Property: For Playwright Paula Vogel, a Well-Rewarded Stage in Life. *Washington Post,* 12 September, G1.

Vogel, Paula. 1996. *Baltimore Waltz and Other Plays.* New York: Theatre Communications Group.

———. 1997. Time to Laugh. Interview with Kathy Sova. *American Theatre,* 14.2 (February), 24.

———. 1998a. *The Mammary Plays: How I Learned to Drive, The Mineola Twins.* New York: Theatre Communications Group.

———. 1998b. The Week in Review: Interview: Paula Vogel. Interview with Matt Wolf. *The Observer,* 21 June, 13.

———. 1999. Interview. In *The Playwright's Voice: American Dramatists on Memory, Writing and the Politics of Culture,* ed. David Savran. New York: Theatre Communications Group.

Witchel, Alex. 1999. After the Prize is the Pressure: Now What?" *New York Times,* 7 February, late ed., sec. 2, 5.

INTERVIEW WITH PAULA VOGEL

Interview conducted by Ann Linden
in March 2001

Ann Linden: I know you've written for other media, but the bulk of your writing has been for the theatre. I wonder if you could say a little bit about why you choose to write primarily for the stage.

Paula Vogel: I have to say that, so far, nothing that I've written has excited me so much as the process of the stage. I actually think of writing for the stage as *not* writing. I think one writes fiction or poems, but playwriting is really about not writing. It's about structuring, about gaps between the language that are really filled in by the collaborators and the process. It's all about indirection rather than a direct statement. It's about not writing. It's about the silence and about what is not said as much as anything on the page. It's a very hard process because to be a playwright is as much an act of diplomacy as it is writing. One of the interesting thoughts about this is, how do you get such a thing as intention followed if it's about indirection, if it's about not writing, if it's about the gaps between the lines? However, then, would a playwright's intention come across on the stage? It's like a three-dimensional chess game in a way. If I say this, will the director go in this direction? If I say this, will the actor respond? And one of the delights of the process is actually *not* having your intention fulfilled, but finding out at times that other people's interpretation or intention is actually much more interesting than what you originally thought of.

AL: You've recently written for Showtime and HBO, yet you've often spoken about the limitations of a Hollywood model of production, in terms of its adherence to the well-made play structure, its exclusion of the writer from the process, etc. How were your experiences with these cable projects?

PV: Well, note that I've been working on an independent or cable model. I haven't done studio pictures, which is not to say that I won't. The economic reality is that either one teaches or one writes for other media in order to stay in theatre. That's just the reality. I have to say, though, that so far my limited experience with this smaller filmmaking—or whatever you want to call cable—has been very, very good. I've been treated well. I've been treated intelligently.

AL: Have you had an active part in the process?

PV: I haven't been allowed an active part in the process in all things—it's not my right to cast or choose directors—but there is input. It's not as bad as I thought. I'm also learning some positive things from the film experience, which is how to write economically, just paying attention to craft, how to move with as much urgency as possible. Things that I believe should apply to theatre as well. I'm looking to subsidize my theatre craft. I'm not looking to get rich. I'm enjoying what I'm doing, and when I don't enjoy it any more I won't do it any more.

AL: In adapting *How I Learned to Drive* from stage to screen, did you have to make a lot of changes, and, if so, were those changes motivated by the medium, the producers?

PV: No, not many changes. Some changes in terms of time. I'd already said all the things I wanted to say in the theatre version, so I wanted to say all the things I couldn't say on the stage by using the camera in a different way. I actually was a little more ruthless in terms of "opening it up" than possibly other writers might have been in adapting it. So, no I haven't felt any stultification that way. It's been remarkably pleasant. I don't know that I would ever want to adapt my own work again in the future. I really want to move on to something new.

AL: Such as writing more scripts originally intended for film or television?

PV: Exactly. Or adapting someone else's work. Or adapting some other genre to the medium. This is much more interesting to me right now.

AL: All of your plays deal on some level with controversial or sensitive issues, but they are also very sophisticated formally, whether you're experimenting with repetition (*The Oldest Profession*) or circularity (*Baltimore Waltz*) or episodic structures (*The Mineola Twins*). I'm wondering how you see form and content working together? Do you think a certain topic requires a certain form or vice versa?

PV: I think that form *is* content. I always have thought that form was content. I've always been more interested, actually, in the formal devices and the structure than in the subject matter, which may seem heretical. But I really am a follower of Viktor Shklovsky, who said that in some ways the subject matter doesn't even matter. It's whether or not we see the subject matter anew that matters.

AL: So in your writing process can you even separate the two? Do you, for instance, generally start with either the idea for a formal experiment or a certain topic?

PV: I interpolate Kenneth Burke and Bert States when I'm teaching, and I concentrate on six different basic plot forms, not that there's any such thing as pure form. But occasionally I'll think, "You know, Vogel, it's been a long time since you've done something linear" or "It's been a long time since you've done something that's kind of epic in form, not in content." And I'll think about that, but in general, something comes to me really as an image. I was always fascinated to hear that Irene Fornes and Sam Shepard work that way as well. An image comes, a moment, and I either work forwards or backwards from that moment. And I think about, what is the best structure to tell this? Very early on I knew I was going to work backwards on *How I Learned to Drive*. Very early on I knew I was going to work in epic form for *Mineola Twins*. I knew that *Baltimore Waltz* was going to be "An Occurrence at Owl Creek Bridge" in dramatic form. It's that sort of thing that's part and parcel of it before I even start working.

AL: You've mentioned the influence that Burke, States, and Shklovsky have had on your work. Are there any feminist theorists or feminist debates that have impacted your work?

PV: I am a very strong feminist. I've always thought of myself as a feminist. I haven't been embraced by seventies or eighties feminist theatre. And that, particularly when I was younger, was very painful. But I've taught in Women's Studies. The difficulty right now—even though I know that I am postmodern—is that I do not read a great deal of theory at the moment, and I've kept out of poststructuralism. I have not read a great amount of, say, Derrida and Lacan, Cixous, or whatever. I read just the basic minimum. And one of the reasons is that I find it impossible to be conscious about theory and then subconscious about my writing. Younger writers can do it. I've seen them. I've had brilliant plays done at Brown where someone was responding to Foucault. I admire that. I am a formalist, which actually means in many ways that I am modern and not postmodern. I think that one gets to the postmodern by deconstructing the modern. And that's what formalism does. If you follow someone like Kenneth Burke or if you follow the Russian formalists all the way to the letter, they're very much active in deconstruction. I sort of see a play travelling through time as unraveling its own devices. I mean, when I think about Bertolt Brecht and the separation of the elements, I literally see the elements separating in terms of the textual elements. The plot and character aren't doing the same thing. But I don't spend a great deal of time thinking about feminist theory because when I do, I find it impossible to write. It's not that I don't embrace feminist theory—I think we all absorb it through the skin. I've absorbed it through my partner, for example, through the work that she does. I've absorbed it through David Savran. I've absorbed it through my students. But quite frankly, I had to let something go, and I let the scholarship and the theory go.

AL: Given the clear feminist sensibility in your plays, it's somewhat surprising that your work was not embraced by earlier feminist theatre.

PV: Well, back when I was starting with things like *Desdemona*, even *Meg* or *The Oldest Profession*, it was seen as being very antifeminist because it was seen as presenting very negative images of women. Back then, interestingly enough, we weren't talking about class and gender or race and gender. It was very much that kind of new wave, National Organization of Women liberal feminism, and lesbianism was a dirty word. Whether or not it was my being completely out as a lesbian back then, very early on, that did it, or whether it was the fact that I don't see how one can separate gender from race, from economics, from class that caused the difficulty, the difficulty was created. Now I think I'm in that weird position where every playwright kind of writes their own path, and somehow or other I went from staged readings to a couple of small productions to suddenly *How I Learned to Drive*. It took me twenty-two plays, but what I didn't do, simply again I think because of geographic location and actually generation, was that I didn't go to WOW Café and I didn't do P.S. 122. And generationally, I wasn't impacted as much by performance. I think it's fascinating, but I'm coming late into that. It's really a strategy for a younger generation. So I think I'm not part of this new wave, either. I'm seen as more traditionally theatrical, which is true. I work in a theatrical process. I work in more traditional structures. I prefer the structures not to be hierarchical. I prefer to work with theatre companies that aren't. So it's interesting. I guess I've sort of fallen between the different models of what feminist theatre is . . . or queer theatre.

AL: You've spoken before about the challenges women and lesbian theatre artists often face. You, of course, achieved a tremendous amount of success with *How I Learned to Drive*. In fact, it was the most-produced play of 1998 in the U.S. Nonetheless, on the list of the ten most frequently produced plays that season, you were one of only two female playwrights. Do you see things changing for women playwrights?

PV: No, I don't. I see it as enormously difficult. And I see us taking a step back, primarily with George [W.] Bush's election. I see it as a constant struggle. I don't see it getting any better, which distresses me, dismays me. I'm aware that I was possibly the only woman produced in the last couple of years in theatre companies, and that's not a good thing. I have to say that I also feel like I'm back to square one with the next play that I do. I think that by and large women playwrights are not given the same leeway in terms of developing different muscles that, say, the critics may give David Mamet. The ability to produce different styles of plays and have an active film career as he has. I don't know that we're given the same leeway. I think we just have to *take* it.

Women and writers of colors are still seen as threats because in essence, when a woman or a writer of color is defining a play world, there's another definition of what our society is, and that's very threatening. I think it's always going to be very hard won. I'm hoping it changes, but I think what has to happen is that the supply of women writers and writers of color has to increase so that there's a greater demand. I think the supply always comes first. A greater supply means looking at not-for-profit theatres and saying, "How accessible is your stage to the community? How accessible is your stage to younger people? How accessible are our universities and our classrooms? What after-school programs are there?" What we're talking about is a field of theatre that, quite frankly, has been one of the most directly hit by Congress, again because of this potential threat. Theatre does indeed show different visions and versions of what our social reality is. So, you want to limit those, and you want to control them—that is, if you're scared of a transformation of society, as I think many politicians are. I think right now that theatre is a cultural battleground. The only thing I can do—and it's a small thing—is try to concentrate on how I can encourage women writers, writers of color, and White male writers who have something different to say—that is, who could be considered noncommercial, who have a different vision of what the surface reality is. And that's the only thing I can think to do, really. Plus, write the next play.

AL: You just mentioned theatre as a social battleground, and you've often talked about your desire to provoke community dialogue through your plays, particularly a political dialogue. Are there certain strategies you consciously employ to provoke such dialogue?

PV: It's no longer conscious. I've loved so many plays that are peculiar and uncomfortable, and I've learned to love being uncomfortable. It's the way I respond. When I go to a movie or go see a play that makes me uncomfortable, I love it. I'm thrilled. I recognize that that's an acquired taste, but it's now automatic and unconscious for me. So, what I do is allow myself to be uncomfortable, or I force myself to be uncomfortable. I must be uncomfortable. There's something wrong with the writing if I'm not literally worrying about the next page and how it's going to turn out. In one sense, what I have to do when I sit down is get completely focused on the formal devices, so that I'll forget, "Oh my god, the audience is going to hate me. No one's going to do this. They're going to string me up." I mean, all the kinds of things that I *do* think when I'm writing something like *How I Learned to Drive*. "I'm going to be stoned. I'm convinced of it." If you think that, you're not going to write the play. And that's why I've really become such a formalist. What I do is concentrate on very specific devices, little technical problems. I write in such a way that it entertains me and makes me laugh, so that I'll keep going on. Because otherwise, if I really thought about it, I wouldn't write it.

AL: Has the feeling of "Oh my god, they're going to stone me" dissipated at all since the success of *How I Learned to Drive*?

PV: No. I'm waiting to be stoned on the very next thing that I'm writing. It doesn't change. And actually, for women, I don't think it *does* change. We *are* likely to be stoned on the very next one. I think being put into a category because of success is just as dangerous as not being able to be categorized.

AL: Perhaps even more so.

PV: Yes, and I'm recognizing the peril of that.

AL: You said earlier that we need to promote younger writers through education. In an interview with David Savran you mentioned that a lot of academic programs kill the thing you love and that your excitement for playwriting may have actually been fostered because you weren't in a playwriting program. As a teacher yourself, how do you approach the subject of playwriting in order to foster rather than smother your student's excitement for the craft?

PV: Well, the first thing that you have to do is do no harm. In essence, apply the Hippocratic oath to teaching. I don't admit anybody to my program whose work I don't love. I may not understand it, but I love it. And I also have to say, "Listen, I'm going to tell you what I think, but what I think may be wrong." Right up front I talk about Georg Büchner. What would have happened if *Woyzeck* had been discovered the year that it was written rather than 125 years later? Would it ever have been produced? No, it would never have been produced. So, how do I know I don't have a young Büchner in my room? I have to make sure that writers know that I may be wrong, but the fact that I'm wrong and how they learn to deal with that is going to help them deal with literary managers and artistic directors. So, a lot of it has to do with finding a way to construct a dialogue about ongoing work that empowers the writer. A lot of it has to do with making sure that there's a diversity of voices around you. A lot of it has to do with thinking of the writing program as a brain trust for writers, not as some infantilization in which the dramaturg gets power. And basically trying to find a place where everyone's aesthetic in the room grows larger rather than smaller. There are ways to do that. It's really not a hard thing to do.

I've often thought that what playwrights need is a community of playwrights. We need a community of playwrights as much as we need actors and a director and actual space. What is happening right now in the usual process is that playwrights are divided and conquered. We're not left to talk to each other. I always think about Racine and Corneille sitting in a little café saying, "I dare you to write *Phèdre*. I'll write *Phèdre* if you write *Phèdre*." The kinds of results that come out of that type of work—which indeed we have done at Brown, we've done every year at Brown—are extraordinary. It's extraordinary to have ten playwrights write the same play. To say to them, "Okay, you have forty-eight hours to write a neoclassical play. Go." and watch what happens with ten different minds. Permission has to be given. Definitions of what a play is have to broaden. I may not understand your work because the fault is in me. But if you help me understand it, my notion of what theatre can be is going to grow. And only playwrights can give that to each other, really.

The time I've spent at Brown has completely spoiled me. It's hard for me, actually, to go into New York. I know I'll see failed work at Brown, but I'll also see extraordinary, sublime moments that I will never see anywhere else. That makes it hard to sit and watch what we call a professional product.

AL: Through your work with young playwrights and your experience with professional theatre, can you identify any trends in contemporary theatre? Can you speculate on future directions American theatre may take?

PV: I can't *really* identify any trends. That's something that we're actually doing when we're really looking at a limited pool, and that tends to emphasize New York. I don't think theatre is New York. The thing that I'm excited about in the towns that I go to or hear about, whether it's Seattle or San Francisco or Providence or Boston, is that these tiny companies are springing up that actually are doing collective playwriting, very much in the notion of poetry slams. That we are getting the "let's produce this by the skin of our teeth" kinds of productions with a playwriting community. I do see that that's taking root, and that's extremely exciting. It hasn't really happened in New York. I think New York is just a much different animal. Actually, that's not true—it *is* happening in small theatre companies in New York. But that's what's happening all around the country. That's the only trend that I can see, and I'm really thrilled about it, because that is very much about giving access to the theatrical process to a younger generation.

There are ten-minute plays going on, all kinds of almost—which is great—theatre as game play. Theatre as communal game play. And that's exactly right. I'm really not interested in seeing a play, necessarily, on a $500,000 budget. Or a $5 million budget. I'd much rather see what somebody does on a thousand dollars. That's where the thrilling work is. Young writers know that if they can do it on a hundred bucks or a thousand bucks, they can certainly do it on five hundred thousand. So, this communal game playing is really an encouraging trend.

MARGARET EDSON: PLAYWRIGHT IN SPITE OF HERSELF

Mead Hunter

A Recipe for Envy

It is simple; it is foolproof. To wit:

1. With no experience in professional playwriting, you embark on writing your first script.
2. After a celebrated off-Broadway production of this first-ever script, you are awarded the 1999 Pulitzer Prize in Drama for a distinguished play by an American author.
3. You resist subsequent offers of play commissions, avowing that you are not currently interested in writing for the theater.

Matters of Fact

In 1991, at the age of 30, Margaret Edson rented an apartment on 35th Street in Washington, DC, above a storefront business called Georgetown Hairstyling. She installed a writing desk there, and then sat down at it with a very particular purpose: to pen an original play. Not just any play, mind you, but one with a definite shape and intent already in mind.

Well aware that playwriting is second only to poetry as the most marginalized form of artistic endeavor in the United States, she nevertheless persevered; after all, if there's virtually no chance anyone is going to produce it, you can scribble away to suit yourself, right?

But someone did elect to produce it: South Coast Repertory (SCR), of Costa Mesa, California, one of the nation's leading crucibles of original work for the stage. This was in 1995.

261

Despite the considerable success of SCR's production (it won six awards from the Los Angeles Drama Critics Circle, including Best Premiere) it would be two more years before another theater undertook a production. At the Long Wharf Theatre of New Haven, Connecticut, in a new production directed by Derek Anson Jones and starring Kathleen Chalfant as the redoubtable Professor Vivian Bearing, lightning struck twice; the play was an unqualified success. In 1998, it opened at New York's Manhattan Class Company (MCC) Theater, and a year later it moved to the Union Square Theater. Subsequently the play garnered a spate of new awards, including the Dramatists Guild Hull-Warriner Award, Drama Desk, New York Drama Critics, Outer Critics Circle, and the Lucille Lortel Award for Outstanding Play.

When word arrived that *Wit* had won the 1999 Pulitzer Prize for Drama, no one was more gobsmacked than Margaret Edson. She was teaching her kindergarten class at the time and was suddenly informed that she was wanted in the principal's office immediately. Such a summons can strike terror into the hearts of adults as much as it does children. Ms. Edson was sure she was in trouble.

An Anatomy of Wit

Vivian Bearing, a formidable English literature professor, specializes in the Holy Sonnets of John Donne, a literary figure so willfully obscurantist that only the most dogged of students survive the university's course on him. Dr. Bearing's investigations into the poet's work are illuminating; she is, by her own admission, "a force." Yet when faced with advanced cancer, she must consider just how much Donne's metaphysics have really taught her about life. To her dismay, Jason Posner, the young physician assigned to her treatment, turns out to be a former student of hers—the sort that takes up a study for the sheer challenge of it. Now, however, he is an ambitious scientist whose passions are reserved for his research rather than for his patients.

Thus does Vivian seem to receive the treatment she deserves. As her treatment becomes more intense, and simultaneously more debilitating, she gradually moves from a position of power to one of dependency. Professor Bearing learns to appreciate human contact, especially as personified by her nurse, Susie Monahan. Over the course of the play, Vivian realizes the insufficiency of mere wit and, in the face of her own impending death, the value of life for its own sake.

Q & A 1

Mead Hunter: How did you conceive of an extraordinary figure like Dr. Bearing? Had you ever met anyone like that?

Margaret Edson: No.

MH: How did you decide she was an authority on Donne, rather than Rilke or Joyce or, for that matter, Shakespeare?

ME: The only possible choice for her is Donne—because he's so difficult and obscure. And also because the Holy Sonnets present themselves as having some insight into the interior lives of human beings. And yet [the Sonnets] get so caught up in their own cleverness that I, for one, have to wonder what insights they really have to offer.

MH: So no native affinity for Donne whatsoever?

ME: No, all that had to come through the research.

MH: And now? How do you feel about him now?

ME: Donne is not the victor in this play. An important moment in *Wit* comes when Vivian Bearing says "no" to John Donne. Her scholar visitor comes in toward the end and says, "Shall I recite something by Donne?" and the audience is thinking "God, no" and Professor Bearing herself moans "nooooo. . . ."

MH: That always gets a big laugh, every time I've seen the play.

ME: Of course, because we're all sitting there thinking the same thing.

MH: So you're not sitting around of a summer's evening and reading Donne for fun?

ME: "Nooooo. . . ."

An Anatomy of Donne

John Donne (1572–1631) was a study in contrasts. Raised as a Roman Catholic in Elizabethan England, he later had to convert to Protestantism just to get a job under King James I's reign. And while he was never the rapscallion voluptuary that his more sensual poems might suggest, he did manage to bite the hand that fed him by eloping with his employer's underage niece.

Correspondingly, his literary oeuvre reflects completely distinct sides of Donne's personality. In fact, some scholars find it convenient to regard him as though he were two separate entities: Jack Donne (witty and risqué lover, writer of the love poems) and Dr. John Donne (austere, almost prudish minister). Perhaps we should not wonder that so many of Donne's religious poems, sermons, and devotions describe a man coming to terms with his own past, forever seeking God's grace in this world—and in the next.

The death of his wife (yes, the same woman with whom he had absconded fourteen years earlier) brought Donne's long-time obsession with death to the surface. Shortly before his death, Donne commissioned an artist to sketch him wrapped in his own burial shroud, standing atop a funereal urn. Donne kept this charcoal sketch of himself at his bedside throughout his final illness.

Coming Soon to a Theater Near You

Currently *Wit* is in production all over the United States and beyond. Notable recent venues, to name only a few, include the Geffen Playhouse in Los Angeles, Oregon Shakespeare Festival in Ashland, the Intiman Theatre in Seattle, and the Vaudeville in London. The script has been translated into numerous foreign languages; none other than Jeanne Moreau directed a recent French production.

Ms. Edson took her high school French teacher to the opening in Paris.

Q & A 2

MH: Have you encountered any hostility from medical practitioners about the play? I mean, has anybody objected to being portrayed in certain ways—such as Jason, with his detached approach to patient care?

ME: Some doctors question it. There was a flurry of correspondence about this very thing in the *New York Times* in the fall of '98. A doctor wrote an essay criticizing the play for that, and then several other people wrote in and criticized her for criticizing it, and there was quite a bit of activity . . .

MH: What about Shakespeare authorities? Has anybody been piqued that the Bard comes in for critical scrutiny in *Wit*?

ME: No, not at all. Only somebody busted me for what I say is a subjective complement, when it's actually a predicate adjective. But then I checked with somebody else who said, no no no, it's a subjective complement.

MH: Is that a lit crit term?

ME: It's a grammatical term. From the beginning of the play, when Dr. Bearing says, "Should I reply 'I feel good,'" using "good" as a subjective complement.

MH: Oh.

ME: I know, I don't understand that part at all. If you want to call it a predicate adjective, fine, it sounds better anyway. But someone came up to me after one of these talks, and said, "No, you were right, it is a subjective complement." So I don't know.

MH: Well, your professor definitely knows the proper use of subjunctive tense, we have to credit her for that.

ME: Like where?

MH: Oh, somewhere early on, she says "if I were fine"—that would be a real "tell," if she had said "if I *was* fine," as virtual everybody does nowadays. I don't think one term or the other is insisted upon anymore, but for someone like Dr. Bearing, that would be a real shibboleth.

ME: This sort of thing has been coming up for me a lot lately, because I've been meeting with translators. It's fun, but challenging; they really come right at me. They'll pick a word out of a page and say, why this word, why does it have to be this one? The Hebrew translator pointed out something: When the Professor says to the young doctor, "what do you say when the patient is frightened, is apprehensive," and the young doctor says, "Of who?" The translator said: "Shouldn't that be 'of whom'"? I said, "Well, this is the United States of America, and here we just do not say 'of whom'."

MH: I know what you mean; it took my Italian tutor several sessions to teach me the difference in the English language between "that" and "which."

ME: There, you see, another difference I don't acknowledge.

MH: Into how many languages has *Wit* been translated now?

ME: Maybe a dozen.

MH: Anything really exotic?

ME: Finnish. I think that's pretty exotic. It's my dream to go see *Wit* performed in a language I don't speak.

MH: Looks like you'll get your wish soon enough. There's a lot going on now, because the national and international rights have just been released, right? Can you even keep track of how many productions are going on these days?

ME: I've been told there's about thirty. All over the country. But right now that release is for regional theaters. Next year, when amateur rights are made available, is when things will get really interesting, I think.

The Rocky Road to International Fame

A partial list of jobs Ms. Edson has held before now:
1. Hot dog vendor
2. Worker in a bar at the end of a dirt road
3. Worker in a French convent in Rome
4. Unit clerk on a cancer and AIDS ward at a research hospital
5. ESL instructor
6. Bicycle shopkeeper
7. Dramatist
8. Kindergarten teacher

Q & A 3

MH: Did you ever have any theater training?

ME: No, not really.

MH: Did you do plays in high school, anything at all?

ME: Yes, I did do that; and I was trying my hand at writing back then, playwriting and all kinds of things. That was where I met Derek Jones, you know, who directed the Long Wharf and New York productions of *Wit*. We did plays back together in high school. He was Touchstone and I was Rosalind in *As You Like It*. In fact, he and I have been in school together since the seventh grade.

MH: So that's when you realized you had this interest in writing?

ME: There never was an interest in that sense; I just knew I wanted to write this particular play.

MH: You've told me that before, and I still hardly know how to credit it. What about now, then? With all the validation you've received, surely you consider yourself a writer now.

ME: No, not at all.

MH: All right, then—please explain how you managed to manifest a full-blown work for the stage.

ME: I wanted to go see this play, which meant that someone had to write it; and finally I realized I would have to write it.

MH: So the story already existed in your head?

ME: It was clear in my mind, yes.

MH: But where did the story come from? I know you had personal experience working in a cancer ward; was that it? Or was it that you wanted to describe a singular figure like Dr. Bearing? Or was it more like the . . . existential situation? I'm fishing for origins because the way you describe it, it's almost as though you channeled this story from on high. I mean that you seemed to receive the story whole and entire, and the transmission of it from you to us was simply a matter of setting it down on paper.

ME: Well, what preceded that was a lot of very serious research; and then what followed that was a ton of cutting. The middle part was the fun part of that.

MH: The middle?

ME: The 10–second spurts of inspiration. There was a ton of work on either side of those.

MH: Did you approach the play in a workman-like way, starting at the beginning and working straight through? Or was it more like you assembled all these different bursts of inspiration?

ME: I was doing the research every day. I had to do all this research on John Donne—I didn't know anything about that field. Also all the medical stuff—I had to get all the details straight about that. But then as I'd be working, some detail would pop into my mind. So I'd make a few notes. And once that detail would pop into my mind, then everything else would become clear.

Some Context

Margaret Edson's stint in the medical profession was brief, but it was evidently instructive, since it provided a setting as well as a cultural context for *Wit*. Ultimately the experience of working as a unit clerk at a major research hospital also informed one of the play's central concerns: people who are so consumed by their work that they forget the humanism inherent in their endeavors.

Ms. Edson's work on the cancer and AIDS inpatient unit was far from taxing; she scheduled appointments, ordered supplies, and generally saw to the unit's clerical infrastructure. Paradoxically, this meant that she was always at the center of the action without actually being caught up in it—and was therefore at a perfect vantage for observing all that went on. From that vantage, she witnessed a great deal.

After a year on the ward she moved on to other endeavors, but the experience of observing the interactions of patients and caretakers haunted her. It occurred to her that people come into a cancer ward or an AIDS unit with specific sets of skills for coping with life . . . and suddenly they may find that those mechanisms no longer work. (The fact that Vivian Bearing is a Doctor of Philosophy, for example, fails to improve her status with her medical doctors.) For Margaret Edson, this exquisitely human situation was what she wanted to depict, and she knew she had to depict it through the most immediate medium she knew: live theater.

Nevertheless, she has often said that the story could be set somewhere besides an inpatient unit and it would still be the same story. According to Ms. Edson, *Wit* is not about medicine or academia or Donne or even Professor Bearing, finally. It's about something John Donne sought all his life but may never have found. It's about redemption.

By the Way

Margaret Edson now teaches first grade. She has no plans to forsake her young charges for the bright lights of Broadway.

Q & A 4

MH: I had meant to start out today by asking you what life is like now that all the hullabaloo has died down. But it sounds like it has not died down at all.

ME: Well, not completely. I'm still doing one or two interviews nearly every evening. But it's starting to quiet down, partly because I'm suppressing it.

MH: What do you mean?

ME: I've been doing a lot of speaking this year, but I just decided not to do any more of that next year.

MH: You mean *Wit*-related speaking? Theaters, health organizations?

ME: Well, I've been speaking to different kinds of organization, but related to *Wit*. More like community-related things. For instance, I spoke to the association of American Colleges and Universities national convention in DC—college administrators and deans. I talked to them about punctuation.

MH: What did you have to say to them about punctuation?

ME: I reviewed the history of punctuation, of course; and then I gave my own feelings about the way the text of the play is punctuated and why that was important. It was a lot of fun; I learned a lot from it.

An Objective Correlative

Late in the play, Professor Bearing recalls a conversation the young Vivian had with her mentor, Professor E. M. Ashford. The venerable teacher has just pointed out to her student that her transcription of Donne's "Holy Sonnet Six," which bristles with exclamation points, amounts to melodrama. As her case in point, Professor Ashford refers to Donne's oft-quoted line, "And death shall be no more, Death thou shalt die":

> Nothing but a breath—a comma—separates life from life everlasting. It is very simple really. With the original punctuation restored, death is no longer something to act out on a stage, with exclamation points. It's a comma, a pause.
>
> This way, the *uncompromising* way, one learns something from this poem, wouldn't you say? Life, death. Soul, God. Past, present. Not insuperable barriers, not semicolons, just a comma. (Edson 1999, 14–15)

Playwright with a Teacup: A Portrait

> At a teahouse in Los Angeles,
> Anachronism and harbinger both at once.
> And here we are.
> Pale gold liquid quavering in our cups.
> She lifts hers with both hands, with ceremony—
> A feint only, she will not sip.
> As the cup floats down to our tiny table,
> Suddenly she says: "How good of you to come out,
> To come all the way out here to see me . . . "
> That's her all over, I will come to find.

So wanting to please.

Yet not easily pleased herself.

Watching with dispassion, an elegant oracle.

Even seated she seems tall as an amazon,

With all the corresponding grace

of that legendary being. Or rather:

a mythical creature, a . . .

    . . . a beautiful, pacific sphinx. Only—

unwittingly so.

Q & A 5

MH: Surely you're aware that there's a lot of curiosity among people as to what sort of person pens a play like *Wit*. Have you managed to enjoy all the attention that comes with personal success?

ME: Well, you know . . . it hasn't really cost anything. I haven't felt wounded or stung or even frustrated by it. I've had interesting conversations with nice people, and made a lot of friends . . . there just hasn't been a negative side to it.

MH: So even when there's something like the doctor in the *New York Times*, who wrote a letter taking issue with the script's portrayal of physicians, that has all been part of the fun for you.

ME: That was interesting, and the response to that was even more interesting, yes.

MH: When word first broke that *Wit* had been awarded the Pulitzer Prize, there was a flurry of e-mail postings on an Internet newsgroup largely made up of playwrights [rec.arts.theatre.plays]. Some posters objected to the award. And initially they tried to base this on quibbles they had with the text itself. One person, I recall, was vehement that Dr. Bearing was dismissive of Shakespeare early on, only to quote him toward the play's end; and someone else responded by saying, "Excuse me, might that be the point?" Volleys went back and forth and back and forth. Did you know about this?

ME: No.

MH: All right, I'll tell you how it ended. There was one brief, two-line post that read something like this—I'm paraphrasing: "*Wit* is a play of great power and majesty. I can't imagine anything deserving the Prize more." And it was signed: Paula Vogel.

ME: Oh, that's wonderful.

MH: She was the last word on *that* subject for a long time. After that it got very quiet in the playwriting newsgroup, at least for a while. Up until then, though, the nature of the criticisms was interesting. Once textual matters dried up, more personal objections came to the fore. A few people complained about Margaret Edson being a first-time playwright—the subtext being, "She hasn't paid her dues." The corollary being: "I've been toiling in this field for decades without recognition, and now this tyro walks off with honors." Rather like an actor with no training walking off with an Oscar.

ME: Well, I'm paying for my dues working for the State of Georgia.

The Classiest Query of All Time

When an unrepresented playwright (i.e., one that lacks an agent) wishes a theater to read her work, she is not without recourse. The time-honored way of striking out on your own and making professional contact without an agent is simply to send a "query letter" to the target theater: typically, a cover letter, synopsis, and sample pages of the script in question.

At the time that I first heard from Margaret Edson, I was the Literary Manager of A.S.K. Theater Projects, reading countless query letters annually. These letters ranged from plaintive to vaguely threatening to being virtual pitches in the Hollywood tradition, and so an unusual query stood out in sharp relief. I will never forget the elegant economy of the letter Ms. Edson wrote, which I quote here in full:

> Dear Mr. Hunter:
>
> Enclosed please find my play *Wit*, which I am sending you at the suggestion of Jerry Patch.
>
> I realize that you have no shortage of scripts to read, and I appreciate you taking the time to read mine.
>
> Sincerely,
>
> Margaret Edson

Synecdoche

One of the most bracing aspects of *Wit* is the way the play's main character, the daunting yet archly droll Professor Vivian Bearing, moves back and forth between absorption in her own past and present, and offering those of us in the audience a wry, metatheatrical commentary on the situation at hand. It is as though by laying bare the scaffolding of drama's stocks-in-trade, Vivian is simultaneously able to bare her soul to us. The following excerpt is from *Wit*'s opening scene, in which Dr. Bearing introduces herself to us by critiquing the standard hospital greeting—"How are you?"—as well as its standard response, "Fine."

> Of course, it is not very often that I do feel fine.
>
> I have been asked, "How are you feeling today?" while I was throwing up into a plastic washbasin. I have been asked, as I was emerging from a four-hour operation with a tube in every orifice, "How are you feeling today?"
>
> I am waiting for the moment when someone asks me this question and I am dead.
>
> I'm a little sorry I'll miss that.
>
> It is unfortunate that this remarkable line of inquiry has come to me so late in my career. I could have exploited its feigned solicitude to great advantage: as I was distributing the final examination to the graduate course in seventeenth-century textual criticism—"Hi. How are you feeling today?"
>
> Of course I would not be wearing this costume at the time, so the question's *ironic significance* would not be fully apparent.
>
> As I trust it is now.
>
> *Irony* is a literary device that will necessarily be deployed to great effect.
>
> I ardently wish this were not so. I would prefer that a play about me be cast in the mythic-heroic-pastoral mode; but the facts, most notably stage-four metastatic ovarian cancer, conspire against that. *The Faerie Queene* this is not.
>
> And I was dismayed to discover that the play would contain elements of . . . *humor*.
>
> I have been, at best, an *unwitting* accomplice. *(She pauses.)* It is not my intention to give away the plot, but I think I die at the end.
>
> They've given me less than two hours.

Local Color
Ms. Edson grew up in Washington, DC, and until recently lived on Capitol Hill there.

Early education took place at Sidwell, where she met Derek Anson Jones; out of that friendship came a determination to see *Wit* produced on the East Coast. Ms. Edson cherishes a photograph of the two of them, taken back when international success was merely a madcap fantasy. In the snapshot you see them at an outdoor café, seated under a broad table umbrella: Maggie in the sunlight, pale and radiant; her friend is in partial shadow, which deepens his already dark skin. The slogan on the umbrella reads simply: WIT. Advertising what, beer? The café? Not Donne's poetry, in any case.

In time, not only did Mr. Jones magnificently direct *Wit*'s first East Coast productions, but he also went on to direct a national tour of *Wit*—before dying, on January 17, 1999, at the age of 38, from complications of AIDS.

Nowadays Ms. Edson lives on a peaceful street in a gracious Atlanta neighborhood. She seems surprised to notice that she does not miss the constant swirl of activity, rumor, and street traffic that is always at the center of our nation's capitol. Her bungalow is freshly painted; the new garden is flourishing; and in the serenely Southern style of her adopted region, she enjoys spending the summer on the front porch.

She plans to live in Atlanta for a long, long time.

Testimonials

The Wall Street Journal: "An original and urgent work of art . . . among the finest plays of the decade."

Newsday: "Exhilarating and harrowing."

New York Times: "A brutally human and beautifully layered new play . . . you feel both enlightened and, in a strange way, enormously comforted."

New York magazine: "A dazzling and humane play you will remember till your dying day."

Los Angeles Times: "*Wit* has acquired a burdensome load of praise, from the Pulitzer Prize on down. Yet [it] shrugs off that burden, just by being the sharp, oddly buoyant work it is."

Q & A 6

MH: Did you ever have any inkling when you sat down to write *Wit* that it would become your pension play?

ME: No. That's a great phrase, though.

MH: I got it from Jeffrey Hatcher, who was talking about Paula Vogel at the time.

ME: Oh, referring to *How I Learned To Drive*?

MH: Referring to any play that surprisingly and beyond all the author's expectations turns out to be what plunks him down in theater history.

ME: Maybe that play is always a surprise.

What Dr. Donne Might Well Have to Say to Ms. Edson

Perhaps they were not so different, after all, as the author of *Wit* supposes. This verse is taken from Donne's *The Canonization*:

> The Phoenix riddle hath more wit
> By us, we two being one, are it.
> So to one neutral thing both sexes fit,
> We die and rise the same, and prove
> Mysterious by this love.

Q & A 7

MH: Have you heard from the John Donne Society yet?

ME: I did turn down an invitation to speak at a conference about John Donne.

MH: That was probably wise.

The Power of Buzz

From the time when our first-timer playwright began sending out unsolicited manuscript copies of her play, up to *Wit*'s premiere, and for years beyond it, Margaret Edson was the darling of literary departments all over the country. Most literary managers worth their salt had read *Wit*; most had loved it; and most assumed that their theaters would never, ever actually produce it.

Fortunately, literary buzz has a way of achieving critical mass. It took only two or three theaters willing to "take a chance" on *Wit* to demonstrate to many American houses just how much they had been underestimating their own audiences.

Q & A 8

MH: Do you have any clue as to why producers were leery of *Wit* for so long?

ME: Oh, of course. It's far easier to understand people's rejection of it than their acceptance. It's too academic; there's too much talk; too depressing; it has a disease-of-the-month; and . . . there are just too many words.

MH: Yet *Wit* is often praised for its economy of language.

ME: Now, yes. But the play that people were originally reading was an hour and a half longer than what's on stage now. Besides, I think that when you're reading it silently, the funny parts don't come through—at the beginning, for example, when she's explaining how great she is, while she's wheeled from one diagnostic procedure to another. When you read it, you don't get a sense of that; all you get is her telling you how great she is; whereas when it's happening, the irony is hilarious and agonizing. Also you get more of a sense of the motion of all these medical procedures going on around her.

MH: You just assume these things were people's objections to your script?

ME: Oh no, I got plenty of rejection letters, I know all about it.

MH: They actually specified that these were problems?

ME: Not always. Usually it was the form letter. And even after the South Coast Rep production, it was the same thing all over again. I couldn't get an agent, couldn't get produced anywhere, for two years.

MH: Which speaks to how parochial American theater can be sometimes—any theater with an interest in new work should have known about the success of the SCR production. So . . . did people say things like, this is virtually a monologue, our audiences won't understand this, that sort of thing.

ME: Yes, and I understood all that. But I never changed it to make it more acceptable.

MH: That's amazing, especially for a new writer. Many writers would willingly wrench their stories out of their orbits to accommodate everybody's opinions if it might mean a production.

ME: I feel very grateful to South Coast Repertory; the only designs they ever had on the play were to make it more true to itself—not to turn it into something else.

MH: And is it still true that you have no interest in writing another play?

ME: Yes.

MH: What if some organization—such as A.S.K.—were to approach you and say, look, here's a few weeks, how about coming out to Los Angeles and simply writing for a few weeks, with no pressure to crank out a new work . . . it's all right if it doesn't lead to a play . . . no one will read it. . . . Maggie, hello? I'm trying to make this sound tantalizing.

ME: Well—in the summer I could do it, when school is out.

MH: Aha, so this is an attractive idea to you.

ME: No.

MH: No?

ME: There's nothing I want to say right now. The place where I want to make a contribution is in the classroom.

MH: So you consider your teaching to be your real vocation?

ME: Completely.

The Impact of Fame on Everyday Life

Among Margaret Edson's innumerable interviews, one notable one is the conversation she had on *News Hour with Jim Lehrer* on April 14, 1999. She was already slightly acquainted with Mr. Lehrer, having attended high school with his daughter.

When he asked her what effect the Pulitzer Prize was having on her pedagogical activities, she responded:

> There are bouquets of flowers all around the [class]room. So, I took that opportunity to teach about the bee dance and how bees communicate with each other about the source of different types of nectar by flying around and then doing the dance to communicate to the other bees about where the good nectar is. So we had a very experiential lesson thanks to all the flowers that people have been sending.

And on into the Future

At this writing, HBO is planning its own production of *Wit*, starring Emma Thompson as the redoubtable Vivian Bearing. Ms. Thompson's co-star will be Tony-winning actress/soprano Audra McDonald, who will play Susie Monahan, the nurse who cares for the imperious Dr. Bearing.

Coda

Though Ms. Edson prizes the time she has spent in academia, friends have observed that in a way, going back to her kindergartners is her way of acknowledging how insufficient it can be to live in a world of wit— as well as the rarefied world of theater that has realized *Wit*.

Q & A 9

MH: What do your students make of your fame?

ME: This year they hadn't really known about it, because there hasn't been much about it locally. But now my picture has been in the paper, since the Alliance [Theatre Company, of Atlanta] is doing *Wit*. So to them—my students—I'm very famous.

MH: But you're famous to them anyway, right?

ME: In their world, I'm a person with a large profile, right. But last year's students got very swell-headed; film crews were coming around— *CBS Sunday Morning* and *ABC News* . . .

MH: And what did your students think was going on?

ME: I told them that it was because I wrote a play, and it was going on in New York, but I was here because I wanted to be with them, so the news people had to come to us. They loved that, they swallowed it whole! But it also happened to be true. So they became very famous. Now they're in the first grade, thinking: Hey, we're not getting half the coverage we got last year!

MH: Last year when all the news was breaking, what did your students want to know about what was happening?

ME: Well, I went to New York and brought back postcards of all the big buildings. Elevators that only go to certain floors—that was very hard for me, I'm from a small town outside of DC. And I told them a lot about the airplane trips, because I made four trips to New York that spring, during weekends. The hard thing was just trying not to miss school.

MH: Gone is gone, I guess; they don't understand when you're not there.

ME: That's right, because I made a promise to them, that I would be there for them, and I can't just be disappearing off to New York every week.

MH: Did they ask you about the content of *Wit*?

ME: A little bit; and then they saw the *CBS Morning Show* with a few scenes from the play. But that raised more questions than it answered.

MH: What sorts of things did they ask?

ME: They weren't too interested in the play; they were more interested in the media attention to themselves. There was a CBS show in February of last year that really showed the class a lot. That was the fun part of it for them.

MH: They became part of your celebrity, as it were.

ME: No, they saw themselves as celebrities in their own right.

On Keeping That Day Job

In February of 2000, Michael Phillips wrote in the *Los Angeles Times*:

> Edson's triumph, above all, is simple. *Wit* gives us a chronicle of a very, very bad experience that we know from the start will not end well. Yet it's a play of small encounters, small revelations and interactions, that add up to a complex life story. It's 'universal,' certainly, but Edson has written specifically and eloquently of an educator's life. It's pure poetic justice that, in [Kathleen] Chalfant's performance, the most moving line is a simple statement of fact: "I'm a teacher."

Note

The "Q & A" sessions are from the author's interview with Margaret Edson in January 2000.

Work Cited

Edson, Margaret. 1999. *Wit*. New York: Faber & Faber, Inc.

DONALD MARGULIES: FROM *BOITSCHICK* TO MAN

Jerry Patch

I wake to sleep, and take my waking slow.
I learn by going where I have to go.

—Theodore Roethke, "The Waking"

Donald Margulies, the last playwright to win the Pulitzer Prize for Drama in the 1990s, was also among the decade's first Pulitzer finalists, in 1991–92, with *Sight Unseen*. His *Collected Stories* was also a finalist in 1996–97, making him the only Pulitzer winner in that period to be a finalist for the award three times. One can understand his belief (and relief) that the Pulitzer Prize awarded him in 1999–2000 for *Dinner with Friends* was as much an honoring of a body of work for the stage as distinction for the play that won:

> I don't think I ever aspired to winning a Pulitzer Prize, but once I became a finalist it suddenly became something that was accessible to me. At this stage of my career, I have a body of work that's been produced on stages across the country, and this kind of national recognition seems to acknowledge not only *Dinner with Friends*, but that collection of plays; for me, it's a validation of all those years working in the theatre.[1]

In that light, *Dinner with Friends* is the most recent piece of an evolving mosaic of plays, one with some common thematic threads but an *ad hoc* variety of styles and strategies. Margulies does not have the master work plan of an August Wilson, the singular voice of a Pinter or

Mamet, or the political urgencies of a Paula Vogel or Tony Kushner to shape and drive his work from play to play. Instead, his theatrical output—now more than a dozen plays, six of which have enjoyed prominent lives on American stages—has come from assessing his own changing vision of himself and the world in which he lives. His approach to playwriting has been perhaps more characteristic of a novelist, or of the visual artist he trained to be.

To date, Margulies has written a fanciful play in which adults play children (*Found a Peanut*), in free verse (Act I of *Resting Place*), an antic mock-musical (*The Loman Family Picnic*), a John Guare-ish comedy of agony (*What's Wrong With This Picture?*), stylized and theatrical naturalism a la Franz Xaver Kroetz (*The Model Apartment*), as well as in more realistic modes (*Sight Unseen, Collected Stories, Dinner with Friends*). To date, his plays can be divided into those by the emerging artist and those by the mature artist; or those by the son and those by the man.

> I was a post Holocaust baby boom Jew who grew up in a Brooklyn ghetto. The Holocaust was a much a part of my household as the depression was. My oldest childhood friend is a child of survivors. I spent a lot of time at his house.

Young playwrights rarely come to their calling with enough imagination or experience to create from whole cloth wholly new plays. Often the ones who have ability appropriate and reconceive works of writers they admire until they've banked enough experiences to shape entire creative worlds of their own. Donald Margulies's early plays came from the lives of his family and neighbors in Coney Island and Sheepshead Bay, some of whom were survivors of the Holocaust who had lived the recent Jewish history that held him in morbid fascination. At age five he asked his neighbor Ida to explain the tattoo on her wrist. At six he watched newsreel footage from the camps and highlights of the trial of Adolph Eichmann on NBC's *Huntley-Brinkley Report*:

> It was the first time I'd seen those images from the liberated camps. They haunted my dreams and fed all kinds of paranoia that stays with me to this day. And there were many survivors in my neighborhood.

He was not of that world, but he lived with and listened to many who had been; and, as he learned, they would never escape it. His perspective on life in those years—that of a young artist/son living in both old and new worlds—became the foundation for his entry into playwriting. "My parents didn't go to synagogue. They went to Broadway."

The proximity of his survivor neighbors and growing up in a secular Jewish household that took its spiritual comfort from American musicals gave Margulies a strong sense of his cultural (if not religious) heritage and a refusal to be defined or limited by it. Like most hyphenate-Americans, he insists on having it both ways. He argues that *Sight Unseen*'s Jonathan Waxman is a man who has lost his sense of himself and who just happens to be Jewish; and he complains about being congratulated for writing a play with no ostensible Jewish characters in it (*Dinner with Friends*).[2]

> The Holocaust was the most stunning event of our time. The legacy of that event, the sheer gravity of it, created an urgency to repopulate the race on the one hand, and on the other to turn away from, or to question the values imposed on the generation born with that legacy. I, for instance, married a gentile woman, which created certain difficulties, but nowhere near as difficult as it would have been had I married her before the death of my parents. Like it or not, you live with these issues on a day-to-day basis.

Donald Margulies in his mid-forties is an artist with a sure sense of who he is and of his place in the theatre. But that identity and security were a long time coming. For years his pursuits were shaped by his drive for acceptance: choosing at age eleven to pursue visual art—for which he was much praised—at the expense of his writing; his switch to writing in college upon hearing an audience's response to his work; his goal of being produced at Joseph Papp's New York Shakespeare Festival before age thirty (done at twenty-nine); and the devastation he felt in the 1980s upon receiving mixed to dismissive reviews of his plays in *The New York Times*. Taken together, they point up Margulies's wish to be embraced by his audiences.

> Some writers are very interested in being an outsider. I am not. I have never relished being the outsider. It has always made me uncomfortable, and set me on forays into the larger world.

The theme of the outsider in American letters is as old as Hester Prynne or Huckleberry Finn, but those characters and the writers who created them were squarely in the American mainstream of their times. Hawthorne and Twain wrestled with the idea and the consequences of what happens when you depart from the mainstream, a likely idea in a century bound by its Puritan heritage. In the last half of the twentieth century, many writers have based their art and their identity—even their celebrity—on their status as outsiders, and have written characters to match. From John Rechy to Tony Kushner, from Ralph Ellison to August Wilson, from Charles Bukowski to Eminem, the statement has been: This is who I am. Take me the way I am—or not at all. Those artists refused to negotiate themselves or their characters, and instead insisted on respect and acceptance.

During the '90s, Margulies began reaching mainstream audiences with plays, issues, and themes they found substantial. In particular, *Dinner with Friends* captured the *zeitgeist* of the married class, succeeding not only in the United States, but in productions in Europe and Asia as well. Some reviewers, especially those writing from desks on alternative weeklies, have criticized *Dinner with Friends* for being too rooted in the mainstream, which seems akin to criticizing a duck for taking to water.

Margulies is not an outsider. He is in the third decade of a marriage to a physician; he is a father; he owns real estate; he teaches at Yale. His bohemian years in Hell's Kitchen during the late 1970s and early 1980s only serve to authenticate his choice to live in the mainstream, where the fact of belonging, of acceptance, is implicit. Yet like most mainstream Americans, he finds himself feeling at times isolated in some eddy or backwater—as an artist, and as a secular Jew. The tension between those in- and outside worlds, a source of anxiety for him in the 1980s, drove his art in *Sight Unseen* and *Collected Stories*:

> No matter who people are in life, they tend to see themselves as mavericks, or misunderstood. It seems a very American attitude to feel apart from the mainstream. Certainly there are those in our society who truly are disenfranchised and on the outside; but then there are people like Jonathan Waxman who steadfastly hold on to antiquated ideas about themselves, ideas which are no longer true. While being interviewed, Jonathan, the controversial artist, is confronted by the idea that he has become the mainstream, an idea he denies. In doing so, he misses the point of his journey—that he has become the other.

Dinner with Friends is clearly a work from the moral center of American culture. Because it is admittedly more interested in how to sustain a marriage than how to end one, for some it has the whiff of the conventional about it. To see Margulies as a flag waver for home and hearth, however, is to misperceive the problem set forth in the play. In Gabe and Karen's world, there are no supports outside themselves to sustain their marriage. They aren't religious or propped up by doting parents. Society no longer cares whether they stay married or not. Margulies has also been criticized for not more explicitly defining the nature of their world in the play, when in fact the spiritual and cultural void the two couples live in is key to their predicament. So when the wheels come off the marriage of Beth and Tom, their friends and alteregos for a decade, Gabe and Karen recognize their own precariousness and momentarily lose their equilibrium.

> The truth that Gabe and Karen finally confront is that marriage is accommodation and compromise. You have to work at marriage all the time. Resentments build and fester. No one is exempt from the abyss.

Writing in 1965, when religion and marriage meant more to many more Americans, Edward Albee presented another confrontation with the abyss in *A Delicate Balance* (Pulitzer Prize, 1967), the apt title of which was both the play's problem and solution. Fifteen years later in *The Real Thing*, Tom Stoppard observed that the way to sustain a relationship was to "shift your weight"—to keep an even keel. The action of Margulies's play demonstrates that maintaining balance in a marriage is an act of choice, and that in a faithless world, a devotion to marriage tantamount to religious belief—at least in one's own marriage—is essential.

Gabe and Karen's way of sustaining theirs in *Dinner with Friends* is to practice routines and rituals that, in performance, become aspects of a secular mass. The most obvious is the back-and-forth game of reassurance they enjoy: "Uh oh." "What." "You know what time it is?" "What." "It's time for me to scare you." "Oh no, please don't," etc. Yet as effective as that game-as-litany is in the play, even more striking is the silence that comes over an audience of couples watching Karen and Gabe deftly make up their bed together, the collaboration as profound a sacrament as the wafer and the wine.

I want people to see things that are familiar to them in a different light; I want to transform the familiar into the unique and extraordinary.

Born in 1954, the second son of a wallpaper salesman and his home-maker wife, Margulies grew up in what he calls "a high rise Jewish ghetto in Coney Island." Any interview with him tends to elicit the story of his family commuter vacations to modest West Side hotels in the the-atre district of New York City to see shows. He calls the first trip at age nine his "seminal experience" in the theatre, but he wouldn't begin to pursue writing for it until midway through college.

Because his talent for drawing as a child earned him praise and iden-tity, he pursued visual art. Encouraged by his parents and teachers, he won scholarships, spending Saturdays and Sundays at the Brooklyn Museum in painting classes. He received an art scholarship to Pratt Institute, a powerful carrot for the lower middle-class Margulies family, and he began to prepare for a career in commercial art.

A growing interest in literature and little chance to pursue it at Pratt caused him to transfer to SUNY Purchase, where he met theatre critic Julius Novick. Under his tutelage, Margulies began to write plays in 1974.

When I saw those first plays performed for audiences, I got the bug. Watching them laugh and get caught up in them was heady stuff.

From 1977–80 Margulies worked as a graphic designer, mostly freelance, designing books and magazines. He was good at it, enjoying considerable success. But he also was invited into various playwrights' groups on the strength of his one-act play, *Pals* (1977), "my Brooklyn/realism/luncheonette play." It gave him identity and permis-sion to pursue playwriting, much as Novick's encouragement had enabled him to begin writing at Purchase. He found a particular home at The Writers Bloc, a group run by playwright Jeffrey Sweet. Actors, directors, and playwrights gathered to read new work. Also attending were Jane Anderson; Anne Meara and Jerry Stiller; Keith, Mark, and Barbara Gordon; William H. Macy; and many more. Margulies credits these groups for giving him his education in theatre—seeing how actors and directors worked, how scenes were structured, and to write with certain actors in mind.

In 1980 he quit a day job as art editor at *Scholastic* magazine to write comedy for Stiller and Meara's show, "HBO Sneak Preview." At night he wrote plays, setting a goal for himself: to be produced at Joseph Papp's Public Theatre before he turned thirty. The HBO day job lasted more than two years, and ever since, Margulies has made his living as a scriptwriter. Coming full circle, one of his most recent assignments was writing the screenplay for *Dinner with Friends* for HBO.

Jewish Repertory Theatre commissioned Margulies to write a stage adaptation of Delmore Schwartz's story, "In Dreams Begin Responsibilities," in 1980. Its production marked his New York debut in 1982. The one-act created no stir; Margulies calls it "a stealth play." *Resting Place*, two related one-acts, followed later that season at Theatre for the New City. In November 1983, Jewish Repertory presented *Gifted Children*, Margulies's first full-length play, which tells of a New York intellectual, suffocating mother and her artist daughter. The daughter returns home pregnant, followed by her artist lover, who is seduced by her mother.

Interestingly, all three of these early plays proved to be studies for Margulies's *Collected Stories* (1996) and point up an aspect of his creative process. His best plays are often truly wrought—the ingredients left frozen, sometimes for a decade or more, before he reconstitutes them into something completely different and new.

Gifted Children attracted the interest of *The New York Times,* where it was resoundingly panned by critic Frank Rich. Six months later, Margulies realized his goal of being produced at the New York Shakespeare Festival's Public Theatre with the premiere of *Found a Peanut*. He and producer Joseph Papp were delighted with all aspects of the production, and looked to the opening with optimism. Mr. Rich's response in *The New York Times* was tepid.

A few months later, Manhattan Theatre Club (MTC) staged the first production of Margulies's *What's Wrong With This Picture?*, marking his third play to be opened in New York within a year. The play is an ultimately rueful comedy about surviving family members sitting *shiva* for their matriarch when she impossibly returns from the dead. Though it sustained a full run to club subscribers and single ticket buyers, Margulies chose not to open the production for critical review.

I didn't feel secure enough about *"Picture?"*—and I was right—that our rendering of the play was definitive, though a lot of the casting was exciting and right, and there were segments that have never played better. But when you present a play people assume that what they are seeing is what you intended them to see. They don't give you the benefit of the doubt, nor should you expect them to. You can't stand up and say, "Nah, I didn't mean for it to look like that." It's irrelevant. So not opening it was really best for me. If Rich had come and panned us, it would have ended my career. To this day, I really believe it would have. I don't know that I could have overcome that.

At that point I was getting my first bids from Hollywood. I had just done a pilot for Norman Lear, and I could have easily gotten on a plane at that point. I didn't because of some burning ambition I had to be a playwright—not a former playwright; Hollywood is filled with former playwrights—and I didn't want to be one, not at thirty, anyway. So it took me a long time—ten years—to earn the good graces of *The New York Times*.

Margulies's mother, Charlene, died suddenly of a heart attack in 1978. His father, Bob, survived her by nine years, dying a grueling death brought on by the complications of medicating his psoriatic arthritis (the disease that afflicted British dramatist Dennis Potter and his protagonist in the television miniseries, *The Singing Detective*). Bob Margulies contracted his disease soon after his wife's death, and Donald saw it as a metaphor for his incapacity in dealing with the loss of Charlene, which devastated his father.

Everything I've written has been a way for me to analyze more of my life through drama. I focused on my own past life and those I knew, my Jewish identity, and the role of the artist. Lately I've written about being a husband and father.

The catalyst for *What's Wrong With This Picture?* was a dream I had shortly after my mother's death. The doorbell rang. I went to answer it and there she was, in a tattered shroud covered in mud. She said, "Look, I don't even want to talk about it—I have to jump in the shower." It was absolutely the voice of my mother—a hilarious and harrowing dream, and so plausible. I started writing something grim with the working title *Somnambulist*. I was too close to the event, the experience of the dream, so I put it aside for three or four years. At that point I began to figure out how to make it my story and not my story.

Following the success of *Sight Unseen* in 1992, Margulies's earlier works were reevaluated, and momentum for a commercial Broadway production of *Picture?* began to grow.

The whole debacle of *Picture?* on Broadway was made possible by my becoming a commodity in the theatre. A lot of talented people were assembled to do the play, so many it was decided that Broadway was the only place for it. I had never aspired to Broadway—ever. But I took a deep breath and said, "Why not? If I had been born a generation earlier, I would have aimed for it." And if it had been a good production, things might have been different. But it wasn't a good production. It happened on its own scheme, its own terms, and I was rendered essentially ineffectual. I had very little voice or clout; mostly I felt like I was hanging out during rehearsal and previews. When it failed, I became clinically depressed. And, yeah, I'm still bitter about it. It's been painful to see that play come and go the way it has.

It's interesting to me to listen to myself talk about the last twenty years and to notice how many times I felt at my "low point," which is a lot. The strength of a good woman has meant a great deal.

Margulies's dark nights in 1985 and 1986 produced his darkest play, *The Model Apartment*, which premiered in Los Angeles in 1988 and was not produced in New York until 1995. Inspired by the survivors he knew growing up in Brooklyn, the play tells of an aging Jewish couple's flight to Florida to escape their monster daughter, Debby. Margulies had been fascinated by the theatrical naturalism he saw in the plays of Franz Xavier Kroetz, especially *Through the Leaves*. That Kroetz was German added to its mystique.

I wanted to write a play that dealt with the legacy of the Holocaust without resorting to any of the now cliched imagery we've come to associate with it. So I looked at the aging survivor population I knew and found something very poignant and potentially dramatic. I remember talking with my friend about his parents resettling in Florida, and being struck by the sheer black comedy of that: when you look at those lives on a continuum and see where they ended up in old age, an old age they were lucky to have—the power of that. And as I was writing the play, I began to sense I was writing a Frankenstein story, and Debby began to emerge as a metaphoric character: the daughter in whom these parents instilled all their hopes, and filled with all of their nightmares, who becomes the receptacle for it all—of history, fantasy, the future hopes, this terrible stew that results in this monstrous girl who won't go away.

Shortly after Bob Margulies's death in 1987, Donald began work on *The Loman Family Picnic*. He had been recollecting aspects of his childhood involving his father he had never before considered; times that, in retrospect, he imagined were difficult for his parents. He decided he could explore them in a play, and settled on the bar mitzvah of the oldest son as the play's event.

> I was just trying to tell my story—a second son living in a cramped apartment with his family in Brooklyn, a beleaguered salesman-father and a mother who did part-time public relations for him. And as I wrote, I realized my story was not the first of its kind.
>
> I remembered seeing *Death of a Salesman* at age eleven on television with Lee J. Cobb and Mildred Dunnock. It was a profound experience, even then. I remember a palpable sense of embarrassment upon seeing things in the play that were so reflective of my own family life. The shame that I felt was very troubling to me, and at the same time I felt a kind of elation that my story was not singular. So, twenty years later, when I was writing my play, I decided to embrace the Miller play rather than ignore it, and acknowledge its position in the culture and its effect on this eleven-year-old kid. So it was late in the process that the title was invented. It was an acknowledgment of what I discovered in writing the play rather than something I began with. Miller's play gave definition to what I had experienced as a child.

Margulies and MTC officials recall that early critics and preview audiences at MTC's Stage II were delighted and moved by *The Loman Family Picnic* in 1989. Mel Gussow, writing in *The New York Times*, was not. This dismissal was particularly difficult. Margulies, having grown up the prodigy and been anointed as most promising, was faced with the fact that he was thirty-five: no longer promising or young in the way he had been. He believed he was in a make or break situation.

In 1988, he had accepted a commission from California's South Coast Repertory (SCR) and set about writing a coming-of-age tale with the working title, *Heartbreaker*. It was an episodic, multiscene and multi-character, picaresque piece with an autobiographical protagonist: a struggling artist who, by Margulies's admission, wasn't very interesting. (Later, he would self-deprecatingly refer to that text as *The Donald Chronicles*.) After working on the play in workshops at SCR in late 1989 and at the Sundance Institute in July 1990, without much success, he shelved the play. We at SCR agreed with Margulies that *Heartbreaker* seemed slight and unsurprising, and supported his move.

Play development is almost always about finding the best way to tell a story onstage that was implicit from the project's beginning. Such was the case with Margaret Edson's *Wit* (Pulitzer Prize, 1999) and Richard Greenberg's *Three Days of Rain* (Pulitzer finalist, 1998), both of which began at SCR, and with *Angels in America: The Millennium Approaches* (Pulitzer Prize, 1993), the development of which I was able to observe on a regular basis. Plays virtually never take on added substance and import as development proceeds; rather, initial visions are clarified and made more stage worthy—or not.

The development of *Heartbreaker* into *Sight Unseen* is unique in my experience. The play became larger, and much more ambitious in theme. Instead of a small tale of coming to manhood, the play expanded into an examination of the persistence of outsider-ship in American life—no matter how successful one became—as well as an ironic testament to the fact that once assimilation begins, there is no going back to what was before.

> The only scenes in *Heartbreaker* which had any dramatic fascination for me were the three in which Jonathan Waxman appeared with his former sweetheart, Patty. Once I began to salvage those scenes—eliminating Waxman's fiance, for instance—it began to improve. Then I had the idea of making Waxman an extremely successful, superstar painter instead of a struggling artist, a rising giant of the type that were around then in American art. I knew something about that because of my visual art back-ground—not that I was of that world, but I knew something about it. So Waxman was still a contemporary of mine, still from Brooklyn, but experiencing a very different trajectory in life from my own.

I just looked for ways to make the material more interesting to me as I invented it—to keep myself surprised. It's what I practice in all my work: starting out with what you know, but changing that and having it become something you can literally play with, making it something you haven't seen in places you haven't been.

Sight Unseen was Margulies's vehicle out of Brooklyn. While Waxman is *from* Brooklyn, most of it is set in England. It led Margulies's writing to a wider world, and also was a bridge from the artist/son plays to the artist/parent plays he has written since.

Collected Stories sprang from a confluence of creative forces in Margulies's life. In 1993 he became fascinated by the issues in the controversy between poet Stephen Spender and novelist David Leavitt (Leavitt appropriated published material from Spender's autobiography, without permission, for his fiction). Margulies had begun teaching and had acquired the perspective of the mentor. He had been a prodigy and, more recently with *Sight Unseen,* had arrived as a front-rank writer, which gave him a perspective on both of the play's characters. And the stories, settings, and characters in *In Dreams Begin Responsibilities, Resting Place,* and *Gifted Children* all provided raw material for Margulies to shape anew in *Collected Stories*.

SCR had again commissioned a play from Margulies during rehearsals of *Sight Unseen*. Some playwrights find the obligation of a commission daunting; Margulies thrives on them, using them as spurs to get his plays written. Still, he was uncharacteristically blocked on the play in early 1995, a period when I was also serving as artistic director of the Sundance Institute's theatre program.

> The writing of *Collected Stories* was a highpoint of my writing life. You invited me to Sundance's lab, even though I didn't have a play. I had twelve pages, and you gave me a big house to write in and two actresses to work with [Kandis Chappell and Maura Vincent]. You and [director] Lisa Peterson and I and sometimes [lab director] David Kranes worked in that little rehearsal room, and the play happened in about ten days. I would write until five in the morning, fax the pages down the hill to the office, get a little sleep, and come to rehearsal. Having those women waiting for pages was a great motivator. It took a couple of years to rev up to that—I had some notes and a couple of monologues—but it was a won-

derful, exciting time for me: writing in a fever. I hadn't had that much time to myself since my son was born in '92, and hadn't been in one of those all-nighter mentalities since college. I went from twelve pages to eighty-seven pages in ten days. Those kinds of discoveries, the experience of finding those solutions, are why I keep doing this. It's thrilling when it happens.

If one asks Margulies to find links between his plays, he responds that most all of them seem to be concerned with loss; and the latest plays, written in his middle years, have grown more concerned with time as an agent of loss. All three of his Pulitzer finalist plays occur over periods ranging from six to seventeen years. He also speaks of how his visual arts training serves his playwriting craft:

> I visualize the structure of each play. *Dinner with Friends* presented itself to me as two triptychs. Act I is a kind of *La Ronde* triptych which leapfrogs one character from scene to scene. The act's event is the revelation of the dissolution of Beth and Tom's marriage. Act II was another triptych—the aftermath—with a scene with the women, one with the men, and then Gabe and Karen's final bedroom scene. But as I was writing it, I was missing something—some dynamic wasn't being injected into the story. I realized there wasn't a scene with all four, and, unless the audience saw the foursome when things were not so fraught, at the beginning and not the detritus—only after I showed them a snapshot of that earlier time would we have a palpable sense of loss. I had to show the foundation.

A third link might stem from the cultural values found in Jewish tradition. Like the learned in a synagogue, Margulies's characters wrestle with ethical and moral issues of our time and all times. One of his particular talents is the ability to give equal voice to every side of unanswerable questions that can only be addressed person by person.

The arrival of the recognition that Margulies has always sought has not made playwriting any easier.

> Whenever I start something new I'm filled with the same terror I experienced when I first set out to write plays. That doesn't go away. You don't become imbued with confidence after recognition and success. In fact, it's more terrifying: more pressure, more expectations, you imagine people standing there with their arms folded, waiting. And with success comes

much greater demands on your time. I spend much more time now managing productions of my earlier work. I'm grateful I was able to write a number of plays which satisfied me before receiving as much attention as I have recently.

He also spends more time taking calls from Hollywood. Margulies, previously in some demand for film and television work, is now much more so.

Will he continue to write in an art form that, compared to media writing, pays miserably—when it pays—and that never guarantees production?

I write for the theatre because it's where my voice can still be the purest it can be as a dramatic writer. Film and television are corporate endeavors that don't allow the purity of the artist's voice to come through. The theatre is a writer's medium completely, albeit maybe a dying one. I don't believe young people are being exposed to it in the way my generation was.

The theatre can only hope Margulies will find enough motivation in hearing his voice purely to continue writing plays. He has the recognition he sought. He needs the money less. Ironically, the Pulitzer Prize for Drama, meant to honor and promote achievement in playwriting, in the last forty years has been more capstone than springboard to the careers of all but a few winning playwrights. Whether it's the increased film offers, less need to succeed, or mounting expectations that cause creative paralysis, only Edward Albee and August Wilson, both multiple winners, have continued to bring forth plays at the level that first won them the prize.

Notes

1. Quotes from Margulies are from the author's interview, January 2001.
2. This reference applies to Kara Manning, "Are We Not Jews?" *American Theatre*, November 2000.

SELECT BIBLIOGRAPHY

Edward Albee

Recent Plays

Albee, Edward. *Who's Afraid of Virginia Woolf?* New York: Atheneum, 1962.

———. *A Delicate Balance.* New York: Atheneum, 1966.

———. *Three Tall Women.* New York: Dutton, 1995.

———. *The Play About Baby.* Produced London 1998, New York 2001.

Criticism and Thought

Bigsby, C. W. E. *American Drama, 1945–1990.* Cambridge, UK: Cambridge University Press, 1992, pp. 126–151.

Gussow, Mel, *Edward Albee: A Singular Journey, A Biography.* New York: Simon & Schuster, 1999.

Kolin, Philip C., Ed. *Conversations with Edward Albee.* Jackson: University Press of Mississippi, 1998.

Kolin, Philip C., and J. Madison Davis, Eds. *Critical Essays on Edward Albee.* Boston: G.K. Hall, 1986.

Paolucci, Anne. *From Tension to Tonic: The Plays of Edward Albee.* Carbondale: Southern Illinois University Press, 1972.

Roudane, Matthew C. *Understanding Edward Albee.* Columbia: University of South Carolina Press, 1987.

Rutenberb, Michael E. *Edward Albee: Playwright in Protest.* New York: Drama Book Specialists, 1969.

Margaret Edson

Recent Play

Edson, Margaret. *Wit*. New York: Faber and Faber, 2001.

Criticism and Thought

Allen, Jamie. "Pulitzer Is Wonderful, But Teaching is Edson's Life,"
    CNN web posting, 3 May 1999.

Lehrer, Jim. "Interview with Margaret Edson." *NewsHour*, 14 April
    1999 (PBS).

Kelly, Jason. "Wit and Wisdom," *Georgetown Magazine*, 1999.

Martin, Adrienne. "The Playwright in Spite of Herself." *American
    Theatre* 16, no. 8, October (1999): 22–25.

Sack, Kevin. "Margaret Edson: Color, Nurses, Letters and John
    Donne," *New York Times* 10 November 1998: E:1.

Gamerman, Amy. "In Kindergarten with Author of 'Wit'," *Wall Street
    Journal*, 12 November 1998: A:28.

Horton Foote

Recent Plays

Foote, Horton. *The Carpetbagger's Children*. Produced by the
    Hartford Stage Company, September 2001.

———. *The Last of the Thorntons*. Woodstock, NY: The Overlook
    Press, Peter Mayer Publishers, Inc., 2000.

———. *Vernon Early*. New York: Dramatists Play Service, 1999.

———. *Getting Frankie Married—and Afterward—And Other Plays*.
    Introduction by James Houghton. Lyme, NH: Smith and Kraus, 1998.

Criticism and Thought

Burkhart, Marian. "Horton Foote's Many Roads Home: An American
    Playwright and His Characters." *Commonweal*, February 26, 1988:
    110–115.

Davis, Ronald L. "Roots in Parched Ground: An Interview with Horton
    Foote." *Southwest Review*, LXXIII (Summer 1988): 298–318.

Freedman, Samuel G. Introduction to *Cousins and The Death of Papa:
    Two Plays from the Orphans' Home Cycle*, New York: Grove Press,
    1989.

Foote, Horton. *Farewell: A Memoir of a Texas Childhood*. New York,
    Scribner, 1999.

Wood, Gerald C., Ed. *Horton Foote: A Casebook*. New York: Garland
    Publishing, 1997.
Wood, Gerald C. *Horton Foote and the Theatre of Intimacy*. Baton
    Rouge: Louisiana State University Press, 1999.

Tony Kushner
Recent Plays
Kushner, Tony. *Angels in America Part One: The Millennium
    Approaches*. New York: Theatre Communications Group, 1994.
———. *Angels in America Part Two: Perestroika*. New York: Theatre
    Communications Group, 1994.
———. *A Bright Room Called Day*. New York: Theatre
    Communications Group, 1994.
———. *Death and Taxes: Hydriotaphia and Other Plays*. New York:
    Theatre Communications Group, 1999.

Criticism and Thought
Bigsby, C. W. *Contemporary American Playwrights*. Cambridge, UK:
    Cambridge University Press, 1999.
Brask, Per. *Essays on Kushner's Angels*. Winnipeg: Blizzard Publishers,
    1995.
Fisher, James. *The Theatre of Tony Kushner: Living Past Hope*. New
    York: Routledge, 2001.
Geis, Deborah, and Steven Kruger, *Approaching the Millennium:
    Essays on* Angels in America. Ann Arbor: The University of
    Michigan Press, 1997.
Kushner, Tony. "Author's Notes," *Thinking about the Longstanding
    Problems of Virtue and Happiness*. New York: Theatre
    Communications Group, 1995.
Rogoff, Gordon. *"Angels in America, Devils in the Wings," Theater*
    24, no. 2 (1993): 21–29.
Vorlicky, Robert, Ed. *Tony Kushner in Conversation*. Ann Arbor:
    University of Michigan Press, 1998.

Jonathan Larson
Recent Play
Larson, Jonathan. *Rent by Jonathan Larson* with text and interviews

by Evelyn McDonnell with Katherine Silberger (New York: William Morrow, 1997).

Criticism and Thought

Asch, Amy. "Jonathan Larson," on-line supplement of American National Biography, edited by John Garraty, copyright © 2000 by the American Council of Learned Societies.

Brantley, Ben. "J.P. Morgan and Some Heavy Site Specificity," *New York Times*, 16 June 1995, sec C, 2.

Istel, John. "Rescuing the Musical," *Village Voice*, 4 July 1995, 73–74.

Kroll, Jack. "Love Among the Ruins," *Newsweek*, 13 May 1996, 54.

Lipsky, David. "Impossible Dream," *US Magazine*, November 1996, 103.

Singer, Barry. "Score One for Wenner," *New York Magazine*, 21 June 1993, 24.

Tommasini, Anthony. "The Seven Year Odyssey That Led to 'Rent,'" *New York Times*, 17 March 1996, Art and Leisure, 7.

www.thesiteforrent.com. The Broadway production's official website.

Donald Margulies

Recent Plays

Margulies, Donald. *Collected Stories*. New York: Theatre Communications Group, 1998.

———. *Dinner With Friends*. New York: Theatre Communications Group, 2000.

———. *Sight Unseen and Other Plays*. New York: Theatre Communications Group, 1995.

Criticism and Thought

Bossler, Gergory. "Donald Margulies," *The Dramatist*, July/August 2000.

Feingold, Michael. "Donald Margulies, or What's an American Playwright?" Introduction to *Sight Unseen and Other Plays*. New York: Theatre Communications Group, 1995.

Schlueter, June. "Ways of Seeing," *Studies in American Drama 1945–Present*, 8, no. 1 (1993): 3–11.

Robert Schenkkan

Recent Plays

Schenkkan, Robert. *Final Passages*. New York: Dramatists Play
   Service, 1993.

———. *Handler*, Oregon Shakespeare Festival, 2001.

———. *The Dream Thief*. Woodstock, NY: Dramatic Publishing
   Company, 1999.

———. *The Kentucky Cycle*. New York: Dutton/Plume, 1993.

Criticism and Thought

Colakis, Marianthe. "Aeschylean Elements in Robert Schenkkan's *The
   Kentucky Cycle*," *Text and Presentation* 16 (1995): 19–23.

Billings, Dwight, Norman Gurney, and Katherine Ledford, Eds.
   *Confronting Appalachian Stereotypes: Backtalk from an American
   Religion*. Lexington: University Press of Kentucky, 1999.

Spencer, Stuart. "Robert Schenkkan," *Bomb* 46, Winter (1994):
   50–53.

"Spotlight on Theater." Prod. John Carr, John Lion, and Kimberly
   Schraf. Videotape. Washington, DC: Kennedy Center, 1995.

Neil Simon

Recent Plays

Simon, Neil. *Laugher on the 23rd Floor. The Collected Plays of Neil
   Simon, Vol. IV*. New York: Simon & Schuster, 1998.

———. *London Suite. The Collected Plays of Neil Simon, Vol. IV*.
   New York, Simon & Schuster, 1998.

———. *Proposals*. New York: Samuel French, 1998.

———. *The Dinner Party*, Produced New York, 2001.

Criticism and Thought

Bryer, Jackson R. "Neil Simon," in *Speaking on Stage: Interviews with
   Contemporary American Playwrights*, ed. Philip C. Kolin and Colby
   H. Kullman. Tuscaloosa: University of Alabama Press, 1996, 58–81.

Henry III, William A. "Reliving a Poignant Past." *Time*, 15 December
   1986, 72–78.

Johnson, Robert K. *Neil Simon*. Boston: Twayne, 1983.

Konas, Gary, Ed. *Neil Simon: A Casebook*. New York: Garland
   Publishing, 1997.

Lipton, James. "Interview with Neil Simon. Playwrights at Work," in *Paris Review*, ed. George Plimpton. New York: Modern Library, 2000.

Walden, Daniel. "Neil Simon's Jewish-style Comedies," in *From Hester Street to Hollywood: the Jewish American Stage and Screen,* ed. Sarah Blacher Cohen. Bloomington: Indiana University Press, 1986, 213–30.

Paula Vogel

Recent Plays

Vogel, Paula. *How I Learned to Drive. The Mammary Plays: How I Learned to Drive, The Mineola Twins.* New York: Theatre Communications Group, 1998, 1–92.

——. *The Mineola Twins. The Mammary Plays: How I Learned to Drive, The Mineola Twins.* New York: Theatre Communications Group, 1998, 93–187.

——. *Hot 'N' Throbbing. Baltimore Waltz and Other Plays.* New York: Theatre Communications Group, 1996, 225–96.

——. *Baltimore Waltz. Baltimore Waltz and Other Plays.* New York: Theatre Communications Group, 1996, 1–57.

Criticism and Thought

Bigsby, Christopher. "Paula Vogel," in *Contemporary American Playwrights*. Cambridge, UK: Cambridge University Press, 1999, 289–329.

Drukman, Steven. "A Playwright on the Edge Turns Toward the Middle." *New York Times,* 16 March 1997, sec. 2, 6.

Rosenfeld, Megan. "One 'Hot' Property: For Playwright Paula Vogel, A Well-Rewarded Stage in Life." *Washington Post,* 12 September 1999, final ed., G1.

Savran, David. "Loose Screws," Introduction to *Baltimore Waltz and Other Plays*. New York: Theatre Communications Group, 1996, ix–xv.

Vogel, Paula. "Interview with David Savran," in *The Playwright's Voice: American Dramatists on Memory, Writing and the Politics of Culture*, ed. David Savran. New York: Theatre Communications Group, 1999, 263–88.

Witchel, Alex. "After the Prize Is the Pressure: Now What?" *New York Times,* 7 February 1999, late ed., sec. 2, 5.

Wendy Wasserstein
Recent plays

Wasserstein, Wendy. *An American Daughter*. New York: Harcourt, 1999.
———. *Heidi Chronicles and Other Plays*. New York: Penguin Books, 1991.
———. *Old Money*. New York: Harcourt, 2002.
———. *Sisters Rosensweig*. New York: Harcourt, 1993.

Criticism and Thought

Barnett, Claudia, Ed. *Wendy Wasserstein: A Casebook*. New York and London: Garland, 1999.
Brenda Murphy, Ed. *The Cambridge Companion to American Women Playwrights*. Cambridge, UK: Cambridge University Press, 1999. 213–31.
Ciociola, Gail. *Wendy Wasserstein: Dramatizing Women, Their Choices and Their Boundaries*. Jefferson, NC: McFarland, 1998.
Bryer, Jackson, Ed. *The Playwright's Art: Conversations with Contemporary American Dramatists*. New Brunswick, NJ: Rutgers University Press, 1995.
Betsko, Kathleen, and Rachel Koenig, Eds. *Interviews with Contemporary Women Playwrights*. New York: Beech Tree Books, 1987.
"Spotlight on Theater." Prod. John Carr, John Lion, Kimberly Schraf. Videotape. Washington, DC: Kennedy Center, 1995.

August Wilson
Recent Plays

Wilson, August. *King Hedley II*, produced Chicago, New York, 2001.
———. *Seven Guitars*. New York: Dutton, 1996.
———. *The Piano Lesson*. New York: Penguin Books, 1990.
———. *Two Trains Running*. New York: Penguin Books, 1993.

Criticism and Thought

Bloom, Harold. *August Wilson*. Philadelphia: Chelsea House Publishers, 2001.

Elkins, Marilyn. Ed. *August Wilson, A Casebook*. New York: Garland Publishing, 1994.

Herrington, Joan. *I Ain't Sorry for Nothin' I Done: August Wilson's Process of Playwriting*. New York: Limelight Editions, 1998.

Nadel, Alan. *Essays on the Drama of August Wilson*. Iowa City: University of Iowa Press, 1994.

Schafer, Yvonne. *August Wilson—A Research and Production Sourcebook*. New York: Greenwood Press, 1998.

Shannon, Sandra. *The Dramatic Vision of August Wilson*. Washington, DC: Howard University Press, 1995.

CONTRIBUTORS

Thomas P. Adler is Professor and head of English at Purdue University, where he has taught for the past thirty years. He has published widely in the area of modern British and American drama, including the monograph *American Drama, 1940–1960: A Critical History,* and, more recently, essays on Hellman, Miller, Williams, and Shepard in four different volumes in the Cambridge Companions Series.

Amy Asch is a musical theatre historian and the archivist for the estate of Jonathan Larson.

Crystal Brian is Associate Professor of Theatre at Quinnipiac University in Hamden, Conn. Brian is also the artistic director of The Lost World, a theatrical production company dedicated to new work by American playwrights. The Lost World has won awards and critical acclaim for West Coast and Equity world premiere productions of plays by Horton Foote, Tina Howe, and Naomi Wallace. Brian is the author of "To Be Quiet and Listen" in *Horton Foote: A Casebook* and is currently completing a critical biography of Horton Foote.

Tom Bryant was dramaturge on *The Kentucky Cycle* throughout its development process and productions at the Intiman Theater, the Mark Taper Forum, the Kennedy Center, and the Royale Theater on Broadway. He has worked extensively as a dramaturge in regional theatre and is most closely associated with the Mark Taper Forum in Los Angeles and the Intiman Theater in Seattle.

Angelika Czekay received her Ph.D. in theatre studies from the University of Wisconsin-Madison, where she is currently an honorary fellow. Some of her research interests include contemporary British drama, feminist theatre, theory, and performance, and the representation of national identity and history in international women's plays. Her articles have appeared in the *Journal of Dramatic Theory and Criticism*, *Western European Stages*, *Theatre Research International*, and in the anthologies *Stirring It* and *The Other Germanies*.

Joan Herrington is an Associate Professor of Theatre at Western Michigan University whose current research focuses on the creative process of playwrights and directors. She has published extensively on August Wilson, including her book *I Ain't Sorry for Nothin' I Done: August Wilson's Process of Playwriting*. Her articles on Wilson, Anne Bogart, and other major theatre artists have appeared in such journals as *Theatre Topics, American Drama, Text and Presentation*, and *The Journal of Dramatic Theory and Criticism*.

Mead Hunter is director of literary programs at A. S. K. Theater Projects, an arts service organization that presented an early reading of *Wit*.

Maggy Lally is a director and teacher who works frequently with young writers and new work. She and Jonathan Larson were classmates in the acting program at Adelphi.

Ann Linden is an instructor at the University of Wisconsin-Madison in the communications department. She is a feminist theatre scholar and has worked professionally as a dramaturge.

Bette Mandl is Professor of English at Suffolk University in Boston. Her articles and reviews have appeared in such journals as *The Eugene O'Neill Review* and *Studies in the Humanities*, as well as in books such as *Modern American Drama: The Female Canon* and *Neil Simon: A Casebook*.

Framji Minwalla teaches in the Drama Department at Dartmouth College. The collection of essays he coedited with Alisa Solomon, *The Queerest Art*, will be published this fall by NYU Press. He is currently at work on a book tentatively titled *History, Politics: Queer Essays on Making and Teaching Theater.*

Jerry Patch has been affiliated with South Coast Repertory (SCR), in Costa Mesa, CA since 1967 and has headed its new play development program since 1980. In that capacity, he served as dramaturge on the development and premiere productions of nearly 150 plays, including Donald Margulies's *Sight Unseen* and *Collected Stories*. Mr. Patch is director of SCR's Pacific Playwrights Festival, held annually in June, and for seven years served as artistic director of the Theatre Program of the Sundance Institute. He currently serves as consulting dramaturge for the Roundabout Theatre in New York.

INDEX